D0931136

Organization Development

A Process of Learning and Changing

Third Edition

W. Warner Burke
Debra A. Noumair

Publisher: Paul Boger
Editor-in-Chief: Amy Neidlinger
Executive Editor: Jeanne Levine
Development Editor: Natasha Wolmers
Operations Specialist: Jodi Kemper
Cover Designer: Alan Clements
Managing Editor: Kristy Hart
Senior Project Editor: Betsy Gratner
Copy Editor: Karen Annett
Proofreader: Debbie Williams
Indexer: WordWise Publishing Services
Senior Compositor: Gloria Schurick
Manufacturing Buyer: Dan Uhrig

For information about buying this title in bulk quantities, or for special sales opportunities (which may include electronic versions; custom cover designs; and content particular to your business, training goals, marketing focus, or branding interests), please contact our corporate sales department at corpsales@pearsoned.com or (800) 382-3419.

For government sales inquiries, please contact governmentsales@pearsoned.com.

For questions about sales outside the U.S., please contact international@pearsoned.com.

First Printing February 2015

ISBN-10: 0-13-389248-4
ISBN-13: 978-0-13-389248-2

Pearson Education LTD.
Pearson Education Australia PTY, Limited
Pearson Education Singapore, Pte. Ltd.
Pearson Education Asia, Ltd.
Pearson Education Canada, Ltd.
Pearson Educación de Mexico, S.A. de C.V.
Pearson Education—Japan
Pearson Education Malaysia, Pte. Ltd.

Library of Congress Control Number: 2014955391

This book is dedicated to the students, participants, and alumni of the Social-Organizational Psychology Program: Ph.D., M.A., Eisenhower Leadership Development M.A. Program (ELDP), Army Fellows Program, Executive M.A. Program in Change Leadership (XMA), Principles and Practices of Organization Development (PPOD), and Executive Education Programs in Change and Consultation in the Department of Organization and Leadership at Teachers College, Columbia University.

Contents

Conclusion

About the Authors

W. Warner Burke is the E. L. Thorndike Professor of Psychology and Education and a founder of the graduate programs in social-organizational psychology at Teachers College, Columbia University. Originally educated as a social-organizational psychologist (Ph.D., University of Texas, Austin), Dr. Burke is currently engaged in teaching, research, and consulting. He teaches leadership and organization change and consultation. His research focuses on multi-rater feedback, leadership, organization change, and learning agility. Dr. Burke's consulting experience has been with a variety of organizations in business/industry, education, government, religious, health care systems, and professional services firms.

Prior to his move to Teachers College, Dr. Burke was Professor of Management and Chair of the Department of Management at Clark University. Prior to the Clark assignment, Dr. Burke was an independent consultant from 1974 to 1976. For eight years he was a full-time professional with the NTL Institute for Applied Behavioral Science, where he was Director for Executive Programs and Director of the Center for Systems Development (1966–1974). For eight years beginning in 1966, he also served as the Executive Director of the Organization Development Network.

Dr. Burke is a Fellow of the Academy of Management, the Association for Psychological Science, and the Society of Industrial and Organizational Psychology. He has served on the Board of Governors of the Academy of Management and the American Society for Training and Development (now Association for Talent Development), and he is a Diplomate in industrial/organizational psychology, American Board of Professional Psychology. From 1979 to 1985 he was Editor of the American Management Association's quarterly, *Organizational Dynamics,* and from 1986 to 1989 he originated and served as Editor of the *Academy of Management Executive*. Dr. Burke is the author of more than 150 articles and book chapters on organization development, training, change and organizational psychology, and conference planning and author, coauthor, editor, and coeditor of 20 books. His latest (2014) book is *Organization Change: Theory and Practice, 4th Edition* (Sage).

Among his many awards are the Public Service Medal from NASA, the Distinguished Scholar-Practitioner Award from the Academy of Management, Lifetime Achievement Awards from the OD Network and Linkage, and the Distinguished Professional Contributions Award from the Society of Industrial and Organizational Psychology.

Debra A. Noumair is Founder and Director of the Executive Masters Program in Change Leadership (XMA), Director of Executive Education Programs in Change and Consultation, Academic Program Coordinator of Graduate Programs, and Associate Professor, in Social-Organizational Psychology in the Department of Organization and Leadership at Teachers College, Columbia University. Professor Noumair is currently engaged in teaching, research, consulting, and coaching; the focus of her work is on applying systems psychodynamics to executive education as well as to organization change at multiple levels with individuals, teams, and organizations. She teaches courses on organization change and consultation and executive coaching.

Dr. Noumair is a coeditor of the Emerald book series, *Research on Organization Change and Development*, and a coeditor of *Group Dynamics, Organizational Irrationality, and Social Complexity: Group Relations Reader 3*. She serves on the Editorial Boards of *The Journal of Applied Behavioral Science* and the OPUS International Journal, *Organisational and Social Dynamics*.

As director of numerous leadership development programs, Dr. Noumair brings her work on individual, group, and organizational dynamics to executives through examining multi-rater feedback and psychological assessments at the individual and group level and through teaching and executive coaching with senior executives nationally and internationally. Much of her executive education work involves partnering with organizations to address the advancement of women through teaching group dynamics and assessment-anchored executive coaching. Dr. Noumair consults to organizations on culture change, senior team effectiveness, intergroup and interorganizational relations, and issues related to diversity at work. A group relations scholar and practitioner, Dr. Noumair is a Fellow of the A. K. Rice Institute. She has consulted to and directed group relations conferences nationally and served on the Board of Directors of the A. K. Rice Institute for nine years.

Dr. Noumair received her bachelor's degree from Boston University and holds masters and doctoral degrees from Teachers College, Columbia University. She is a member of the American Psychological Association, the Academy of Management, and the Organization Development Network.

Preface

I wrote the first two editions of this book on organization development (OD) in 1987 and 1994, respectively. The significant change for this third edition is the addition of my coauthor, Debra Noumair. We have been colleagues at Teachers College, Columbia University, for two decades and have worked together on numerous projects and several courses within our social-organizational psychology programs, which she now directs.

It was clear that the second edition, slightly more than 20 years old, was dated. It was also clear that some more recent perspectives and additions were in order, such as integrating covert processes into organization diagnosis, consulting to loosely coupled systems, and coaching and OD. Although massive change in the field has not occurred in the last two decades, plenty of change has evolved. Therefore, instead of the 11 chapters in the second edition, we now have 14, and with an exception or two (history remains the same), all other chapters have been revised, some significantly, such as Chapters 2, 12, and 14. A chapter-by-chapter summary follows, but a few words of clarification first: the intended audience for this book and some personal biases.

We have three audiences in mind: (1) the manager, executive, or administrator—that is, a potential user of organization development; (2) the practitioner in the field—that is, a user who may need some guidelines for his or her practice either as a consultant internal to an organization or as an external consultant working with a consulting firm or as an independent practitioner; and (3) the student—one who may in the future use the information provided in either of roles (1) or (2).

And now a brief word of clarification: Although we believe we have been reasonably objective in defining and describing OD, the theories underlying the field, and the way practitioners typically work, we do have a bias. While defining OD, we also present what we think OD *should* be; that is, a clear goal of change in the organization's culture. An organization's culture is the single greatest barrier to change for any system, whether profit-making or nonprofit, government, educational, or religious institution. Not everyone will agree with this bias, but agreement or disagreement should not prevent a reasonable understanding of how we have described the concepts and practices of organization development.

What follows is a summary statement of the content for each of the 14 chapters organized in three parts plus a Conclusion.

Part I, "The Field of Organization Development"

Chapter 1, "What Is Organization Development?," presents an actual case based on a consulting assignment, which succinctly illustrates the primary characteristics of OD practice, although taking into account what OD should be (our bias), it does not exemplify what OD really is.

Chapter 2, "Organization Development Then and Now," is significantly revised and focuses on the impact of the external environment on OD. It first summarizes the previous second edition with the nine significant changes between 1969 and 1994 and then covers nine newer trends that are under way as of 2014 and likely will be influential for the foreseeable future.

Chapter 3, "Where Did Organization Development Come From?," remains essentially the same as before and traces the roots or forerunners of the field as well as briefly describes ten theories related to organizational behavior that underlie OD practice.

Chapter 4, "Organization Development as a Process of Change," covers the fundamental models of change that guide OD practitioners and, using another actual case to illustrate, also covers the phases of consultation that OD practitioners follow in their practice.

Part II, "Understanding Organizations: Diagnosis"

Chapter 5, "Defining the Client: A Different Perspective," addresses the question of who the client is, which might seem obvious, but isn't. This perspective considers the client in terms of relationships.

Chapter 6, "Understanding Organizations: The Process of Diagnosis," describes some of the most common frameworks or organizational models that OD practitioners use after they have conducted their interviews and perhaps administered questionnaires, made their observations, and read some documents and then attempted to make systematic sense out of what often at first seems a mass of confusing data.

Chapter 7, "The Burke-Litwin Model of Organizational Performance and Change," extends and builds on the previous chapter by describing our own way of thinking about organizations and changing them. The significant change that occurred at British Airways during the latter half of the 1980s is explained to illustrate how the Burke-Litwin model was used as a framework.

Chapter 8, "Understanding Organizations: Covert Processes," is a new chapter that addresses those organizational issues that exist beneath the surface—the "undiscussables," matters of collusion, and what might be referred to as the collective unconscious. Central to the chapter is an actual case that brings these issues to the surface and provides a framework for integrating covert processes with OD models, tools, and practice.

Part III, "Changing Organizations"

Chapter 9, "Planning and Managing Change," explains what OD practitioners do after the diagnostic phase and includes many of the primary steps involved in managing change as well as theory about organizational culture change. With change in general being more rapid than ever and with organizations being more differentiated than ever, we end the chapter with two caveats—we may not have as much time to plan our change effort as we would like, and we can no longer assume that most organizations today follow the organizational model of General Motors in the days of Alfred P. Sloan (1946), *the* model of its day for corporate America.

Chapter 10, "Understanding and Changing Loosely Coupled Systems," another new chapter, compares and contrasts loosely coupled systems with tightly coupled systems and explores the complexities of attempting to change a loosely coupled system, a network or political party, for example. Social network analysis is a popular and useful tool for understanding loosely coupled systems. Other political tools and interventions, such as large group techniques that can be useful for changing a loosely versus tightly coupled system, are explored.

Chapter 11, "Does Organization Development Work?," presents some summary evidence that OD does work, brings the evidence up to date, highlights the issues in evaluating OD efforts, and provides the key reasons in support of conducting an evaluation.

Chapter 12, "The Organization Development Consultant," is significantly revised and covers OD consultant roles and functions, abilities required of an OD practitioner, OD values, ways to become an OD consultant, self as instrument, and reflective practice. This chapter also addresses the shift toward integrating OD skills into line functions and managerial and leadership roles in organizations.

Chapter 13, "Coaching and Organization Development," another new chapter, covers the field of coaching and its relation to OD. Although coaching as a process of teaching and learning has been around for centuries, as a distinct field within organizations and primarily for executives, managers, and supervisors, it is comparatively new. There are different roles and functions of coaching and OD practitioners need not only be aware of these processes, but also incorporate coaching into organization development and change.

Conclusion

Chapter 14, "Organization Development and the Future," is significantly revised and provides an overview of current and future trends in OD and then summarizes four primary trends currently under way and likely to influence the field of OD in the foreseeable future. These four are dialogic OD, leadership development, positive psychology, and agility both organizational and individual. The chapter ends with an overall summary.

Writing a book—even one that is a revision, a third edition of an earlier one—requires long hours of digging into the more recent and relevant literature, concentrating on what needs updating, what new topics need to be added, and what is not necessary to incorporate into this latest edition. But the long hours have been rewarding because new learning for us has been realized. This learning has come from both new theory concepts and research, as well as from new and different practice. The joy comes from seeing how theory and research can influence practice and how practice can inform what new research and theory needs to be conducted. Completing this third edition therefore strengthens our self-identity of being scholar-practitioners.

And, finally, with respect to helping us to bring this book to the printed page, we wish to express our deep gratitude to Ms. Ambar Ureña for her skill at typing and use of the computer, her administrative abilities, and most important, her positive, can-do attitude.

New York, NY   W. Warner Burke

Debra A. Noumair

1

What Is Organization Development?

The term *organization development,* or OD, the label most commonly used for the field, has been in use since at least 1960. In the '60s and early '70s, jokes about what the abbreviation OD meant were common. Today, few people in the world of large organizations associate OD with overdose, olive drab, or officer of the day, however. Organization development as a field may not yet be sufficiently known to be defined in the dictionary or explained in the *Encyclopedia Britannica,* but it has survived some turbulent times and will be around for the foreseeable future. Although not defined in these well-known standards for definitions, organization development is defined in the *Encyclopedia of Management Theory,* Volume Two (Kessler, 2013) albeit requiring more than five double-columned pages. Moreover if we do check Webster's dictionary and look for the definition of *development,* we will find that part of the definition is as follows:

- Evolve possibilities
- Make active
- Promote growth
- Make available or usable resources the organization has
- Move from an original position to one that provides more opportunity for effective use

In other words, we could hardly do better attempting to find a more appropriate lead-in to what OD means.

Explaining what OD is and what people do who practice OD continues to be difficult nevertheless because the field is still being shaped to some degree and because the practice of OD is more of a process than a step-by-step procedure. That is, OD is a consideration in general of how work is done, what the people who carry out the

1

work believe and feel about their efficiency and effectiveness, rather than a specific, concrete, step-by-step linear procedure for accomplishing something.

An example should help to explain. The following case represents a fairly strict, purist stance for determining what OD is and what it is not.

A Case: Organization Development or Crisis Management?

The client organization was a division of a large U.S. manufacturing corporation. The division consisted of two plants, both of which manufactured heavy electrical equipment. The division was in trouble at the time I (Burke) was hired as an OD consultant. There were quality and control problems and customers were complaining. The complaints concerned not only poor quality, but also late delivery of products—inevitably weeks, if not months, later than promised. Several weeks prior to my arrival at the divisional offices, a senior vice president (VP) from the corporation's headquarters had visited with the division's top management team, a group of six men. The corporate VP was very much aware of the problems, and he was anything but pleased about the state of affairs. At the end of his visit, he made a pronouncement, stating in essence that, unless this division was "turned around" within six months, he would close it down. This ultimatum would mean loss of jobs for more than 1,000 people, including, of course, the division's top management team. Although the two plants in this division were unionized, the corporate VP had the power and the support from his superiors to close the division if he deemed it necessary.

For several months before this crisis, the division general manager had taken a variety of steps to try to correct the problems. He had held problem-solving meetings with his top management team; he had fired the head of manufacturing and brought in a more experienced man; he spent time on the shop floor talking with first-line supervisors and workers; he authorized experiments to be conducted by the production engineers to discover better methods; and he even conducted a mass rally of all employees at which he exhorted them to do better. After the rally, signs were placed throughout the division announcing the goal: to become number one among all the corporation's divisions. None of these steps seemed to make any difference.

The general manager also sought help from the corporate staff of employee relations and training specialists. One of these specialists made several visits to the division and eventually decided that an outside consultant with expertise in organization development could probably help. I was contacted by this corporate staff person, and an exploratory visit was arranged.

My initial visit, only a few weeks after the corporate vice president had made his visit and his pronouncement, consisted largely of (1) talking at length with the general manager, (2) observing briefly most of the production operations, (3) meeting informally with the top management team so that questions could be raised and issues explored, and, finally, (4) discussing the action steps I proposed. I suggested we start at the top. I would interview each member of the top management team at some length and report back to them as a group what I had diagnosed from these interviews; then we would jointly determine the appropriate next steps. They agreed to my proposal.

A couple of weeks later, I began by interviewing the six members of the top management team (see Figure 1.1) for about an hour each. They gave many reasons for the division's problems, some of the presumed causes contradicting others. What became apparent was that, although the division's goals were generally understandable, they were not specific enough for people to be clear about priorities. Moreover, there were interpersonal problems, such as conflict between the head of marketing and the head of employee relations. (The marketing manager believed that the employee relations manager was never forceful enough, and the employee relations manager perceived the marketing manager as a blowhard.) We decided to have a two-and-a-half-day meeting of the top management team at a hotel some 90 miles away to work on clarifying priorities and ironing out some of the interpersonal problems.

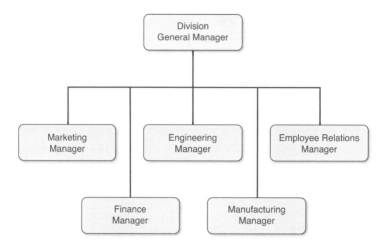

Figure 1.1 Organization Chart: Top Management Team of Manufacturing Division

The off-site meeting was considered successful because much of what we set out to accomplish was achieved—a clearer understanding of the problems and concerns and an agenda for action. The crucial problem did indeed surface. A layer or two of the organizational onion had been peeled away, and we were finally getting at not only some causes but specifics that we could address with confidence that we were moving in the right direction. The key problem that surfaced was the lack of cooperation between the two major divisional functions—engineering and manufacturing.

As the organization chart in Figure 1.1 shows, the division was organized according to function. The primary advantages of a functional organization are clarity about organizational responsibilities because of the division of labor and the opportunities for continuing development of functional expertise within a single unit. The disadvantages also stem from the distinct divisions of responsibility. Because marketing does marketing and manufacturing manufactures, the two rarely meet. In this case, the problem was between engineering and manufacturing. The design engineers claimed that the manufacturing people did not follow their specifications closely enough, while the manufacturing people claimed that the design engineers did not consider that the machinery for manufacturing was old and worn. Because of the condition of the machinery, the manufacturing people were not able to follow the design engineers' specifications to the desired tolerances. Each group blamed the other for the drop in overall product quality and for the delays in delivery of the product to the firm's customers.

This kind of conflict is common in organizations that are organized functionally. The advantages of such organizations are clear, of course, but a premium is placed on the need for cooperation and communication across functional lines. Moreover, the pressures of daily production schedules make it difficult for managers to pull away and clearly diagnose the situation when conflicts occur between functions. Managers spend a great deal of time fighting fires—that is, treating symptoms rather than causes. An outside consultant who is not caught up in this day-to-day routine can be more objective. Thus, my primary role as consultant to this division was diagnostician.

The next step was to deal with this problem of intergroup conflict. Another off-site meeting was held about a month later with the top six people from engineering and their equivalent number from manufacturing. These men were predominantly engineers, either design engineers assigned to the engineering function or production engineers working in the manufacturing operation. These two functions were supposed to interact closely. The design engineers sent blueprint-like plans to manufacturing for production of the specified electrical equipment. The manufacturing people reiterated their complaint that the design tolerances were too stringent for their worn-out machinery to handle. Meeting the design specifications would require purchasing new machinery, but the cost was prohibitive. "And besides," they added, "those design guys never set foot on the shop floor anyway, so how would they know whether we complied with their specs or not?"

These comments and the attitudes they reflect are illustrative and common. Communication is rarely what it should be between groups in such organizations. It is also common, perhaps natural, for functional groups to distance themselves from one another to protect their own turf.

Using a standard OD intergroup problem-solving format, I worked with the two groups to understand and clarify their differences, to reorganize the two groups temporarily into three four-person, cross-functional groups to solve problems, and to plan specific action steps they could take to correct their intergroup problems. The object in such a format is to provide a procedure for bringing conflict to the surface to enable those affected to understand it and manage a solution more productively. An initial exchange of perceptions allows the parties to see how each group sees itself and the other group. Next comes identification of the problems that exist between the two groups. Finally, mixed groups of members from both functions work together to plan action steps that will alleviate the conflict and solve many of the problems. See "Conflict in Organizations" (Burke, 2014a) for a detailed description of this process and see Figure 1.2 for a summary of its application in this case.

The outcome of this intergroup meeting clearly suggested yet another step. A major problem needing immediate attention was that the manufacturing group was not working well as a team. The design engineers produced evidence that they often got different answers to the same design production problem from different manufacturing people. Thus, the next consulting step was to help conduct a team-building session for the top group of the manufacturing function. Approximately two months after the intergroup session, I met off-site for two days with the production engineers and general foremen of manufacturing. In this session, we set specific manufacturing targets, established production priorities, clarified roles and responsibilities, and even settled a few interpersonal conflicts.

By this time, I had been working with the division on and off for close to nine months. After my team-building session with the manufacturing group, I was convinced that I had begun to see some of the real causes of the divisional problems; until then, I had been dealing primarily with symptoms, not causes. I noticed, for example, that the first-line supervisors had no tangible way of rewarding their hourly workers; they could use verbal strokes—"Nice job, Alice," or "Keep up the good work, Joe"—but that was about it. They could use negative reinforcement, however, if they so chose—for example, threatening a one- or two-week layoff without pay if performance did not meet standards. This type of action was within the bounds of the union contract.

Procedure to Resolve Conflict

Participants

Manufacturing Department   Engineering Design Department
      (six people)   (six people)

Step 1: Identify Perceptions

Each department's six representatives work as a group and separately
from other departments to generate three lists: how we see ourselves,
how we see them, and how we think they see us.

Step 2: Exchange of Perceptions

Meeting as total community of twelve, each departmental group of six
presents its lists of perceptions to the other departmental group.

Step 3: Problem Identification

Employing information presented in Step 2, the two groups, again
working separately, identify the primary problems that exist
between the two departments.

Step 4: Problem Exchange

Each group presents its problem list to the other group.

Step 5: Problem Consolidation

The total group, or representatives from each department, consolidate
the two lists into one.

Step 6: Priority Setting

Together the twelve people rank the problems listed from most to
least important.

Step 7: Group Problem Solving

The total community is reorganized into three cross-departmental,
temporary problem-solving groups. Each of the three groups, consisting
of four people, two from manufacturing and two from engineering
design, takes one of the top three most important problems
and generates solutions.

Step 8: Summary Presentations

Each of the three groups presents its solutions to the other two groups.

Step 9: Follow-Up Planning

Final activity in total community of twelve is to plan
implementation steps for problem solutions.

Figure 1.2 Example of Intergroup Problem-Solving Process

The hourly employees were paid according to what is called a
measured day-work system. Their pay was based on what an industrial
engineer had specified as an average rate of productivity for a given
job during an eight-hour day. Incentive to produce more for extra pay
was not part of the system.

I suggested to the division general manager that a change in the reward system might be in order. At that suggestion, the blood seemed to drain from his face. He explained that the present president of the corporation was the person who, years before, had invented the measured day-work system. He did not believe in incentive systems. The division general manager made it clear that he was not about to suggest to the corporate president, the big boss, that the measured day-work system should perhaps be scrapped. I discussed this matter with my original corporate contact, the staff specialist. He confirmed the origin of the reward system and stated that changing the reward system was not an option. I became extremely frustrated at this point. I thought that I had finally discovered a basic cause of divisional, if not corporate, production problems, but it became apparent that this root of the problem was not going to be dug up. The next step I nonetheless recommended in the overall problem-solving process—to change some elements of the reward system for hourly employees, if not the entire system—was not a step the division general manager was willing to take. The corporate staff person was also unwilling to push for change in this aspect of the system. My consulting work with the division ended shortly thereafter.

The point of this consultation case is as follows: What I used as a consultant was the standard methodology of organization development, but the project was *not,* in the final analysis, organization development. Having described the case, I will now use it as a vehicle for clarifying what OD is and what it is not.

Definitions

In the consultation, I used OD methodology and approached the situation from an OD perspective. The methodological model for OD is *action research;* data on the nature of certain problems are systematically collected and then action is taken as a function of what the analyzed data indicate. The specific techniques used within this methodological model (few of which are unique to OD) were as follows:

1. *Diagnosis.* Interview both individuals and groups, observe the situation, then analyze and organize the data collected.

2. *Feedback.* Report back to those from whom the data were obtained on the organization's collective sense of the organizational problems.

3. *Discussion.* Analyze what the data mean and then plan the steps to be taken as a consequence.

4. *Action.* Take those steps.

In OD language, taking a step is making an *intervention* into the routine way in which the organization operates. In the consultation case, there were three primary interventions: team building with the division general manager and the five functional heads who reported directly to him, intergroup conflict resolution between the engineering and manufacturing groups, and team building with the top team of the manufacturing group.

The case does not qualify as an effort in OD because it meets only two of the three criteria for OD as they have been defined (Burke & Hornstein, 1972, p. xviii). For change in an organization to be OD, it must (1) respond to an actual and perceived need for change on the part of the client, (2) involve the client in the planning and implementation of the change, and (3) lead to change in the organization's culture.

As a consultant, I was able to meet the first two criteria, but not the third. For cultural change to have taken place in this case, the reward system would have to have been modified. The bias presented in this book is that *organization development is a process of fundamental change in an organization's culture.* By fundamental change, as opposed to fixing a problem or improving a procedure, we mean that some significant aspect of an organization's culture will never be the same. In the case described, it was the reward system. In another case, it might be a change in the organization's management style, requiring new forms of exercising authority, which in turn would lead to different conformity patterns because new norms would be established, especially in decision making.

Now that we have jumped from a specific case to more general concepts, perhaps we should slow down and define some terms. Any organization, like any society, has its own unique culture. A given culture consists of many elements, but the primary element is the unique pattern of norms, standards, or rules of conduct to which members conform. Other significant elements of an organization's culture are its authority structure and way of exercising power, values, rewards and way of dispensing them, and communication patterns.

Our definition of culture emphasizes norms and values because doing so gives us an operational understanding of culture: conforming patterns of behavior. Norms can be changed. The changed behavior is a different conformity. This position, albeit perhaps limited, is nevertheless consistent with Kurt Lewin's thinking concerning change in a social system (Lewin, 1958; see Chapter 3, "Where Did Organization Development Come From?," of this book).

Edgar Schein (1985) defines culture at a *deeper* (emphasis added) level, as

> *basic assumptions* and *beliefs* that are shared by members of an organization, that operate unconsciously, and that define in a basic "taken-for-granted" fashion an organization's view of itself and its environment. These assumptions and beliefs are learned responses to a group's problems of *internal integration.* They come to be taken for granted because they solve those problems repeatedly and reliably. This deeper level of assumptions is to be distinguished from the "artifacts" and "values" that are manifestations or surface levels of the culture but not the essence of the culture (pp. 6–7).

According to Schein's definition, I—as the consultant in the manufacturing case—was dealing with surface levels. And this is true—almost. The OD practitioner's job is to elicit from the client implicit norms, those conforming patterns that are ubiquitous but are just below the surface, not salient. These behaviors are *manifestations* of basic assumptions and beliefs as Schein notes, and may not be the essence but constitute more operational means for dealing with organizational change. These issues concerning covert data are addressed in Chapter 8, "Understanding Organizations: Covert Processes."

At the outset of an organization consultation, it is practically impossible for an OD practitioner to deal with data other than fairly superficial behavior. To discover the essence of organizational culture, the practitioner must establish not only good rapport with members of the client organization, but also a sound basis for trust. If organization members are reluctant or even unwilling to talk openly, the OD practitioner may never discover the true culture. To find out why its members behave the way they do, the OD practitioner must therefore truly engage the client organization's members. This is done by asking discerning and helpful questions and by showing genuine interest in the members as people and in what they do, what they are responsible for, what their problems are, and what helps or hinders them from making the kind of contribution they want to make as well as what will be beneficial to the organization. Engaging people in this way is an *intervention* into the organization, not simply observation.

Schein (1991) terms this form of organizational consultation and research *clinical research*. He maintains that one cannot understand the culture of an organization via the traditional scientific model; that is, making observations and gathering data without disturbing the situation. It is practically impossible to collect data without disturbing the situation. The classic Hawthorne studies, as Schein appropriately points out, demonstrated rather clearly that changes observed were due more to the researcher's presence than to any of the other modifications in the workers' environment; for example, change in lighting.

Schein's point, therefore, is this: To discover the essence of culture, the practitioner must *interact* with the client—ask questions, test hypotheses, and provide helpful suggestions. He states that "once the helping relationship exists, the possibilities for learning what really goes on in organizations are enormous if we learn to take advantage of them and if we learn to be good and reliable observers of what is going on" (p. 5).

In summary, the OD practitioner begins with asking about and observing norms and values in the client organization. Inherent in this process is building rapport and trust with the client organization as well as testing the values and norms presented and observed. Gradually, then, the OD practitioner becomes clearer about the essence of the culture and can sort out what needs to be maintained, if not strengthened, and what needs to change.

For an organization to develop (see definitions of *development* in the opening paragraph of this chapter), then, change must occur, but this does not mean that *any* change will do. Using the term *development* to mean change does not, for example, mean growth. Russell Ackoff's distinction is quite useful and relevant to our understanding of what the *D* in OD means:

Growth can take place with or without development (and vice versa). For example, a cemetery can grow without developing; so can a rubbish heap. A nation, corporation, or an individual can develop without growing.... [Development] is an increase in capacity and potential, not an increase in attainment.... It has less to do with how much one has than with how much one can do with whatever one has (Ackoff, 1981: 34–35).

OD, therefore, is a process of bringing to the surface those implicit behavioral patterns that are helping and hindering development. Bringing these patterns of conformity to organization members' conscious awareness puts them in a position to reinforce the behaviors that help development and change those that hinder. OD practitioners help clients to help themselves.

More specifically, OD practitioners are concerned with change that integrates individual needs with organizational goals more fully; change that improves an organization's effectiveness through better utilization of resources, especially human resources; and change that involves organization members more in the decisions that directly affect them and their working conditions.

At least by implication and occasionally directly, we shall define OD several times throughout this book. The following general definition provides a starting point: Organization development is a planned process of change in an organization's culture through the utilization of behavioral science technologies, research, and theory.

What if an organization's culture does not need any change? Then OD is neither relevant nor appropriate. Organization development is not all things to all organizations. It is useful only when some fundamental change is needed. Then how does one recognize when fundamental change is needed? Perhaps the clearest sign is when the same kinds of problems keep occurring. No sooner does one problem get solved than another just like it surfaces. Another sign is when a variety of techniques is used to increase productivity, for example, and none seems to work. Yet another is when morale among employees is low and the cause can be attributed to no single factor. These are but a few signs. The point is that OD ultimately is a process of getting at organizational root causes, not just treating symptoms.

To be clear: Much of what is called OD is the use of OD techniques—off-site team building, training, facilitation of ad hoc meetings; providing private and individual feedback to managers and executives; and so on—but not in our purist definition. According to our definition, organization development provides fundamental change in the way things are done, modifying the essence of organizational culture. Many, perhaps most, practitioners, therefore, are conducting sessions and processes that rely on OD technology—and that's fine. But using OD techniques is not necessarily providing organization development.

A Total System Approach

The target for change is the organization—the total system, not necessarily individual members (Burke & Schmidt, 1971). Individual change is typically a consequence of system change. When a norm, a dimension of the organization's culture, is changed, individual behavior is modified by the new conforming pattern. Organization development is a total system approach to change.

Most practitioners agree that OD is an approach to a total system and that an organization is a sociotechnical system (Trist, 1960). Every organization has a technology, whether it is producing something tangible or rendering a service; a subsystem of the total organization, technology represents an integral part of the culture. Every organization is also composed of people who interact to accomplish tasks; the human dimension constitutes the social subsystem. The emphasis of this book is on the social subsystem, but both subsystems and their interaction must be considered in any effort toward organizational change.

The case at the beginning of this chapter illustrates the sociotechnical qualities or dimensions of an organization. The problem between the engineering and manufacturing groups was both technical (out-of-date machinery) and social (lack of cooperation). The case also illustrates another important point. A cardinal rule of OD is to begin any consultation with what the client considers to be the problem or deems critical, not necessarily what the consultant considers important. Later, the consultant can recommend or advocate specific changes, but the consultant begins as a facilitator.

Whether the consultant's role should encompass advocacy as well as facilitation is in dispute within the field of OD. Practitioners and academicians are divided according to their views of OD as contingent or as normative. The contingent camp argues that OD practitioners should only facilitate change; according to their view, the client determines the direction of change, and the OD practitioner helps the client get there. The normative camp, significantly smaller, argues that, although the approach to OD should be facilitative at the beginning, before long the practitioner should begin to recommend, if not argue for, specific directions for change. We place ourselves in the normative camp, the minority. Although we are taking a position, we shall make every attempt to be comprehensive and as objective as possible in our coverage of OD.

In the consultative case introduced previously, I (Burke) dealt almost exclusively for more than nine months with what the client considered to be the central problems and issues. As I became more confident about what I considered to be not just symptoms but causes, I began to argue for broader and more directed change. Until then we had been putting out fires, not stopping arson. Although the organization was correcting problems, it was not learning a different *way* of solving problems—that is, learning how to change, the essence of OD. This essence has been elaborated on by Argyris and Schön (1978), who call it *organizational learning*, and by Senge (1990). According to Senge, for organizational learning to occur, members and especially managers and executives must develop systems thinking. To understand complex managerial problems, one has to visualize the organization as a whole, how one aspect of the system affects another within an overall pattern. These ideas are highly compatible and consistent with what we mean by OD.

When a consultant takes a position, regardless of how well founded, he or she risks encountering resistance. This obviously happened in the case I described earlier. I didn't consult much longer than the first nine months. As it turned out, I did help; the division did turn around in time to keep the corporate vice president from acting on his threat to close the plant unless quality and delivery time were improved. As a consultant, I take satisfaction in this outcome. From an OD perspective, however, I consider that my work was a failure. That assessment stems from two perspectives, one concerning research and the other concerning values.

Research evidence regarding organizational change is now very clear. Change rarely if ever can be effected by treating symptoms, and organizational change will not occur if effort is directed at trying to change individual members. The direction of change should be toward the personality of the organization, not the personality of the individual. My knowledge of the research evidence, my realization in the consultation case that a modification in the organization's reward system was not likely, and my acceptance that OD, by definition, means change led me to conclude that, in the final analysis, I had not accomplished organization development.

The values that underlie organization development include humanistic and collaborative approaches to changing organizational life. Although not all OD practitioners would agree, decentralizing power is part of OD for most organizations. In the consultation case, it seemed that providing first-line supervisors with more alternatives for rewarding their workers positively not only was more humanistic but would allow them more discretionary and appropriate power and authority for accomplishing their supervisory responsibilities. Changing the reward system was the appropriate avenue as far as I was concerned, but this change was not to be and, for my part, neither was OD.

By way of summary, let us continue to define what OD is by considering some of the field's primary characteristics. The following five characteristics serve as a listing so far; thus we have just begun:

1. Our primary theoretical father is Kurt Lewin. We begin summarizing his work in Chapter 3, "Where Did Organization Development Come From?," and continue in Chapter 4, "Organization Development as a Process of Change." His "field theory" is derived from physics and states that human behavior can be understood as reactions to forces in our environment that influence us one way or the other. But it is not just environmental forces. Each of us as individuals have a personality the sum total of who we are as human beings. Lewin puts these two elements, personality and environment, together in a simple formula—Bf P/E: Behavior is a function of the interaction between personality and how one perceives his or her

environment. Thus, we cannot understand human behavior unless we take into account *both* personality and context. The organization serves as context and the organizational member has a personality. As OD practitioners, we must attempt to understand individual behavior through the eyes of that individual, how she or he interprets the context and how the person's personality helps to explain her or his behavior accordingly. There is much more to Lewin but his formula explaining behavior is fundamental. As authors of this book, we are in part Lewinians.

2. Besides field theory, there is system theory to which we subscribe. Organizations are open systems with input, throughput, and output with a feedback loop. This means that we consider the roots of organizational issues and problems to be primarily systemic in nature, thus the problems we seek to solve do not reside with individuals who are idiots but with systems that are idiotic.

3. Our work in OD must be data-based; otherwise, we come across as opinionated with no real basis for our opinions. Our data may be either qualitative or quantitative, preferably both, and grounded in what we learn from clients.

4. Our clients have the solutions to their problems. They may not know it at the outset; therefore, our job is to help our clients find the solution—not hand a solution to them.

5. And perhaps most important of all, we are values-based regarding OD practice, but there are many values to which we subscribe, and it is therefore important for us to know what our priorities are. Is treating people respectfully more important than resolving conflict? And when does the bottom line and/or meeting our budget demands take precedence?

Conclusion

What we have just stated is likely to raise many more questions than answers. But we have only begun. Let us move on now to more clarity and, we hope, answers. In the next chapter, we explore a broader context for OD as a way of clarifying further the work of OD practitioners and the domain of their work for the future.

2

Organization Development
Then and Now

The purpose of this chapter is to consider trends in the external environment that have had and will have a significant impact on organization development. To specify these important trends, this chapter revisits in a condensed form the original Chapter 2 from 1994 and then in the second half addresses what has happened since in terms of major events in the last 20 years, for example, 9/11, followed by current trends and movements in our society that have implications for organization development (OD).

Some Significant Changes Between 1969 and 1994

Perhaps the most significant event to affect the field of OD, at least from an economic if not competence perspective, was the oil embargo and recession of 1972–1973. Organizations cut back, especially in the "soft" areas of training and human resource development. Many OD consultants had to change labels. The less experienced and less competent were weeded out. By 1994, OD practitioners, especially those who survived the economically tough times around 1973 and remained in OD, were more competent. Those newer to the field had taken advantage of the greater pool of knowledge about OD to quickly learn the concepts and skills required to practice OD effectively.

With respect to organizational dynamics and approaches to management in general, there were at least nine significant shifts between 1969 and 1994 (see Table 2.1).

Table 2.1 Significant Shifts in Organizational Dynamics and Management Between 1969 and 1994

From	To
Growth	Consolidation
Moderate speed	Warp speed
Moderate complexity	High complexity
Strategic planning	Strategic implementation
Consultant jargon	Popular, accepted concepts
Management	Leadership
Unilateral, top-down management	Multilateral, participative management
Little concern for ethics	High concern for ethics
Micro	Macro

From Growth to Decline to Consolidation

Perhaps the biggest change is that organizational growth, while not a thing of the past, was far more limited by 1994. Growth was limited to certain industries and entrepreneurial activities and was not nearly as widespread as during the 1960s. Moreover, competition in 1994 was far keener than a quarter of a century before and occurred not just from around the corner, but worldwide. The pressure on many businesses was to become *global;* they must not only be more efficient, but also be able to compete more effectively.

In addition to the global movement, *consolidation* was a primary goal of corporate management by 1994. Executives were working harder to determine their corporations' core business and then to shed those divisions that did not fit the defined core. It also seemed that core or not, many businesses were being shed simply because of their inadequate profitability.

Another form of consolidation is the merger or acquisition. This form of consolidation occurred in the pharmaceutical industry, which had traditionally involved a great many firms with a strong market leader. Merck & Co., the market leader at the time, accounted for less than 20 percent of the world market; the remainder of the market was divided among hundreds of other players. In such an industry, some joining up became the logical thing to do (Burke & Jackson, 1991; Burke & Biggart, 1997).

The movement from managing growth toward managing consolidation had implications for the organization consultant. In 1969, we did a lot of team building; today, even more is required. Consultants needed to be highly knowledgeable and skilled about such matters as:

- The psychological consequences of "downsizing"—layoffs—on both employees who are let go and those who remain. (See, for example, Brockner, 1988; and Brockner et al., 1986.)

- Downsizing with the least amount of psychological pain (Brockner, 1992).

- Designing and managing flatter organizational structures. The old maxim that an optimum span of control is 7, 8, or 9 is just that—*old*. OD consultants needed to know how to help managers deal with 15, 20, or even 50 direct reports, not a mere 7 subordinates. This meant, for example, that they must be knowledgeable about semiautonomous and self-managed work groups (Hackman, 1989).

- Defining core competencies required to execute a corporation's core businesses. This required on the part of OD consultants (1) knowledge about the business and (2) the ability to determine (by means of interview, observational, and analytical skills) whether individual organizational members possess the requisite competencies.

- The particular nature of the client's business itself, the larger industry in which the business is a player, and the primary factors that cause ups and downs in that industry, such as seasonal differences, changing government regulations, and changing technology. A chief executive officer (CEO) at the time said that the number-one value of his human resource chief (a Ph.D. I/O psychologist) was the fact that he knows, studies, and cares about the business.

This list provides only a taste of the knowledge and skills OD consultants needed to work effectively in the world of leaner, flatter, tighter, and bottom-line focused organizations.

Implication for OD: Practitioners are expected to be competent about how to lead and manage organization change.

Time: From Moderate to Warp Speed

Everything seemed to be at a faster pace those days, even organization change. Change occurred rapidly when precipitated by traumatic events, such as a leveraged buyout, an acquisition, a sudden downturn in the market, or a scandal. Even organizational cultures seemed to change more rapidly. Although not everyone was convinced that culture can be changed at all, we were convinced. Having been involved from 1985 to 1990 in the effort of British Airways (BA) to change from a government agency to a private corporation, it is clear that significant change in BA's culture did indeed occur (Goodstein & Burke, 1991; Burke, 2014b) in just five years.

In a related effort that shaped a newly merged culture from two different businesses (in somewhat the same industry) and two different nationalities (British and American), the time required was less than three years (see Burke & Jackson, 1991; Bauman, Jackson, & Lawrence, 1997).

Unequivocal documentation of the comparative times needed for culture change is not possible and is less to the point than the fact that applying what we have learned about culture change (see, for example, the book by Kotter & Heskett, 1992) may expedite change. It is clear that executive clients expect faster change. Moreover, CEOs themselves today rarely have five or more years to manage such a change.

Those of us who claimed to be organization consultants needed to be knowledgeable about the nature of organization culture (see such books as Deal & Kennedy, 1982; Sashkin & Kiser, 1993; Schein, 2004; Frost et al., 1991) and skillful in applying such knowledge (see, for example, Lawler & Worley, 2006; Nadler et al., 1992).

Unlike the way many of us were trained, we could not wait for more evidence before offering advice or direction to clients. Although the client may have seemed to have been moving too rapidly, without sufficient documentation, even half-cocked, we as consultants were expected to respond, to help. Managers then and today are admonished to be innovative, to take risks, and to act more quickly.

Implication for OD: Like our clients, we must be willing to take risks as well.

From Moderate Complexity to Even Greater Complexity

Complexity has been with us for quite some time—and remains. In the late '80s, Kanter (1989), for example, expressed complexity in the form of paradoxes. Her list from back then is amazingly relevant for our organizational world today. Consider the following demands facing managers and executives that she listed back then:

- Be entrepreneurial and take risks—but don't cost the business anything by failure.
- Continue to do everything you're currently doing, even better—and spend more time communicating with employees, serving on teams, and launching new products.
- Speak up, be a leader, set the direction—but be participative, listen well, and cooperate.
- Succeed, succeed, succeed—and raise terrific children.

Corporations as well face escalating and seemingly incompatible demands, according to Kanter:

- Get "lean and mean" through restructuring—while being a great company to work for and offering employee-centered policies, such as job security.
- Encourage creativity and innovation to take you in new directions—and "stick to your knitting."
- Communicate a sense of urgency and push for faster execution, faster results—but take more time to deliberately plan for the future.

We add to the list of paradoxes, several slanted more toward the OD consultant's world:

- We organizational and psychological consultants are becoming specialists even as organizational conceptualization is moving more toward systemic and holistic thinking.
- Organization members experience more stress than ever due to change and, consequently, have a desire for some stability, yet chaos is more likely to be the new norm.

- With tougher times facing most organizations, *how* one manages is as important as achieving results.

- Organizational members cry out for leadership and direction, yet demand more participation.

- There is more talk than ever about vision, mission, new directions, values, and promises to customers, yet one of the most significant issues concerning top management today is that so many managers and executives do *not* "walk the talk," as the expression goes.

- Competition in business is keener than ever, yet there is a clear movement afoot, especially in mature industries, to join with the enemy via strategic alliances and joint ventures—witness IBM and Apple, at the time.

- OD consultants seem to be moving more toward "traditional management consulting" (that is, concern with business matters) and traditional consultants seem to be moving more toward the "soft" domains (that is, concern with process issues).

These baffling contradictions can not only be confusing, but at times perhaps immobilizing, yet it is important in our complex world of OD to embrace paradox and seeming inconsistencies. Turning to the natural sciences can be helpful to our understanding. The theorizing of Ilya Prigogine (Nicolis & Prigogine, 1977) and the subsequent writings of Erich Jantsch (1980) are relevant to our understanding of change. They state that to understand evolution, you must focus more on disequilibrium than on equilibrium, the implication being that change is not linear. Jantsch also contended that evolution is accelerating, just as the overall process of change appears to be. This theory has been heralded by some as a paradigmatic shift comparable to Einstein's move away from Newton.

Just as Einstein's theory of relativity wrested the physical sciences away from Newton's static ideas of gravity, Jantsch's ideas challenge us to view movement, relativity, and change in living systems as *constant*. He argued that all living things are always coevolving, yet maintaining a "relativity" to one another. Both Jantsch and Prigogine believed that the disequilibrium and perturbation that arise from time to time in living things are actually a kind of "molting," a shedding of the old within organisms as they strive to attain a higher level of existence. These perturbations, activities of disequilibrium, are signs of positive change that lead to self-organization rather than to decline. (See Chapter 5, "Defining the Client: A Different Perspective," for more elaboration on the work of Prigogine and Jantsch as well as that of Fritjof Capra.)

From an organization change perspective, this theory reminds us of Greiner's (1972) ideas about the life cycle of organizations as well as the work of Adizes (1979). At times, organization change should occur like a perturbation or a leap in the life cycle of the organization, not as an incremental process. The management of the change should be incremental, but not always the initiation of the change itself.

Implication for OD: Accepting the complexity of paradox and being grounded in theory beyond organizational theory may be helpful to our understanding of organization development and change.

From Strategic Planning to Strategic Implementation

Strategic planning was not passé at the time, but executives had to learn that planning is about 10 percent of the effort to change an organization, whereas implementing the plan, the tougher part of the job by far, requires the remaining 90 percent of the effort. Here, the work of Lawler and Worley (2006) in their book, *Built to Change,* is useful. They emphasize that strategic planning as we have known it, a planned event that often is conducted once a year, is inappropriate for today's fast-paced world of business. Rather, strategic planning should be a daily process—not an event—and the more appropriate term, therefore, needs to be *strategizing,* which puts the focus on constant change (and "changing"), not a singular once-in-a-while activity. Thus, managing change is, as a routine, the emphasis today (see Chapter 7, "The Burke-Litwin Model of Organizational Performance and Change").

Implication for OD: The more an OD effort is aligned with the organization's strategy, the better.

From Consultant Jargon to Popular, Accepted Concepts

The language of organizations has changed. Years ago, clients would ask what was meant by *culture;* today, they use the term before we do. *Value* is another term that clients use before we do as well as *vision, mission, climate,* and *leadership.* We welcome this language change, yet are uneasy about it because even after many years of OD, we are not certain that we truly understand these terms or concepts. Do clients really understand these terms they so loosely bandy about?

Clients today use OD jargon quite easily, yet are very uneven in their level of understanding and commitment to the action the words betoken. Thus although they all may use the words, not all act on them. Even though most use the terms, some remain skeptical about, if not resistant to, change.

Implication for OD: Clients may not always know in depth the words about change that they use, but assume that they are more sophisticated than a decade or so ago.

From Management to Leadership

In 1969, leadership was not mentioned very often. It was not considered unimportant, but the term simply was seldom used. Today, leadership and its distinctions from management are discussed and debated frequently (see, for example, Bennis & Nanus, 1985; Burke, 1986; Zaleznik, 1977). The leadership function is not only highlighted more today, but it is also emphasized by many in the context of bringing about organizational change.

Implication for OD: Initiating change needs leadership; implementing change needs management.

From Unilateral, Top-Down Management to Multilateral, Participative Management

Organizational members today are less tolerant of the arbitrary use of power than was true in the past. And while conflict resolution and effectiveness in lateral relations were acknowledged as important in 1969, they are viewed by most executives as critical for effective organizational functioning today. This shift is due in part to (1) more decentralized authority and flatter hierarchies, where getting work done depends more on influence skills than on the exercise of power as a function of status or position; (2) the emphasis being given

to collaborative, joint approaches to labor-management relations as opposed to adversarial ones; and (3) the occurrence of mergers and acquisitions, where achieving integration or at least some degree of smooth working relationships is important. This trend is covered in more depth in Chapter 10, "Understanding and Changing Loosely Coupled Systems."

Implication for OD: Remember the OD mantra: "involvement leads to commitment."

From Little Concern for Ethics to a High Concern for Ethics

In part, at least, increased competition has no doubt caused some managers to cut corners. Scandals either occur more frequently today or they are more likely to be exposed than was true in the past. Many managers are therefore caught in the vise (if not paradox) between meeting targets more rapidly than ever before and with less cost and emphasizing high quality. The two do not have to be mutually exclusive. In fact, managers are perhaps more wary about short-term measures, knowing that in the long run a large price will be paid one way or the other. Yet, they feel the pressure.

OD consultants are on occasion put in the position of serving as conscience for the client. This is an uncomfortable role, to be sure, but can be quite helpful. Sometimes managers simply need to be reminded of the ethics of a situation. When reminded, they often feel relieved that someone will support their doing the right thing. We cover this topic again later in the chapter.

Implication for OD: Although we may differ about a definition of OD, in the end it is about being values-based.

From a Micro Perspective to a Macro Perspective

The shift from micro to macro perspective since 1969 is perhaps more specific to the practice of OD than to management or organizational dynamics in general. In the 1960s, OD practitioners viewed organizational issues mostly in terms of individuals and small groups (sensitivity training, T-groups, management development), whereas today OD practitioners take a larger, more systematic perspective (reward systems, strategic planning, structure, management information systems). This shift is far more realistic for purposes of organizational change.

Implication for OD: A recent study comparing values of OD practitioners reported in 1994 compared with 2014 (Shull, Church, & Burke, 2014) showed that OD practitioners have shifted yet again but now back to micro activities; for example, leader development, coaching, and training. This is a concern because OD is usually defined as systemic change; that is, more macro than micro.

The nine shifts described here are not the only ones since 1969, but they are the most significant for OD. OD practitioners are in the business of change and they involve people in decisions and activities that directly affect them. These nine shifts concern in various ways organization change and differences in the way people are managed.

The New Corporation

To broaden our context regarding changes since 1969, let us consider briefly the work of John Naisbett. Naisbett's best seller *Megatrends* (1982) caused readers to think about the changing nature of organizations. His later book, coauthored with Patricia Aburdene (Naisbett & Aburdene, 1985), was more to the point of organizational shifts, however. The following list is their observations of how the corporation was being reinvented at that time:

1. The best and brightest people will gravitate toward those corporations that foster personal growth.
2. The manager's role is that of coach, teacher, and mentor.
3. The best people want ownership—psychic and literal—in a company; the best companies are providing it.
4. Companies will increasingly turn to third-party contractors, shifting from hired labor to contract labor.
5. Authoritarian management is yielding to networking, people-style management.
6. Entrepreneurship within the corporation—"intra-preneurship"—is creating new revitalizing companies inside out.

7. Quality will be paramount.
8. Intuition and creativity are challenging the "It's all in the numbers" business-school philosophy.
9. Large corporations are emulating the positive and productive qualities of small business.
10. The dawn of the information economy has fostered a massive shift from infrastructure to quality of life (pp. 45–46).

It seems clear that Naisbett and Aburdene's observations regarding the future of the corporation had a prescient quality with the possible exception of their last two—large corporations emulating a small business and a shift to quality of life—their "reinventions" of the corporation are fairly accurate. And even though characterized by considerable foresight, the work of Naisbett and Aburdene was in the early to mid-1980s. Much has happened since then and since the publication of the second edition of this book in 1994. Thus, the remainder of this chapter is devoted to events, trends, and movements since 1994 that have affected our world, in general, and OD in particular.

Significant Changes Since 1994

What follows is our current list of nine trends or movements since 1994 that no doubt have emerged over the past two decades or so as consequences one way or the other from big events. At the top of the events list would be 9/11, followed by long-standing wars in Iraq and Afghanistan, the 2008 financial crisis, the emergence of the Tea Party, the election of the first African American as president of the United States, and climate change. This is not a complete list by any means, but more of an illustration of how much has changed and how significant and impactful these events have been. But with respect to these big events since 1994, and our list of trends since then to follow, it is not clear what is cause and what is effect. To link a trend, say, more caution regarding major business decisions, to the 2008 financial crisis might be an attractive hypothesis, but such a suggestion would be purely speculative and probably unwarranted. Our main objective, then, is to identify trends irrespective of the causes behind them but rather to provide context and to draw an implication or two for OD now and in the future.

Before plunging into our inventory of trends and movements over the past 20 or so years, let us consider briefly one other declaration for the purpose of providing additional context—the constancy of change. Change has always been with us, a constant of life, so what is new? The growing recognition and *acceptance*, finally, of this constancy. Instead of two inevitabilities—death and taxes—we now have added a third—change.

With these matters of context as background, let us now move to the foreground of changes since 1994 or what might be labeled as shifts, trends, or movements in our society that have implications for OD. In other words, these nine trends are not *the* nine; rather, they emerged for us as the ones that may be the most impactful regarding OD. Thus, for each case, we end with *"Implication for OD"* as we did in the section on trends between 1969 and 1994. In no particular order, the following sections explore the nine trends that we think are important for the field.

Agile, Nimble, and Quick

With competition being as tough as ever, technology that is ever-changing, and consumer preferences seeming to bend with the wind, organizations whether in the corporate world, government agencies, nongovernment organizations (NGO), or nonprofits, in general, are expected to be responsive and quick to do so. A spate of books covering this ability to be nimble and agile has brought to the table advice, admonitions, and ideas about the subject. Brief summaries of those books are provided in Chapter 14, "Organization Development and the Future," which will be part of our coverage about the future.

Understanding agility over the past five years more deeply has led to several faculty and doctoral students in the social-organizational psychology program at Teachers College, Columbia University, attempting to measure behaviorally the concept of learning agility for more than five years. So by adding this work, we are not just making observations and commentary, but have joined the trend ourselves. Learning agility, an intriguing concept, is not easy to define, much less measure. There are two primary components—the key idea or *concept* and one's *motivation*. The concept of agility means being agile particularly when confronted with a new and different situation. The learning aspect concerns whether what one has learned from experience, how one thinks and behaves, is applicable to the new and different situation and if not, what does one then do? Motivation concerns one's willingness to take risks in attempting to deal with a novel situation when not knowing exactly what to do. In addition to risk-taking is seeking feedback about how one is doing regardless of how threatening this action might be to one's self esteem. Other relevant terms include flexibility, speed, and avoiding being defensive—that is, justifying one's actions regardless of the uniqueness of the situation. Learning agility, therefore, is the combination of *motivation*, willingness to engage and stay engaged with a novel situation, and the *skill* to discern quickly the consequences of one's actions and then determine what to do next in order to continue the process of learning.

This brief coverage of learning agility is expanded in Chapter 14 regarding the future. Thus, because of its importance, agility, being quick and nimble, is covered twice, here in terms of a clear trend that has implications for OD and again in our final chapter, where agility is one of four important considerations for the future.

Implication for OD: This trend is highly compatible with the objectives and values of OD. After all, OD people are usually advocates of change; thus, helping people in the workplace to be more agile is fundamental to the practice. This means finding ways and means behaviorally for organizational members to learn to feel more comfortable with embracing ambiguity and to experiment and take risks with new and different ideas. And assuming that increased agility leads to greater organizational adaptability and less rigidity, which in turn can lead to more innovation, perhaps we in the field should go so far as to be advocates for enhancing these kinds of behaviors.

The Haves Versus the Have Nots

This trend of more and more of a chasm between the highly wealthy and the rest of us strikes at the heart of individual beliefs and values. When 1 percent control most of the wealth in the world and when "CEOs enjoy incomes that are on average 295 times that of the typical worker, a much higher ratio than in the past, without any evidence of a proportionate increase in productivity" (Stiglitz, 2014, p. SR 7), people pay attention. Supposedly we in the United States live in a democracy, not an oligarchy. Moreover, the financial crisis of 2008 raised issues about how money is made and accumulated. It is not that the value system of OD practitioners resides in the domain of socialism, but it does advocate fairness and social justice. Incidentally, this issue of inequity is not merely one for profit-making corporations. Discrepancy and inequity exist as well in universities, health-care systems, religious institutions, and in the U.S. Congress. The economist and Nobel laureate, Joseph Stiglitz, quoted above, argues that the problem of inequality is more about politics than economics. It is a matter of ensuring that the haves pay their fair share of taxes. He goes on to state that "We are not embracing a politics of envy if we reverse a politics of greed....[it's] the right to justice for all." (Stiglitz, 2014, p. SR 7).

Implication for OD: Later in the book, Chapter 12, "The Organization Development Consultant," addresses more specifically values that underlie the field of OD. For now, it is important to understand that high on the list of values are fairness and equity in the workplace. In the early stages of OD work, facilitation is more the norm than advocacy. Except for declaring our "point of view" about how we normally work (follow a particular framework or model of organization change, for example), we typically facilitate what the client wants. At some later stage, however, we may choose to take a position about what the organization should do. In the case described in Chapter 1, "What Is Organization Development?," after several months of work, the consultant argued for changing the organization's reward system. The client resisted such a change and the consulting work with that organization soon ended. It may be, nevertheless, that in this growing world of inequity, confronting such issues could be considered appropriate, at least from the standpoint of acting consistently with OD values. But the tactic in this case would not necessarily be one of declaring that the CEO's compensation is way out of line, making it nothing more than a moral issue, but instead stating that the compensation discrepancy does no doubt lead to a feeling of unfairness on the part of employees, which may affect morale and a decrease in motivation and in turn eventually have an impact on organizational performance; that is, the bottom line. This kind of consultant action combines an inequity problem with a very practical business issue.

Cautious Decision Making

Organizations of all types are more cautious about making decisions requiring large expenditures. This is particularly true of corporations. Major companies are "sitting on" tons of cash. Perhaps the financial crisis of 2008 is the culprit here, but time has passed with no further crises—at least none in the world of finance. Mergers and acquisitions are back in vogue, thus some of the dormant money is being spent on buying other companies. This return to mergers and acquisitions is in spite of the dismal record regarding these kinds of deals; that is, the consequences are more likely to result in "wealthy destruction" than wealth enhancement—see, for example, Moeller, Schlingemann, and Stulz (2005) in the academic literature and a more recent summary article in *The New York Times* by Sommer (2014).

Implication for OD: Practitioners in OD can help to promote the fact that knowledge exists about what works and what doesn't when attempting to integrate two organizations for the first time; that is, a merger but much more often an acquisition. Serving on a National Research Council task force for the Academy of Science, Burke and Biggart (1997) conducted a study of interorganizational relations, including mergers and acquisitions. They found that upwards of 75 percent of mergers and acquisitions fail; that is, fall short of accomplishing the goals set forth in justifying the decision to come together. Their study included a summary of what contributes to success regarding a merger or acquisition, for example, having a clear vision about the "new" organization and what can be expected, and what contributes to failure, for example, an imbalance of power between the two parties. In other words, when an organization does decide to spend its cash reserves on an acquisition, OD professionals can help to make it a success.

Another opportunity for an OD practitioner to capitalize on this trend would be to advocate the organization's investing in its people. There might be an opportunity to "sell" a program or initiative that would help the organization to have more competent employees.

Some examples include improving procedures and criteria for selecting high potentials for leadership, establishing a long-term program for leader development, revising the performance management and reward system to focus not only on results but on *how* those results are achieved as well, and perhaps a program on group and cross-cultural dynamics. Experienced OD practitioners are likely to be primed to deliver on these kinds of people development possibilities.

Emphasis on Innovation

As long as the United States has been a sovereign nation, there has been an emphasis on innovation. When he was president and commander in chief of the U.S. Army, Abraham Lincoln was constantly interested in new weapons for the war. We remain a nation of innovators. Yet with global competition continuing to increase and the math and science scores of our schoolchildren not being sufficiently a match for children in other countries, the pressure on being innovative is on the rise. Interestingly, we could have a problem with caution regarding major decisions compared with this innovation trend because the latter requires at least some degree of risk-taking. Even though risk-taking is involved, it takes different forms depending on the type of innovation that is being pursued. There are at least three forms or levels of innovation for organizations: (1) things, (2) the ways work is done in the organization, and (3) competition for the organization within its industry. Innovation with things means developing new or improved products and services. IDEO is a successful consulting firm that provides innovation for client organizations by designing a new or modified product or service for their clients. A second form of innovation is to change ways and means of working in order to compete more effectively in the organization's markets. Improving quality by way of a Six Sigma program would be an example. A third form is to change the way an organization competes in its respective industry. An example of this third form is represented by the work of Clayton Christensen (1997) and Christensen and Raynor (2003). Christensen's assessment of competition within industry groups rests on the notion that successful companies doing everything right— serving customers well, constantly improving the ways they conduct their business, and so on—are susceptible to competitors who are minor players entering their market(s) with cheaper products that are lower in quality; yet over time, these smaller competitors begin to encroach into the larger company's territory. The larger, more successful company continues to do business the way they have been for years. Why should they change? Their ways work. But this "disruptive innovation," as Christensen calls it, gradually gains a competitive edge and then wreaks havoc for the larger, more successful company. Examples of companies that got caught in this disruption include Sears, Digital Equipment Corporation, Xerox, and AT&T.

In passing, it should be noted that even though Christensen's books have been best sellers and that he has disciples everywhere, his theory of change has been criticized as founded on panic, anxiety, and shaky evidence. A primary critic, historian Jill Lepore, puts it this way:

> Disruptive innovation is a theory about why businesses fail. It's not more than that. It doesn't explain change. It's not a law of nature. It's an artifact of history, an idea, forged in time; it's the manufacture of a moment of upsetting and edgy uncertainty. Transfixed by change, it's blind to continuity. It makes a very poor profit (Lepore, 2014, p. 36).

Businesses do fail for lack of innovation, but these failures may not occur quite the way that Christensen depicts them. The point is that with more emphasis on innovation, we must get it right.

Implication for OD: Innovation involves change. OD is about change. This trend is, therefore, good for OD—of the three forms or levels of innovation described above, the latter two are more within the practice of OD. Improving products and services involves design skills that most OD practitioners do not have. OD practitioners can be useful in helping to change ways of doing things, processes, and procedures because these factors are endemic to the organization's culture. OD practitioners must be culture experts. Off-site team-building sessions can be appropriate activities for changing processes, so can resolving intergroup conflict, and work-out sessions.

With respect to the third area of innovation, the organization's relation to its industry, OD practitioners can be helpful here as well. Any OD effort should begin with an assessment of the organization's external environment. What forces "out there" are having an impact on the organization—industry competitors, government regulations, changes in technology, and so forth? Helping executives to craft scenarios about which forces to tackle and how to deal with them is a worthy endeavor and should be done early in an OD process— see Chapter 2 in Lawler and Worley (2006) for ideas and suggestions for conducting environmental scenarios followed by "strategizing" in Chapter 3.

More often than not, OD practice involves innovation, or at least it should. The work is about change, whether an effort is transformational or one that focuses on improving what exists.

Greater Dispersion of Power and Politics

At a global level with the possible exceptions of North Korea, certain nation states in Africa, and arguably Russia, power is not as concentrated in one person or office as in the past. And the political world is in many respects deadlocked with little agreement among parties and thus unable to get important issues on the agenda, much less move legislation forward. These statements are not meant to be hyperbolic; moreover, there is evidence to support them. The primary evidence comes from a book, *The End of Power*, by Moisés Naim (2013). The subtitle of the book conveys the range of coverage— *From Boardroom to Battlefields and Churches to States, Why Being in Charge Isn't What It Used To Be*. Naim attributes these shifts in power, or revolutions, to the "3Ms"—*more, mobility*, and *mentality*. Here are brief definitions and the main point for each:

- *More*. Profusion is the operative concept. There is more of everything, everywhere—more people, cities, countries, armies (large and small), political parties, goods and services with more businesses selling them, more weapons, computers, criminals, and iPhones. Naim also notes that the more people have, the more they want. People are living longer, and with many exceptions, are enjoying healthier lives. What's the point? "*When people are more numerous and living fuller lives, they become more difficult to regiment and control*" (Naim, 2013, p. 58— italics in the original).

- *Mobility*. People are on the move. Migration continues at a rapid pace with people searching for a better life. As noted above, there are more cities with urbanization accelerating, particularly in Asia. Borders between countries (take Europe, for example) are becoming more porous. Social media facilitate this increase in mobility. Practically everyone has access to the Internet. What's the point? *With such mobility and access to information, people are harder to control*.

- *Mentality.* This shift or revolution is all about expectations that people around the globe now have. This is especially true for the middle class, which is expanding in the less-developed countries, but shrinking in the more wealthy countries (see the previous section on the haves and have nots). Where expansion is occurring, there is a consequent quest for more education. And with greater education, expectations, or developing a mental set of having a *right* for more, increase. Rising expectations create demands. What's the point? *For people holding positions of power, it is becoming more and more difficult for them to meet expectations that their constituents have and will have in the future.*

All one has to do is travel the world to see that Naim is largely correct in what he proclaims. In addition, the Endnotes of his book that provide support for his points comprise 20 pages. Power may not be ending, but it is changing, becoming more dispersed with less of the qualities of command and control and authoritarianism.

Implication for OD: Involvement of individuals in the making of decisions that directly affect them and a bias toward participative management have been long-standing values and arguments of professionals in the field of OD. Sharing power and shared leadership are further manifestations of these values and biases. Thus, the dispersion of power is largely welcomed by OD professionals. But there are at least two resultant issues. One concerns loosely coupled systems where power is dispersed and, therefore, understanding how to work with these kinds of organizations where hierarchy barely exists if at all, as in say, a network, is highly important. In our OD practice, it is clear that we know more about how to loosen a tightly coupled system than to tighten a loose one. Chapter 10 is devoted to this issue.

A second issue concerns the nature of authority. Getting things done with people requires dealing with the reality of the exercise of power, which in turn involves leadership, management, and authority in one form or another. Knowing how to deal with issues of authority is critical to the success of any OD effort. The fundamental question is: Who among us is authorized to do our bidding? When *authorizing* someone, what does that process entail and what does it look like? Authorizing means that someone or a number of people are "given the right" (the operative term) by the larger group or system to make decisions on behalf of that larger system. Authorizing or giving the right may be temporary or more permanent, but the expectation is that having been given this right should not be taken for granted. These are the kinds of issues and questions that must be addressed by OD practitioners as the revolution of power in the world shifts.

More Emphasis on Talent Management

We can remember the day when TM stood for "transcendental meditation"; today, it is *talent management*. Organizations around the world are competing for talent. Our information age demands that employees have more than one skill, are interpersonally competent, and know something. If they do not know something, they at least know how to find what they need to know, and this does not mean always relying on Google or Wikipedia. It may mean attending a workshop or conference, taking a course, or pursing a graduate degree.

The management of talent follows a cycle:

- *Selection.* Understanding the criteria for finding the talent desired and needed and then actively recruiting them

- *Development.* Providing a variety of job/role experiences along with feedback and coaching regarding how they are doing so that learning can occur

- *Measurement.* Performance on the job as well as multi-rater feedback and assessment

- *Deployment.* Further assignments to ensure further growth and development especially cross-cultural experiences to learn from regarding issues of diversity and/or global opportunities

- *Incentives.* Providing incentives within a larger reward system that is competitive in the labor market

Implication for OD: Talent management is a natural for OD practitioners. Combining TM with OD, one in support of the other, means that OD is linked to the life force of the organization, its mission and strategy, and how to implement these organizational activities in the best possible way for the initiation and sustainment of change for the future. For example, it was critical to the success of the change at British Airways (BA) (see Chapter 7) to hire, place, and develop people who would be highly customer-focused and service-oriented. Because the airline industry, particularly for the front-line people—ticket counter agents, gate attendants, and cabin crew—is largely about emotional labor (dealing with customers at times under stressful circumstances), it is essential to get the right people in the right jobs.

The BA example is about talent in general and for large segments of the organization's members, but what if we are linking talent management to high potentials in the organization? This is often the case in large corporations. This differentiation raises the issue of high potentials versus those who are not yet valuable to the organization. A value of OD is that all organizational members should be treated equally in many important ways—involvement, engagement, provided with opportunities for growth and development, to name a few. TM based on high potentials is by definition discriminatory, so do we have a situation of OD versus TM? Church (2013) has addressed this question. His research indicated that high potentials in terms of engagement and related processes were not that different from others in management positions at least in the consumer products company that he studied. So, it may be that TM and OD can coexist peacefully. Parenthetically, Church (2014) in a more recent article provides such a possibility in his coverage of "the role of OD in strategic talent management." Following Church's (2013) lead, it would be enlightening to conduct similar studies in other organizations that are identifying high potentials and treating them differently.

The Ever-Changing World of Technology

There are at least four major developments in technology that have meaning for OD practitioners: *social media*, including the underlying foundation of the Internet and e-mail, of course, *data analysis, simulations*, and *information retrieval*.

The *social media* has been transformative. Part of the attraction of Twitter, Facebook, and so on is both the speed of contacts—we can reach one another in a matter of seconds—and the breadth of contacts with the possibility, for example, of forming networks for multiple purposes, like sharing common interests such as backpacking, scientific domains, the ever-popular spelunking, and so on, and the sharing of information among professional groups, not to mention the sharing of jokes, cartoons, and a favorite photograph or video. Smartphones, especially, have had an impact on organizational life; for example, colleagues will text each other in real time in meetings. It has given new meaning to what we think of as "undiscussables" or issues that are under the table (Marshak, 2006).

Data Analysis: Three terms that are highly relevant for OD capture this technology trend—Big Data, People Analytics, and algorithm. The term *algorithm* is not new, of course. It is in the dictionary and is defined as a set of rules for solving a problem in a finite number of steps, then finding the most significant common divisor, a "common denominator." It involves programming a computer to solve a specific problem. In this case, an algorithm is applied to Big Data and People Analytics, for purposes of solving complex problems. Big Data means what you would assume it to mean—BIG—huge volumes of data that are gathered into one or more sets to understand a problem more clearly than we could have done before; that is, "information that can't be processed or analyzed using traditional processes or tools" (Zikopoulos, Eaton, deRoos, Deutsch, & Lapis, 2012, p. 3). Enter algorithms. Now consider a situation for a company that may be puzzling. The overall economy, let's say, is on the rise, other companies in the same industry appear to be doing well, and consumer confidence is increasing, yet the company of interest has products where sales are flat with some even sinking, and competitive companies with similar products are doing well. Why? Using a Big Data approach, one would amass information about such factors as economic status, age range, educational level, degree of mobility, and so forth of the company's consumers; which products of the competitors are selling well and where geographically; inflation rate within the overall economy; new technology in the industry; and so on. One would then enter all of these data into an algorithmic computer program and search for commonalities, if any, across many sources. If common divisors emerge, they may provide clues as to what action to take.

People Analytics is about applying Big Data to issues, problems, and operations in general that concern human resources, typically in large organizations. One of the first People Analytics examples, and perhaps best known, is Billy Beane, the general manager of the Oakland Athletics major-league baseball team. Beane applied information from large data sets to make decisions about which players to hire and which to reject. His success story is told in a book, *Moneyball*, by Michael Lewis (2004). In addition to hiring decisions, People Analytics can be applied to problems of turnover, poor performance, and determining important criteria for finding and hiring highly talented, and perhaps specialized, people. For more depth about how Big Data and People Analytics relate to and can become a part of OD, see the article by Church and Dutta (2013).

Simulations have been around for quite some time. Business cases where participants make decisions that are judged against financial performance criteria are common today especially in business schools. But now we have simulations that are more sophisticated, more of an interactive process between the participants and the computer program and among the participants, and criteria for performance that are based, for example, on what we know about managing change that leads to a successful outcome grounded in what works and what doesn't. Points for participant teams are allocated accordingly.

With the advent of Google Scholar and other sources from the Internet, we rarely have a need to visit the library—we can have instant *information retrieval*. If it is an article, we can find it, and download it if we desire, in a matter of minutes. If it's a book, we can order it from Amazon and have a tangible copy in our hands within a day or two, or more immediately, as an e-book. We operate today in an age where information quickly retrieved cannot only be valuable, but powerful as well, for example beating the competition to the punch, or accessing the digital footprint of someone you are trying to recruit for a key position.

Implication for OD: To what extent does networking on Facebook, for example, spill over into the workplace, the organization, and if so, does it matter? Obtaining information from Twitter might be useful for the organization such as in the arena of marketing. What seems to be some primary interests of people in certain age groups and areas of the country? The point for OD practitioners is to be cognizant of and sensitive to any relationship between networks in the social media and informal networks in the organization and to note any overlap. If overlap exists, does it matter? With the example of texting in real time, OD practitioners must explore not just patterns of communication, but modes of communication as well. It is a matter of determining what influence social media have on people in their working lives.

With respect to *data analysis,* OD practitioners must be data analysts both in terms of data that are quantitative and data that are qualitative. Unless the organization is largely based on science and/or engineering, not that many organizational members are likely to be adept at analyzing data, especially survey data and data based on ratings like those in the category of multi-rater feedback. Although one does not have to be the greatest of statisticians, it is important to know a few things to help clients make sense of and to draw meaning from a large, complicated set of data, such as which numerical outcomes are significant and which are not, what aspects of the respondents' demographics (gender, race, ethnicity, nationality, sexual orientation, age, number of years working in the organization, level of position in the organization, etc.) relate to what outcomes (motivation, performance, job satisfaction, etc.) if any relationship at all.

As noted, the world of simulation for learning purposes has become more sophisticated, and thus it behooves the OD practitioner to learn about these forms of learning and development for organizational members. And, finally, with respect to information retrieval, access to information required to conduct OD more effectively is now at our fingertips.

Diversity

We (the authors) live and work in New York City, one of the most diverse cities in the world. Diversity is manifested and enjoyed in a great variety of food and drink, arts and entertainment, languages, and cross-cultural experiences. Living in a diverse environment, however, does not make leveraging the strengths of diversity or managing the complexity of diversity any easier. With so much diversity, classifying people when responding to a census form, for example, can be frustrating. A woman, age 41, from Puerto Rico, was asked to identify her ethnicity and then her race. She considered herself to be "all of these." Annoyed and exasperated, "she checked Hispanic, and then identified herself as white, black, and 'some other race'" (Vega, 2014, p. A12). To say that the world is becoming even more diverse via marriage, immigration, and life/work experiences is an understatement. While understanding and being tolerant of human differences is desirable for living and working together harmoniously, classification may be becoming less important. Moreover, research evidence regarding diversity and performance is anything but obvious. There is evidence that groups with heterogeneous learning styles outperform those with homogenous learning styles. In other words, group members with similar preferences for how to learn do not perform on a variety of tasks as well as those groups with members having a mix of learning styles (Kayes, Kayes, & Kolb, 2005). But for groups composed of a mix of, for example, gender, age, ethnic background, and more macro demographic factors, the picture is much more complicated. No study shows that the greater the demographic diversity of a work group, the higher (or lower for that matter) the group's performance. Simple dispersion of group members does not predict group performance. Studies have classified people demographically, for example, gender, age race, ethnicity, or according to job-related attributes, such as differences in education or functional background, or according to personality, attitudes, and values. None of these classifications relate directly to work group performance. In other words, there is no reliable link between the positive and negative effects of diversity to types of diversity. These statements are based on an extensive review of the research literature between 1997 and 2005 conducted by van Knippenberg and Schippers (2007). These researchers argue that determining the true effects of diversity on performance runs deeper than the more general dimensions of gender, education, or personality. With diversity serving as context, such variables as status and power differentials may be more important to study. Rather than study dispersion per se, women compared with men, as van Knippenberg and Schippers suggest, investigating the degree of difference is more important. A ten-member group of eight men and two women is not the same as one composed of eight women and two men. Although this is gradually changing, for now women in the Western world are more accustomed to being in the minority than men are. Thus, the dynamics within the group would differ and in turn have a differential impact on performance. Such research would tap into subtle differences of diversity and help to explain their influence on outcomes. Although the gender study just mentioned has probably not been done, studies of these more subtle differences have been conducted. For example, "the degree and nature of interdependence between group members moderates [that is, has an effect on] the relationship between work group diversity and outcomes [that is] cooperative interdependence would thus be expected to be associated with effects of diversity that are more positive" (van Knippenberg & Schippers, 2007, p. 529). For example, Chatman and colleagues (Chatman, Polzer, Barsade, & Neale, 1998; Chatman & Spataro, 2005) demonstrated that when groups with collectivistic norms emphasized cooperation rather than independence and competition, diversity was associated more with positive, as opposed to negative, group process and performance.

The point is that the term *diversity* covers a lot of territory, and when it comes to understanding the relationship between the concept of diversity and performance, it is the subtle, less-obvious aspects of dissimilarities that are far more important than whether group members are old or young, female or male, extravert or introvert, and so on.

Implication for OD: Assuming current trends will continue, half of the population in the United States by around the year 2050 will be a composite of Latino, African American, and Asian. This means that OD practitioners must become as astute as possible about the implications of these population shifts in the workplace. Although we can consider diversity at the organizational level; for example, its impact on the organization's culture, the extent to which top executives incorporate issues of diversity into their planning and decision making particularly regarding mission and strategy, and the organization's stance about how it wants to be seen in the local community, and beyond if a global operation; that is, not only tolerant of but seeking to employ a diverse workforce, the primary focus for the OD practitioner is at the work group level. There are at least two reasons for this argument. One is the fact that by far most of the research on diversity has been conducted with groups not at the organizational level. Therefore, what knowledge we have to apply to our practice is predominantly at the group level. Second, the work group is where the action is on a daily basis in organizations. The OD practitioner, then, needs to be highly skilled in team building, perhaps still the cornerstone of OD anyway; conflict management and resolution, including intergroup conflict; and group dynamics in general, helping work groups (face-to-face and virtual, in real time and asynchronously) to deal with issues of boundaries, authority, roles, and the tasks at hand—not to mention expertise in how to run an effective meeting.

Dominance of Large Consulting Firms

Organization development operates within the larger world of organization change, or referred to as managing change, and this larger world is getting larger. This is not to say that individuals who prefer to work on their own can no longer do so. Nor are we claiming that there is no room in the organization change consulting arena for the boutique firms, say a company or partnership of 20 or so people. In fact, those boutiques that compete well can indeed grow. What we are saying is that this competitive process is more prolific and difficult now and is likely to remain so for the foreseeable future. Why, you may ask? One reason is probably due to the complexity of the change process itself. It is now well known that the failure rate of organization change efforts is significant—beyond 70 percent (Burke, 2011b). Moreover, it is more commonplace today for executives at the top of organizations, whether a consumer products company or a medical complex, to have experienced failure, or at least to have had an experience that could be described as "less than a success." Thus, there is a growing appreciation among executives, especially those at the top of large bureaucracies, that help is needed. And the larger and more complicated the organization, the more executives are likely to turn to a large consulting firm with a variety of expertise that can deal with complexities more effectively than a solo operator or small boutique. Those potential clients are therefore more likely to seek help from Accenture, Deloite, Korn Ferry, Mckinsey, and other big firms that have been around for a while. Another possible reason is simply competition. The larger firms compete with one another, of course, and got bigger often via acquisitions of smaller firms, and in any case, are more aggressive regarding sales and marketing than smaller players. This trend is quite clear and is likely to continue.

Implication for OD: For those OD practitioners who are external consultants rather than internal employees and are solo, more experience, as is usually the case, would be beneficial. However, an advantage for a boutique firm is to have specialties that few others have. For the smaller firms, attempting to be all things for all clients is not a good idea. Otherwise whether internal or external, working in large firms is the alternative, which means that OD practitioners in this category, employed by the larger organization, must be team players working together in groups to serve large-system clients. The implication here is that until one has more time in, developing one's emotional intelligence and capacity to work collaboratively is what can help to hold one in good stead in the short term (and the long term). In the world of consulting, there is little room for the young practitioner who may want to run her or his own show.

Conclusion

The field of organization development does not exist in a vacuum. The work is influenced by larger societal issues and trends every day. In the first part of this chapter, the trends from 1969–1994 in the second edition of this book were condensed. The latter part of the chapter addressed trends since 1994. By including the "*Implication for OD*" points for all the trends, we have leapt ahead of ourselves and in some cases touched on areas we cover in more depth in later chapters, such as being nimble and agile and issues of power and politics. Treat our hastiness as forthcoming attractions, the next of which is to cover the important origins of the field.

3

Where Did Organization Development Come From?

Evolution is a better term than *birth* to characterize the beginnings of organization development (OD) as a singular event. This chapter thus traces the evolution of OD from its forerunners and selected theoretical roots.

Before OD

Even in evolution, we must start somewhere. There was no "big bang" or "blessed event" in OD, but considering three forerunners or precursors will help us to understand the beginnings; that is, where OD came from. These three precursors are sensitivity training, sociotechnical systems, and survey feedback.

Sensitivity Training

From a historical perspective, it would be interesting to know how many events, inventions, and innovations that occurred around 1946 had lasting impact through the subsequent decades. Apparently once World War II ended, people felt free to pursue creative endeavors. Both sensitivity training, later "housed" at the National Training Laboratories (NTL), and a similar yet different version of human relations training independently founded at the Tavistock Institute in London, began about that time.

On the U.S. side, sensitivity training, or the T-group (*T* for training, or laboratory training), all labels for the same process, consisted and still consists today of small-group (eight to ten people) discussions in which the primary, almost exclusive source of information for learning is the behavior of the group members themselves. The feedback participants receive from one another regarding their behavior becomes a source of personal insight and development. Participants also learn about group behavior and intergroup relationships.

T-groups are educational vehicles for individual change. During the late 1950s, when this form of education began to be applied in industrial settings for organizational change, the T-group became one of the earliest so-called interventions of organization development.

Sensitivity training began to be used as an intervention for organizational change. Members of the small T-groups were either organizational "cousins"—from the same overall organization but not within the same vertical chain of the organization's hierarchy—or members of the same organizational team, so-called family groups. Douglas McGregor of the Sloan School of Management at the Massachusetts Institute of Technology (MIT) conducted this kind of training at Union Carbide. Similar events at Esso (now Exxon Mobil) and at the Naval Ordnance Test Station at China Lake, California, represented the early forms of organization development, which usually took the form of what we now call team building (Burck, 1965; McGregor, 1967).

During the same period, circa 1959, McGregor and Richard Beckhard were consulting with General Mills. Working on what we now call a sociotechnical systems change, they helped to change some of the work structures at the various plants to introduce more teamwork and decision making at the shop-floor level. Although they fostered more "bottom-up" management, they didn't want to call what they were doing *bottom-up.* Nor were they satisfied with *organization development,* the label that became the name for the work Herb Shepard, Harry Kolb, Robert R. Blake, and others were doing at the Humble Refineries of Esso. Nevertheless, McGregor and Beckhard called what they were doing organization development. Meanwhile across the Atlantic at the Tavistock Institute, the label sociotechnical systems stuck.

Sociotechnical Systems

In the United Kingdom at about the same time that sensitivity training began in the United States, Eric Trist and Ken Bamforth of the Tavistock Institute were consulting with a coal-mining company. They found that coal was mined by teams of six. Each team selected its own members and performed all tasks from extraction of the coal to loading to getting it to the surface. Teams were paid on the basis of group effort and unit productivity, not individual effort, and tended to be quite cohesive.

Problems arose with the introduction of new equipment and a change in technology that changed the way work was conducted. Individual, not group, labor became the norm. As work became more individualized and specialized and jobs more fractionated, productivity decreased and absenteeism increased.

Trist and Bamforth suggested combining the essential social elements of the previous team mode of work with the new technology. When the company's management implemented their suggestions, productivity rose and absenteeism decreased. The specifics of this early work, including the documented measurements and outcomes, are reported in Trist (1960) and Trist and Bamforth (1951). Similar work was done by A. K. Rice, another Tavistock consultant and researcher, in two textile mills in Ahmedabad, India (Rice, 1958).

The approach pioneered by the Tavistock consultants is based on the premise that an organization is simultaneously a social and a technical system. Whether they produce something tangible or render a service, all organizations have technology, a subsystem of the total organization and an integral part of the culture. All organizations also are composed of people who interact around a task or series of tasks, and this human dimension constitutes the social subsystem. The emphasis of OD is typically on the social subsystem, but it should be clear that both subsystems and their interaction must be considered in any effort toward organizational change.

Survey Feedback

Organization development has been influenced by industrial/ organizational psychology. This influence is perhaps manifested most in the third precursor to OD, survey feedback. Rensis Likert, the first director of the Institute for Social Research of the University of Michigan, started by founding the Survey Research Center in 1946. Kurt Lewin had founded the Research Center for Group Dynamics at MIT. With his untimely death in 1947, the Center was moved to the University of Michigan later that year. These two centers initially constituted Likert's institute. The two primary thrusts of these centers, questionnaire surveys for organizational diagnosis and group dynamics, combined to give birth to the survey feedback method. As early as 1947, questionnaires were being used systematically to assess employee morale and attitudes in organizations.

One of the first of these studies, initiated and guided by Likert and conducted by Floyd Mann, was done with the Detroit Edison Company. From their work on the problem of how best to use the survey data for organization improvement, the method we now know as survey feedback evolved. Mann was key to the development of this method. He noted that, when a manager was given the survey results, any resulting improvement depended on what the manager did with the information. If the manager discussed the survey results with his subordinates yet failed to plan certain changes for improvement jointly with them, nothing happened—except, perhaps, an increase in employee frustration with the ambiguity of having answered a questionnaire and never hearing anything further.

Briefly, the survey feedback method involves, first, the survey, collecting data by questionnaire to determine employees' perceptions of a variety of factors, most focusing on the management of the organization. The second step is the feedback, reporting the results of the survey systematically in summary form to all people who answered the questionnaire. Systematically, in this case, means that feedback occurs in phases, starting with the top team of the organization and flowing downward according to the formal hierarchy and within functional units or teams. Mann (1957) referred to this cascade as the "interlocking chain of conferences." The chief executive officer, the division general manager, or the bureau chief, depending on the organization or subunit surveyed, and his or her immediate group of subordinates receive and discuss feedback from the survey first. Next, the subordinates and their respective groups of immediate subordinates do the same, and so forth downward until all members of the organization who had been surveyed hear a summary of the survey and then participate in a discussion of the meaning of the data and the implications. Each functional unit of the organization receives general feedback concerning the overall organization and specific feedback regarding its particular group. Following a discussion of the meaning of the survey results for their particular group, the boss and his or her subordinates then jointly plan action steps for improvement. Usually, a consultant meets with each of the groups to help with data analysis, group discussion, and plans for improvement.

This is a rather orderly and systematic way of understanding an organization from the standpoint of employee perceptions. Processing this understanding back into the organization so that change can occur, with the help of an outside resource person, not only was a direct precursor to and root of organization development, it is an integral part of many current OD efforts.

Current OD efforts using survey feedback methodology do not, however, always follow a top-down, cascading process. The survey may begin in the middle of the managerial hierarchy and move in either or both directions, or may begin at the bottom and work upward, as Edgar Schein (1969) has suggested. For more information about and guidelines for conducting survey feedback activities, see David Nadler's book (Nadler, 1977).

Finally, it should be noted that there are other forerunners or precursors to OD. A case in point is the activity prior to World War II at the Hawthorne Works of Western Electric. There, Mayo (1933), Roethlisberger and Dickson (1939), and Homans (1950) established that psychological and sociotechnical factors make significant differences in worker performance.

The work at Hawthorne and its consequent impact occurred some two decades prior to the three precursors we chose to discuss in some detail. Thus, sensitivity training, sociotechnical systems, and survey feedback had a much greater and more direct influence on the beginnings of OD.

Theoretical Roots

Organization development has other roots in the area of concepts, models, and theories. What follows is a synopsis of some of the thinking of a fairly select group of people who have helped to provide most of the theoretical and conceptual underpinnings of OD. Ten theorists or conceptualizers were selected to represent the theory associated with OD because no single theory or conceptual model is representative or by itself encompasses the conceptual field or the practice of OD. We have instead a group of minitheories that have influenced the thinking and consultative practice of OD practitioners; each helps to explain only a portion of organizational behavior and effectiveness.

Ten theory categories were selected because they best represent the theory we do have within the field of OD. Some prominent names in the field of OD were not included because their contributions have been more descriptive than theoretical (an example is Blake and Mouton's 1964 *Managerial Grid*). The selection is a matter of judgment and could be debated. In fact, I (Burke) have heard Frederick Herzberg state that he did not associate himself with the field. B. F. Skinner probably never heard of organization development. In other words, these theorists did not elect themselves into OD. We have chosen them because we believe their thinking has had a large impact on the practice of OD.

Need Theory—Maslow and Herzberg

According to Maslow (1954), human motivation can be explained in terms of needs that people experience to varying degrees all the time. An unsatisfied need creates a state of tension, which releases energy in the human system and, at the same time, provides direction. This purposeful energy guides the individual toward some goal that will respond to the unsatisfied need. The process whereby an unsatisfied need provides energy and direction toward some goal is Maslow's definition of motivation. Thus, only unsatisfied needs are motivating; a satisfied need creates no tension and therefore no motivation.

Maslow contended that we progress through a five-level need system one level at a time. The hierarchy represents a continuum from basic or physiological needs to safety and security needs to belonging needs to ego-status needs to a need for self-actualization.

It is on this last point, a single continuum, that Herzberg parts company with Maslow. Herzberg (1966; Herzberg, Mausner, & Snyderman, 1959) maintains that there are two continua, one concerning dissatisfaction and the other concerning satisfaction. It may be that the two theorists are even more fundamentally different in that Herzberg's approach has more to do with job satisfaction than with human motivation. The implications and applications of the two are much more similar than they are divergent, however.

Herzberg argues that only the goal objects associated with Maslow's ego-status and self-actualization needs provide motivation or satisfaction on the job. Meeting the lower-order needs simply reduces dissatisfaction; it does not provide satisfaction. Herzberg calls the goal objects associated with these lower-level needs (belonging, safety, and basic) hygiene or maintenance factors. Providing fringe benefits, for example, prevents dissatisfaction and thus is hygienic, but this provision does not ensure job satisfaction. Only motivator factors, such as recognition, opportunity for achievement, and autonomy on the job ensure satisfaction.

Herzberg's two categories, motivator factors and maintenance or hygiene factors, do not overlap. They represent qualitatively different aspects of human motivation.

One other point of Herzberg's is important: He states that not only does the dimension of job dissatisfaction differ psychologically from job satisfaction, but it is also associated with an escalation phenomenon, or what some have called the principle of rising expectations: The more people receive, the more they want. This principle applies only to job dissatisfaction. Herzberg uses the example of a person who receives a salary increase of $1,000 one year and then receives only a $500 increase the following year. Psychologically, the second increase is a cut in pay. Herzberg maintains that this escalation principle is a fact of life, and that we must live with it. Management must continue to provide, upgrade, and increase maintenance factors—good working conditions, adequate salaries, and competitive fringe benefits—but should not operate under the false assumption that these factors will lead to greater job satisfaction.

Job enrichment, a significant intervention within OD and a critical element of quality-of-work-life projects, is a direct application of Herzberg's theory and at least an indirect one of Maslow's.

Expectancy Theory—Lawler and Vroom

Expectancy theory (Lawler, 1973; Vroom, 1964) has yet to have the impact on organization development that need theory has had, but it is gaining in acceptance and popularity. This approach to understanding human motivation focuses more on outward behavior than on internal needs. The theory is based on three assumptions:

1. People believe that their behavior is associated with certain outcomes. Theorists call this belief the *performance-outcome expectancy.* People may expect that if they accomplish certain tasks, they will receive certain rewards.

2. Outcomes or rewards have different values (*valence*) for different people. Some people, for example, are more attracted to money as a reward than others are.

3. People associate their behavior with certain probabilities of success, called the *effort-performance expectancy.* People on an assembly line, for example, may have high expectancies that if they try, they can produce 100 units per hour, but their expectancies may be very low that they can produce 150 units, regardless of how hard they may try.

Thus, people will be highly motivated when they believe that their behavior will lead to certain rewards, that these rewards are worthwhile and valuable, and that they are able to perform at a level that will result in the attainment of the rewards.

Research has shown that high-performing employees believe that their behavior, or performance, leads to rewards that they desire. Thus, there is evidence for the validity of the theory. Moreover, the theory and the research outcomes associated with it have implications for how reward systems and work might be designed and structured.

Job Satisfaction—Hackman and Oldham

Hackman and Oldham's (1980) *work design model* is grounded in both need theory and expectancy theory. Their model is more restrictive in that it focuses on the relationship between job or work design and worker satisfaction. Although their model frequently leads to what is called job enrichment, as does the application of Herzberg's motivator-hygiene theory, the Hackman and Oldham model has broader implications. Briefly, Hackman and Oldham (1975) contend that there are three primary psychological states that significantly affect worker satisfaction:

1. Experienced meaningfulness of the work itself
2. Experienced responsibility for the work and its outcomes
3. Knowledge of results, or performance feedback

The more that work is designed to enhance these states, the more satisfying the work will be.

Positive Reinforcement—Skinner

The best way to understand the full importance of the applications of B. F. Skinner's (1953, 1971) thinking and his research results is to read his novel, *Walden Two* (1948). The book is about a Utopian community designed and maintained according to Skinnerian principles of operant behavior and schedules of reinforcement. A similar application was made in an industrial situation in the Emery Air Freight case ("At Emery Air Freight," 1973). By applying Skinnerian principles, which are based on numerous research findings, Emery quickly realized an annual savings of $650,000. Skinner was neither an OD practitioner nor a management consultant, but his theory and research are indeed applicable to management practices and to organizational change. For Skinner, control is key. If one can control the environment, one can then control behavior. In Skinner's approach, the more the environment is controlled, the better, but the necessary element of control is the rewards, both positive and negative. This necessity is based on a fundamental of behavior that Skinner derived from his many years of research, a concept so basic that it may be a law of behavior, that people (and animals) do what they are rewarded for doing. Let us consider the principles that underlie this fundamental of behavior.

The first phase of learned behavior is called *shaping,* the process of successive approximations to reinforcement. When children are learning to walk, they are reinforced by their parents' encouraging comments or physical stroking, but this reinforcement typically follows only the behaviors that lead to effective walking. *Programmed learning,* invented by Skinner, is based on this principle. To maintain the behavior, a schedule of reinforcement is applied and, generally, the more variable the schedule is, the longer the behavior will last.

Skinner, therefore, advocates positive reinforcement for shaping and controlling behavior. Often, however, when we consider controlling behavior, we think of punishment ("If you don't do this, you're gonna get it!"). According to Skinner, punishment is ineffective. His stance is not based entirely on his values or whims, however. Research clearly shows that, although punishment may temporarily stop a certain behavior, negative reinforcement must be administered continuously for this certain process to be maintained. The principle is the opposite of that for positively reinforced behavior. There are two very practical concerns here. First, having to reinforce a certain behavior continuously is not very efficient. Second, although the punished behavior may be curtailed, it is unlikely that the subject will learn what to do; all that is learned is what *not* to do.

Thus, the way to control behavior according to Skinnerian theory and research is to reinforce the desirable behavior positively and, after the shaping process, to reinforce the behavior only occasionally. The implication of Skinner's work for organizations is that a premium is placed on such activities as establishing incentive systems, reducing or eliminating many of the control systems that contain inherent threats and punishments, providing feedback to all levels of employees regarding their performance, and developing programmed-learning techniques for training employees.

The application of Skinner's work to OD did not occur systematically until the 1970s. Thus, his influence is not as pervasive as is Maslow's, for example. Skinner's behavior-motivation techniques as applied to people also raise significant questions regarding ethics and values: Who exercises the control, and is the recipient aware? Thus, it is not a question of whether Skinner's methodology works, but rather how and under what circumstances it is used.

The Group as the Focus of Change—Lewin

The theorist among theorists, at least within the scope of the behavioral sciences, is Kurt Lewin. His thinking has had a more pervasive impact on organization development, both direct and indirect, than any other person's. It was Lewin who laid the groundwork for much of what we know about social change, particularly in a group and by some extrapolation in an organization.

According to Lewin (1948, 1951), behavior is a function of a person's personality, discussed primarily in terms of motivation or needs, and the situation or environment in which the person is acting. The environment is represented as a field of forces that affect the person. Thus, a person's behavior at any given moment can be predicted if we know that person's needs and if we can determine the *intensity* and *valence* (whether the force is positive or negative for the person) of the forces impinging on the person from the environment. Although Lewin borrowed the term *force* from physics, he defined the construct psychologically. Thus, one's *perception* of the environment is key, not necessarily reality. An example of a force, therefore, could be the perceived power of another person. Whether or not I will accomplish a task you want me to do is a function of the degree to which such accomplishment will respond to a need I have and how I perceive your capacity to influence me—whether you are a force in my environment (field).

Lewin made a distinction between *imposed* or induced forces, those acting on a person from the outside, and *own* forces, those directly reflecting the person's needs. The implications of this distinction are clear. Participation in determining a goal is more likely to create own forces toward accomplishing it than is a situation in which goal determination is imposed by others. When a goal is imposed on a person, his or her motives may match accomplishment of the goal, but the chances are considerably more variable or random than if the goal is determined by the person in the first place. Typically, then, for imposed or induced goals to be accomplished by a person, the one who induced them must exert continuous influence or else the person's other motives, not associated with goal accomplishment, will likely determine his or her behavior. This aspect of Lewin's theory helps to explain the generally positive consequences of participative management and consensual decision making.

Another distinction Lewin made regarding various forces in a person's environment is the one between *driving* and *restraining* forces. Borrowing yet another concept from physics, quasi-stationary equilibria, he noted that the perceived status quo in life is just that— *a perception.* In reality, albeit psychological reality, a given situation is a result of a dynamic rather than a static process. The process flows from one moment to the next, with ups and downs, and over time gives the impression of a static situation, but there actually are some forces pushing in one direction and other, counterbalancing forces that restrain movement. The level of productivity in an organization may appear static, for example, but sometimes it is pushed higher, say by supervisory pressure, and sometimes it is restrained or even diminished by a counterforce, such as a norm of the work group. *Force-field analysis* is used to identify the counterbalancing forces that determine situations.

Change from the status quo is therefore a two-step process, according to Lewin. Step 1 is to conduct a force-field analysis, and step 2 is to increase or decrease the intensity of a force or set of forces. Change can be fostered by adding to or increasing the intensity of the forces Lewin labeled *driving forces*—those forces that push in the desired direction for change. Or change can be fostered by diminishing the opposing or restraining forces. Lewin's theory predicts that the better of these two choices is to reduce the intensity of the restraining forces. By adding forces or increasing the intensity on the driving side, a simultaneous increase would occur on the restraining side, and the overall tension for the system—whether it is a person, a group, or an organization—would intensify. The better choice, then, is to reduce the restraining forces.

This facet of Lewin's field theory helps us to determine not only the nature of change but how to accomplish it more effectively. Lewinian theory argues that it is more efficacious to direct change at the group level than at the individual level.

If one attempts to change an attitude or the behavior of an individual without attempting to change the same behavior or attitude in the group to which the individual belongs, then the individual will be a deviate and either will come under pressure from the group to get back into line or will be rejected entirely. Thus, the major leverage point for change is at the group level—for example, by modifying a group norm or standard. According to Lewin:

> As long as group standards are unchanged, the individual will resist change more strongly the farther he is to depart from group standards. If the group standard itself is changed, the resistance which is due to the relation between individual and group standard is eliminated (1958, 210).

Adherence to Lewinian theory involves viewing the organization as a social system, with many and varied subsystems, primarily groups. We look at the behavior of people in the organization in terms of (1) whether their needs jibe with the organization's directions, usually determined by their degree of commitment, (2) the norms to which people conform and the degree of that conformity, (3) how power is exercised (induced versus own forces), and (4) the decision-making process (involvement leading to commitment).

Changing Values Through the Group—Argyris

It is not possible to place the work of Chris Argyris in one category, one theory, or one conceptual framework. He has developed a number of minitheories, whose relationship and possible overlap are not always apparent. He has always focused largely on interpersonal and group behavior, however, and he has emphasized behavioral change within a group context, along the same value lines as McGregor's (1960) Theory Y. The work described in *Management and Organizational Development* (Argyris, 1971) best illustrates this emphasis.

Argyris's early work (1962) emphasized the relationship of individual personality and organizational dynamics. To improve satisfaction in this relationship, the organization must adjust its value system toward helping its members to be more psychologically healthy, less dependent on and controlled by the organization. The individuals must become more open with their feelings, more willing to trust one another, and more internally committed to the organization's goals.

In his thinking, research, and writing during the late 1960s and early 1970s, Argyris became more clearly associated with organization development. His thrust of this period was in (1) theorizing about competent consultation, and especially about the nature of an effective intervention and (2) operationalizing organizational change in behavioral terms by McGregor's Theory Y (Argyris, 1971). Argyris (1970) contends that, for any intervention into an organization-social system to be effective, it must generate valid information, lead to free, informed choice on the part of the client, and provide internal commitment by the client to the choices taken.

Later, Argyris turned his attention to the gaps in people's behavior between what they say (he calls it espoused theory) and what they do (theory in action). People may say that they believe that McGregor's Theory Y assumptions about human beings are valid, for example, but they may not act accordingly. Argyris goes on to argue that as people become more aware of these gaps between their stated beliefs and their behavior, they will be more motivated to reduce the differences, to be more consistent.

In collaboration with Don Schön, Argyris studied and elaborated the learning process involved in obtaining greater self-awareness and organizational awareness about human effectiveness (Argyris and Schön, 1978). Argyris and Schön argue that most organizations accomplish no more than *single loop learning*, that problems are solved or fixed and a single loop of learning is accomplished. To improve an organization significantly and to ensure its long-term survival and renewal, however, change must occur in more fundamental ways. Although problems must be solved in a single loop, new ways of learning how to solve problems must be learned as well. Another loop is thus added to the learning cycle—what Argyris and Schön refer to as *double loop learning*. This process of learning is analogous to if not the same as the way OD is sometimes defined as a planned process of change in the organization's culture—how we do things and how we relate to one another.

The Group Unconscious—Bion

Most people believe that everyone has an unconscious: Freud has clearly had an effect. Wilfred Bion believed, as others do, that there is also a group unconscious—a collective unconscious that is more than the sum of the individual unconscious. Bion gave compelling but complex arguments for this theory (Bion, 1961; Rioch, 1970).

Bion believed that every group is actually composed of two groups, the work group and the basic-assumption group; that is, every group behaves as if it were two groups, one concerned with group accomplishment and rational actions, the other concerned with activity that stems from the unconscious and is irrational. Bion did not mean simply that a group is both rational and irrational. He went far beyond this commonly accepted dichotomy.

The *work group* is the aspect of group functioning that is concerned with accomplishing what the group is composed to do, the task at hand. The work group is aware of its purpose, or at the outset knows that its initial task is to establish clarity of purpose. The work group is sure about, or quickly becomes sure about, roles and responsibilities in the group. The work group is also clearly conscious of the passage of time and the procedures and processes needed to accomplish the task.

How many times have you been a member or leader of a group that fit such a description? I suspect that it has not been very often, if ever. Bion stated that groups do not behave in this clearly rational and sensible way because there is always another group operating simultaneously—the *basic-assumption group*.

Bion theorized that all groups function according to basic assumptions, that groups operate as if certain things are inevitable. Perhaps an analogy will help to explain. In the early days of automobiles, many people made the basic assumption that no motorized vehicle could go faster than a horse, and these people acted accordingly. In fact, some of them eventually lost money because they bet heavily on their assumption. The point is that they acted as if their beliefs were true and inevitable.

There are three types of basic-assumption groups: the dependency group, the fight-flight group, and the pairing group. The *dependency* group assumes that the reason the group exists is to be protected and to be assured of providence by its leader. The group members act immaturely, childishly, and as if they know little or nothing as compared with the leader. The leader is all-powerful and wise. In the dependency group, the leader is typically idolized. However, because we mortals are neither omnipotent nor omniscient, group members soon realize that they must seek someone new to depend on and the cycle then repeats itself with a new leader.

The *fight-flight* group assumes that it must preserve itself, that its survival is at stake, so group members act accordingly. Taking action is the key to survival, as in the proverbial army command: "Do something even if it's wrong!" It is the *group* that must be preserved, so individuals may be sacrificed through fight or abandonment (flight). The leader's role in this basic-assumption group is clear: to lead the group into battle or retreat. The best leader is one who acts in a paranoid manner, assuming that "They're out to get us, gang!" Eventually and inevitably, the leader will not meet all the group's demands, at which point the group panics and searches for a new leader.

In the *pairing* group, the assumption is that the group's purpose is to give birth to a new messiah. The leader in this case is purely incidental, and the group must quickly get on with the business of bringing forth the new savior. Two members therefore pair off to procreate. The two may be both male, both female, or male and female, but the basic assumption is that when two people pair, the pairing is sexual in nature, even though it may take the innocent form of establishing a subcommittee. Although new life and hope may be provided, the new messiah, as with the Christian Messiah, will soon be done away with. All the basic-assumption groups behave as if the leader must be replaced or, to use Bion's more dramatic and graphic terminology, as if the leader must be crucified.

Although the work group and the basic-assumption group are functioning simultaneously, their degree of activity varies. At times, the work group is predominant and at other times the basic-assumption group holds sway.

Bion was never an OD practitioner; he was a psychotherapist. His theory, however, is applicable to interventions with teams, consultation with leaders, and diagnosis of possible processes of collusion. For a direct application and extension of the latter group or organizational dynamic, see Harvey's "The Abilene Paradox" (1974), an extension of Bion's theory that explains collusive behavior on the part of members of a group.

For the OD practitioner serving as a consultant to an organizational team, Bion's theory is particularly useful for diagnosing internal problems, especially those concerning team members' relationships with the leader. For example, when subordinates defer to the boss for most if not all decisions, a basic-assumption mode of dependency may be occurring, with the work group mode being submerged. Calling this process to the attention of the group may break the basic-assumption mode and help to facilitate the group's task accomplishment. An OD practitioner might intervene with a comment like, "We seem to be looking to (the boss) for practically all of our problem solutions," and follow up with a question such as, "Don't we have experience among us that we could tap into more?" Helping a work group to stay focused on its task is a way of preventing flight and another example of how to apply Bion's theory.

Bion's work, not surprisingly, has spawned additional theorizing. Two other basic assumption groups have been postulated. They are *oneness* and *me-ness*. In the *oneness* group (Turquet, 1985), the assumption is that if group members surrender their individuality in service of joining a powerful union with an omnipotent force, they will feel existence, wholeness, and well-being, at one with the all-powerful other. An example of basic-assumption *oneness* is a religious cult in which the group is bound together by its veneration of a person or an ideal.

As proposed by Lawrence, Bain, and Gould (1996), basic-assumption *me-ness* is the opposite of oneness. In basic-assumption me-ness, group members act as if there is no group because if there were a group, it would represent all that is negative in group life. Individuals focus on their own personal boundaries and engage solely in instrumental transactions as they fear that joining the group would lead to becoming part of an undifferentiated mob. The me-ness basic assumption is hypothesized to be a reflection of postindustrial society in which the perceived demands of the external environment are such that one must deny their existence and focus exclusively on one's inner reality.

Participative Management—the One Best Way—Likert

Likert is best known for two concepts: the linking pin notion of management and the four-system model of organizations. He is also known for his unequivocal advocacy of participative management as the approach to be taken by managers, regardless of organizational type. Likert's method for organization development is survey feedback. We shall consider each of these concepts briefly.

Likert's (1961) idea of the linking pin originated from his desire to design organizations in a more decentralized form without eliminating the hierarchical structure. He also wanted to incorporate more opportunity for group activity, especially group decision making, in the managerial process. Thus, each manager is simultaneously a member of two groups, one in which he or she manages and is the leader and one in which he or she is a subordinate and follows the leadership of a boss. By being a member of both these hierarchical groups, the person becomes a key *link* within the vertical chain of command. This linkage manifests itself primarily in activities involving communication and resolution of conflict. The manager-subordinate, therefore, is the primary conduit for information and facilitates the resolution of conflict, by virtue of the linking position, when there are differences between the two vertically connected organizational groups. An organization chart is drawn so that groups overlap vertically rather than in the more traditional way, as separate boxes connected only by lines.

Likert (1967) described four major models or systems of organization design: the autocratic, the benevolent autocratic, the consultative, and the participative. He used seven organizational functions to describe the four models differentially: leadership, motivation, communication, interaction and influence, decision making, goal setting, and control. His "Profile of Organizational Characteristics," a diagnostic questionnaire, is organized according to these seven functions and four models. Organizational members' answers to the questionnaire provide a perceptual profile of the organization. The profile is derived from the respondents' views of how the seven functions are managed and depicts which of the four systems seems to be predominant, at least in the eyes of the respondents.

Likert not only argued that there is one best way to manage, he also espoused one best way to conduct an OD effort. His method is survey feedback; his survey instrument, the Profile of Organizational Characteristics, organizes feedback for analysis according to the four-system model of organizational management. In an OD effort, then, Likert's approach is highly data-based, but the diagnosis is largely limited to the functions he deems important. Once the survey data are collected, they are given back in profile form to organizational family units—to a boss and his or her team—as described earlier.

Although organizational change agents may be uncomfortable with Likert's one best way and may prefer an approach that is more contingent and perhaps more flexible, they can be very sure of the direction and the objectives of the change effort.

It All Depends—Lawrence and Lorsch

For an organization to operate efficiently and effectively, one person cannot do everything, and every organizational member cannot do the same thing. In any organization, therefore, there is a division of labor. Lawrence and Lorsch (1967, 1969) call this *differentiation*. In an organization with many divisions, some people must provide coordination, so that what the organization does is organized in some fashion. Lawrence and Lorsch label this process *integration*. Their approach is sometimes referred to as a theory of differentiation-integration. A more appropriate label, however, and the one they prefer, is *contingency theory*. They believe that how an organization should be structured and how it should be managed depend on several factors, primarily the organization's environment, or its marketplace. The central elements of the Lawrence and Lorsch contingency theory are differentiation, integration, the organization-environment interface, and the implicit contract between the employees and management.

Differentiation means dividing up tasks so that everything that needs to be done is accomplished. To determine the degree of differentiation in an organization, Lawrence and Lorsch consider four variables:

1. *Goal certainty.* Are goals clear and easily measured or ambiguous and largely qualitative?
2. *Structure.* Is the structure formal, with precise policy and procedures, or loose and flexible, with policy largely a function of current demand?
3. *Interaction.* Is there considerable interpersonal and intergroup communication and cooperation or very little?
4. *Timespan of feedback.* Do people in the organization see the results of their work quickly or does it take a long time?

The more that units within an organization differ from one another along these four dimensions, the more differentially structured the organization is. Some units may be very sure of their goals while others are not so sure, and some units may follow strict and precise work procedures while other units are still trying to formulate working procedures. It should be clear, therefore, that highly differentiated organizations are more difficult to coordinate. In a pyramidal organization, the coordination and the resolution of conflict are handled by the next higher level of management. When organizations are simultaneously highly differentiated and decentralized with respect to management, Lawrence and Lorsch argue that integrator roles are needed, that certain people must be given specific assignments for coordinating and integrating diverse functions. These people may or may not be in key decision-making positions, but they ensure that decisions are made by someone or by the appropriate group.

How should an organization be structured, differentiated, and centralized (pyramidal) or decentralized? We already know the answer: It depends. But on what does it depend? Lawrence and Lorsch argue that it depends primarily on the organization's environment, on whether the environment is complex and rapidly changing, as in the electronics industry, or relatively simple (one or two major markets) and stable (raw materials forthcoming and predictable and market likely to remain essentially the same in the foreseeable future). The more complex the environment, the more decentralized and flexible management should be. Lawrence and Lorsch's reasoning is that, the more rapidly changing the environment, the more necessary it is that the organization have people monitoring these changes, and the more they should be in a position to make decisions on the spot. When the organization's environment is not particularly complex and when conditions are relatively stable, management should be more centralized because this way of structuring is more efficient.

Lawrence and Lorsch consider matters of conflict resolution because conflicts arise quickly and naturally in a highly differentiated organization and the management of these conflicts is critical for efficient and effective organizational functioning. Moreover, if the organization is highly differentiated and decentralized, conflict is even more likely.

Finally, how well an organization operates is also a function of the nature of the interface between management and employees. Lawrence and Lorsch recognize the importance of individual motivation and effective supervision. They tend to view motivation in terms of expectancy, believing that employees' motivation (and morale) is based on the degree to which their expectations about how they should be treated are actually met by management in the work environment.

In summary, Lawrence and Lorsch, contingency theorists, advocate no single form of organizational structure or single style of management. The structure and the style depend on the business of the organization and its environment—how variable or how stable it is.

Lawrence and Lorsch have been among the most influential theorists for OD practitioners. Considering contingencies before acting has proven to be a popular approach to OD.

The Organization as a Family—Levinson

Harry Levinson believes that an organization operates like a family, with the chief executive officer taking the role of all-powerful parent, either father or mother, depending on the culture and structure of the organization. According to Levinson, all organizations "recapitulate the basic family structure in a culture." The type of organization Levinson understands best is the family-owned business, and his theory about organizations and how they operate and change has its roots in Freudian psychology (Levinson, 1972a, b).

Levinson does not look at organizations exclusively through psychoanalytical glasses, however. He is well aware that structure, the type of business, and the outside environment affect the internal behavioral dynamics of organizations. More important for Levinson's diagnosis of an organization, however, is the nature of the organization's personality (we might call it culture). He believes that an organization has a personality, just as an individual does, and that the health of an organization, like that of a person, can be determined in terms of how effectively the various parts of the personality are integrated. He refers to this process as *maintaining equilibrium.* Levinson also believes that implicit psychological contracts exist between management and employees, based on earlier experiences from family life. If the employees behave themselves (are good boys and girls), the parents (management) will reward them appropriately. Thus, the psychological contract is characterized by dependency. Note that this aspect of Levinson's theory is similar to Argyris's theory.

Continuing the psychoanalytic paradigm, Levinson theorizes that the chief executive officer represents the ego ideal for the organizational family and that this ideal, for better or for worse, motivates the kinds of people who are attracted to the organization in the first place, the interaction patterns among people in the organization, especially in matters of authority, and the kinds of people who are promoted. If a chief executive officer stays in office for a long time, the personality of the organization slowly crystallizes over the years; those who aspire to the ego ideal stay in the organization, and those who do not leave. Accordingly, Levinson believes that history is a critical factor in diagnosing an organization.

In summary, as a consultant, Levinson uses the clinical case method in diagnosis, intervenes primarily at the top of an organization, and bases his theory on psychoanalysis. In his own words:

> You've got to take into account all the factors in an organization, just as you gather all the main facts of a person's life in taking a case history. But you need a comprehensive theory like psychoanalysis to make sense of all the facts, to make it hang together in a useful way (1972a, 126).

Conclusion

At the risk of oversimplification, we have summarized ten theories by categorizing them according to perspective, emphasis, and application. A summary of these factors is given in Table 3.1. Keep in mind that there is no single, all-encompassing theory for organization development. What we have are several minitheories that help us understand certain aspects of organizational behavior and OD. Taken together and comparatively, they become more useful to the practitioner who must cope with an ever-changing, complex, total organization.

Thus, OD comes from many sources and has its roots in more than one methodology and in a variety of theories and concepts. The background provided in this chapter, though varied, nevertheless has commonality. The trunk from these roots might be expressed as the attempt to improve an organization with methods that involve people and to create conditions whereby the talents of these people are used more effectively.

Table 3.1 Summary of Primary OD Theorists According to Their Perspectives, Emphases, and Applications

Perspective	Theorist	Emphasis	Application
Individual	Maslow and Herzberg	Individual needs	Career development, job enrichment
	Vroom and Lawler	Individual expectancies and values	Reward system design, performance appraisal
	Hackman and Oldham	Job satisfaction	Job and work design, job enrichment
	Skinner	Individual performance	Incentive systems, reward system design
Group	Lewin	Norms and values	Changing conformity patterns
	Argyris	Interpersonal competence and values	Training and education
	Bion	Group unconscious, psychoanalytic basis	Group behavior diagnosis

Perspective	Theorist	Emphasis	Application
System	Likert	Management style and approach	Change to participative management
	Lawrence and Lorsch	Organizational structure	Change contingent on organizational environment
	Levinson	Organization as a family, psychoanalytic basis	Diagnosis of organization according to familial patterns

4

Organization Development as a Process of Change

Recall the definition of organization development (OD): a planned process of change in an organization's culture through the utilization of behavioral science technology and theory. The focus of this chapter is on the process of change and on utilization of theory.

Although the practice of OD may be based on portions of several theories from the behavioral sciences, as stated in the previous chapter, there is no single, all-encompassing theory of OD. This no doubt constitutes a weakness of the field, but it is not surprising because it is a very young field, having its origins around 1959, and is based on several disciplines. Nevertheless, most practitioners agree that three models are the underlying and guiding frames of reference for any OD effort: (1) the action research model; (2) Lewin's three-step model of system change—unfreezing, moving, and refreezing; and (3) phases of planned change as delineated by Lippitt, Watson, and Westley (1958).[1] These models are not mutually exclusive, and all stem from the original thinking of Kurt Lewin.

Action Research

The words *action research* reverse the actual sequence (Brown, 1972). In practice, research is conducted first and then action is taken as a direct result of what the research data are interpreted to indicate. As French and Bell (1978) have pointed out, action research came from two independent sources, one a person of action, John Collier, who was commissioner of Indian Affairs from 1933 to 1945, the other a person of research, Kurt Lewin. Collier worked to bring about change in ethnic relations and was a strong advocate of conducting research to determine the "central areas of needed action" (Collier, 1945). He coined the label action research.

Although Lewin was an academic—a scholar, theoretician, and researcher—he was just as eminent a man of action (Marrow, 1969). Moreover, he pulled it all together when he stated that there is "no action without research, and no research without action" (Lewin, 1946). Lewin and his colleagues and students conducted many action research projects in several different domains: community and racial relations, leadership, eating habits, and intergroup conflict. The action research project that is perhaps most relevant to OD was conducted by John R. P. French (a student of Lewin's and subsequently a professor at the University of Michigan) and his client, Lester Coch. Their famous study of workers' resistance to change in a pajama factory not only illustrated action research at its best but provided the theoretical basis for what we now call participative management (Coch & French, 1948).

Wendell French (1969); Frohman, Sashkin, and Kavanagh (1976); and Schein (1980) made the action research model directly applicable and relevant to the OD process. Figure 4.1 shows French's adaptation.

Lewin's Three-Step Procedure of Change

According to Lewin (1958), the first step in the process of change is *unfreezing* the present level of behavior. To reduce prejudice, for example, the unfreezing step might be catharsis (Allport, 1945) or participation in a series of sensitivity training sessions (Rubin, 1967). For organizational change, the unfreezing step might be a series of management training sessions in which the objective for change was a more participative approach (Blake, Mouton, Barnes, & Greiner, 1964; Shepard, 1960) or data feedback from a survey that showed serious problems in the managerial process of the organization (Bowers, 1973; Nadler, 1977). With respect to the change at British Airways (BA) (see Chapter 7, "The Burke-Litwin Model of Organizational Performance and Change"), it was the double whammy of (1) Prime Minister Thatcher declaring that BA would become a private, stock-owned, profit-making company and no longer a government agency and (2) the new CEO Colin Marshall's reduction of the workforce from 59,000 to 37,000. These kinds of actions do indeed get people's attention and tend to unfreeze the system.

The second step, *movement,* is to take action that will change the social system from its original level of behavior or operation to a new level. This action could be organization structuring (Foltz, Harvey, & McLaughlin, 1974), team development (Beckhard & Lake, 1971), or any number of what OD practitioners call interventions.

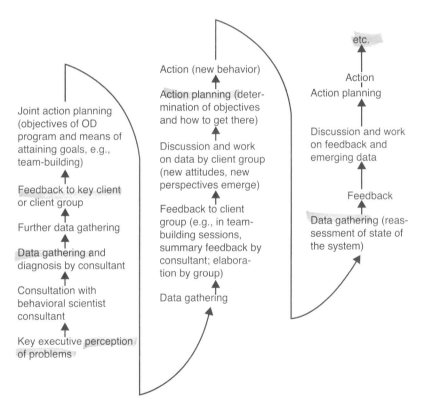

Figure 4.1 Action-Research Model for Organization Development

Source: W. L. French, "Organization Development: Objectives, Assumptions, and Strategies," © 1969 by the Regents of the University of California. Reprinted from the *California Management Review*, Volume XII, No. 2, p. 26 by permission of The Regents.

The *refreezing* step involves establishing a process that will make the new level of behavior "relatively secure against change" (Lewin, 1958). Refreezing may include different conforming patterns, or new forms, such as collaboration rather than competition (Davis, 1967; Tannenbaum & Davis, 1969), a new approach to managing people (Marrow, Bowers, & Seashore, 1967; Seashore & Bowers, 1970), or a new reward system that will positively reinforce the desired behavior change (Lawler, 1977; Lawler & Worley, 2006; Burke, 2014b).

Thus, according to Lewin, bringing about lasting change means initially unlocking or unfreezing the present social system. This might require some kind of confrontation (Beckhard, 1967) or a process of reeducation. Next, behavioral movement must occur in the direction of desired change, such as a reorganization as in the BA story. Finally, deliberate steps must be taken to ensure that the new state of behavior remains relatively permanent. Changing the performance appraisal and reward systems at BA were the primary interventions to reinforce the new managerial behaviors (openness in communication, teamwork, trust building, etc.). These three steps are simple to state but not simple to implement. Lippitt, Watson, and Westley (1958) and Schein and Bennis (1965; see especially Chapter 10 in their book) have helped to clarify these steps by elaborating on them.

Schein's Elaboration of Lewin's Three-Stage Model

As Schein points out: "These stages overlap and may occur very rapidly, but they are conceptually distinct, and it is important for the helper [OD practitioner] to be aware of what stage he is working in" (Schein, 1987, p. 93).

Stage 1. Unfreezing: Creating Motivation and Readiness to Change

Schein describes three ways of unfreezing an organization:

- *Disconfirmation or lack of confirmation.* Organizational members are not likely to embrace change unless they experience some *need* for it. Embracing change typically means that people are dissatisfied with the way things are—quality is below standard, costs are too high, morale is too low, or direction is unclear, for example.

- *Induction of guilt or anxiety.* This is a matter of establishing a gap between what is current but not working well and some future goal that would make things work better. When people recognize a gap between what *is* and what would be better and more desirable, they will be motivated via guilt or anxiety to reduce the gap. But disconfirmation and induction are not enough to accomplish the unfreezing stage, according to Schein. One more process is necessary.

- *Creation of psychological safety.* To face disconfirmation, experience guilt or anxiety, and be able to act or move, people must believe that moving will not bring them humiliation or loss of self-esteem. People must still feel worthy, psychologically safe. The consultant must therefore be concerned with people not losing face and must take care that when people admit that something is wrong, they will not be punished or humiliated.

Stage 2. Changing

This stage entails what Schein calls *cognitive restructuring*; that is, helping people to see things differently and to react differently in the future. There are two main processes for accomplishing this stage:

- Identifying with a new role model, mentor, boss, or consultant to "begin to see things from that other person's point of view. If we see another point of view operating in a person to whom we pay attention and respect, we can begin to imagine that point of view as something to consider for ourselves" (Schein, 1987, p. 105).

- Scanning the environment for new, relevant information. A brief, personal consulting example should help to clarify this point of Schein's. In working with the chairman of a company and the president or CEO, the three of us explored many reasons for their conflict with one another. To help with reducing some of this conflict, we worked hard on clarifying roles and responsibilities. In addition, the consultant (Burke) volunteered to bring to them other chairman-president/CEO models from other client organizations, some that worked very well and some that did not. This process was an activity of bringing to the two of them new, relevant information that might help them move forward with the changes needed in the relationship.

Stage 3. Refreezing

This final stage is one of helping the client integrate the changes. Schein sees this stage in two parts—self and relations with others:

- Personal refreezing is the process of taking the new, changed way of doing things and making it fit comfortably into one's total self-concept. This process involves a lot of practice—trying out new roles and behaviors, getting feedback, and making adjustments until the new way of doing things feels reasonably comfortable.

- Relational refreezing is the process of assuring that the client's new behavior will fit with significant others. In a system, when one begins to do things differently, will this difference quickly and, in any case, eventually affect others with whom the person interacts? If you and I interact frequently and I change, to maintain the relationship you will have to change as well, at least to some extent to maintain the relationship. This process involves openly engaging with others about the new way of doing things, to help them see why the change is better than the old way. The process applies Stages 1 and 2 to others to get to Stage 3.

Phases of Planned Change

The Lippitt, Watson, and Westley (1958) model of planned change expands Lewin's three steps to five phases. They use the word *phase* deliberately because *step* connotes a discrete action or event rather than the more likely reality, that step 1 has probably not been completed when step 2 is being taken, and so forth. The five phases are:

1. Development of a need for change (Lewin's unfreezing)
2. Establishment of a change relationship
3. Working toward change (Lewin's changing)
4. Generalization and stabilization of change (Lewin's refreezing)
5. Achieving a terminal relationship

Lippitt, Watson, and Westley viewed the change process from the perspective of the change agent. Their concept of change agent is a professional, typically a behavioral scientist, who is external or internal to the organization involved in the change process. In OD terms, this person is the OD practitioner or consultant. Lippitt and his colleagues go on to state:

> The decision to make a change may be made by the system itself, after experiencing pain (malfunctioning) or discovering the possibility of improvement, or by an outside change agent who observes the need for change in a particular system and takes the initiative in establishing a helping relationship with that system (Lippitt, Watson, & Westley, 1958, p.10).

With respect to Phase 1, development of a need for change, Lippitt, Watson, and Westley suggest that the unfreezing occurs in one of three ways: (1) A change agent demonstrates the need by, for example, presenting data from interviews that indicate a serious problem exists, (2) a third party sees a need and brings the change agent and the potential client system together, or (3) the client system becomes aware of its own need and seeks consultative help.

By establishment of a change relationship, Phase 2, the authors mean the development of a collaborative working effort between the change agent and the client system. Lippitt and his colleagues make an important point when they note that "often the client system seems to be seeking assurance that the potential change agent is different enough from the client system to be a real expert and yet enough like it to be thoroughly understandable and approachable" (p. 134). Striking this balance is critical to effective consultation in OD.

Most of their elaboration on Lewin's three steps is in the moving phase, or, as Lippitt and his colleagues call it, working toward change. There are three subphases to this third major phase:

1. *Clarification* or diagnosis of the client system's problem consists primarily of the change agent's collecting information and attempting to understand the system, particularly the problem areas.

2. *Examination* of alternative routes and goals involves establishing goals and intentions of action and also includes determining the degree of motivation for change and the beginning of a process of focusing energy.

3. *Transformation* of intentions into actual change efforts is the *doing* part—implementing a new organization structure, conducting a specific training program, installing a new record system, and the like.

Refreezing, or the generalization and stabilization of change, is the fourth major phase. The key activity in this phase is spreading the change to other parts of the total system. This phase also includes the establishment of mechanisms or activities that will maintain the momentum that was gathered during the previous phases. Lippitt and his colleagues call this a process of institutionalization. Hornstein, Bunker, Burke, Gindes, and Lewicki (1971) view this as both normative and structural support for the change. Normative support means that, in the refreezing phase, organization members are conforming to new norms. To ensure this form of institutionalization, organization members must be involved in planning and implementing the action steps for change. Involvement leads to commitment—in this case, commitment to new norms. Structural support may take the form of new organizational arrangements—that is, new reporting and accountability relationships, as reflected in a new organization chart—or the placement of guardians of the new culture, the new conforming patterns. These guardians, or facilitators, of the new culture are people whose job it is (1) to monitor the state of the organization's effectiveness, (2) to see that the information that is monitored is reported to the appropriate people in the organization, (3) to provide help in understanding the information, especially in the diagnosis of problems, (4) to assist in the planning and implementation of action steps for further changes, and (5) to provide additional expertise in helping the organization to continue to change and renew where appropriate. Their primary responsibility, therefore, is to help regulate change as an organizational way of life. Hornstein and his colleagues go on to state:

> Initially, this role is typically fulfilled by an outside consultant to the organization. Frequently, he attempts to work in conjunction with some person (or persons) inside the organization. If the internal person is not trained in OD, the external consultant will usually encourage the internal person(s) and other key individuals in the organization to develop their own resources in this area (Hornstein et al., 1971, p. 352).

In other words, the more the consultant can arrange for OD-trained people to be permanent organization members, the more likely the initiated change is to last and become institutionalized as a way of life.

For the final phase, Lippitt and his colleagues argue for the achievement of a terminal relationship. What they mean is that the relationship between the change agent and the client must end. They contend that it is common for clients to become dependent on change agents and that change agents' ultimate goal is to work themselves out of a job. The underlying value of this model for change is that it creates within the client system the expertise to solve its own problems in the future, at least those problems that fall within the same universe as the original change problem.

Summary of Action Research Methodology

Lewin's three-stage model has been a fundamental aspect of OD practice for a long time (Lewin, 1947). Most OD practitioners as a rule think and act according to these three steps or stages or phases. Remember they overlap and are therefore not discrete. More recently, there has been some criticism that Lewin's model is no longer apropos and, for example, is a bit too simplified for modern times; see Dawson (1994), Hatch (1997), and Kanter, Stein, and Jick (1992). Bernard Burnes (2004), citing theory and evidence, has responded to these criticisms. He summarized the criticisms into four categories and responded to each:

- *Criticism 1.* The three-step model is too simplistic and mechanistic. Burnes's response: Lewin did not view change as linear and unidimensional; social settings are in a state of constant change. So, Burnes's response is that this criticism is a misreading of Lewin's ideas and theory.

- *Criticism 2.* Lewin only addressed incremental and isolated change projects, not transformational change. Burnes's response: This criticism is more about speed than the scope of change. Moreover, incremental changes over time can lead to transformation. Because Lewin concentrated on behavioral change at all levels, individual, group, and organizational time and effort are required. The critics do seem to agree that transformation occurs with structural and technical changes, which can be achieved fairly rapidly but not with cultural change requiring new behavior. The culture change at BA (see Chapter 7), which was largely based on acquiring new behavior, took the better part of five years.

- *Criticism 3.* Lewin ignored issues of power and politics as well as conflict within organizations. Burnes's response: He found this criticism strange. After all, Lewin was significantly involved in race relations, religious intolerance, value differences, problems of status and caste, economic discrimination, political leadership, and leadership in general. And as Burnes points out, the original treatise on the bases of social power was written by French and Raven (1959). French was a student of Lewin's and the same French of Coch and French (1948) and Raven, a social psychologist, was highly influenced by Lewin's theory and research (Raven, 1993).

- *Criticism 4.* Lewin was an advocate of top-down, management-driven approaches to change and essentially ignored bottom-up change. Burnes's response: Actually, Lewin's sympathies were obviously with the underdog, the disadvantaged and those who were discriminated against. Lewin worked with a wide range of groups and organizations and he consistently emphasized learning and participation of everyone concerned.

Burnes concludes that these four criticisms are for the most part unwarranted. There is little substantiation to support them. His further conclusion, which captures much of the man, Lewin, and his contributions, are best conveyed in Burnes's own words:

> Looking at Lewin's contribution to change theory and practice, there are three key points to note. The first is that Lewin's work stemmed from his concern to find an effective approach to resolving social conflict through changing group behavior (whether these conflicts be at the group, organizational or societal level). The second point is to recognize that Lewin promoted an ethical and humanist approach to change, that saw learning and involvement as being the key processes for achieving behavioural change. This was for two reasons: (a) he saw this approach as helping to develop and strengthen democratic values in society as a whole and thus acting as a buffer against the racism and totalitarianism which so dominated events in his lifetime; (b) based on his background in Gestalt psychology and his own research, he saw this approach as being the most effective in bringing about sustained behavioural change. The last point concerns the nature of Lewin's work. Lewin's Planned approach to change is based on four mutually-reinforcing concepts, namely Field Theory, Group Dynamics, Action Research and the 3-Step model, which are used in combination to bring about effective change. His critics, though, tend to treat these as separate and independent elements of Lewin's work and, in the main, concentrate on his 3-Step model of change. When seen in isolation, the 3-Step model can be portrayed as simplistic. When seen alongside the other elements of Lewin's Planned approach, it becomes a much more robust approach to change (Burnes, 2004, pp. 995–996).

The Generic Model for Organizational Change

The four models covered so far in this chapter—action research; Lewin's three steps of unfreezing, moving, and refreezing; Schein's elaboration of Lewin's three stages; and Lippitt, Watson, and

Westley's five phases of planned change—are all part of a generic model for bringing about organizational change. This is not accidental, of course, because all four models are based on the original thinking of Kurt Lewin.

The generic model might be described as a process by which a consultant collects information about the nature of an organization (the research) and then helps the organization to change by way of a sequence of phases that involve those who are directly affected—the organization members themselves. This more general model consists of the following elements:

1. An outside consultant or change agent
2. The gathering of information (data) from the client system by the consultant for purposes of understanding more about the inherent nature of the system, determining major domains in need of change (problems), and reporting this information back to the client system so that appropriate action can be taken
3. Collaborative planning between the consultant and the client system for purposes of change (action)
4. Implementation of the planned change, which is based on valid information (data) and is conducted by the client system, with the continuing help of the consultant
5. Institutionalization of the change

To summarize and integrate the four models of change that we have considered thus far, Figure 4.2 shows a comparison of Lewin's (1958) three steps; the action research model provided by Wendell French (1969) and Schein (1980, 1987); and Lippitt, Watson, and Westley's (1958) phases of planned change. As shown in the figure, the action research model for OD is the main reference point for comparison.

It should be noted that earlier thinking about planned change, especially Lippitt et al. (1958) emphasized the role of the change agent as data collector, data interpreter, feedback provider, and so on. The change agent was depicted as doing practically everything. Current practice of OD emphasizes the role of the practitioner more in terms of *facilitation*, helping the client to do many of these activities themselves (Schein, 1987). Organizational development consulting is distinct in this regard from management consulting, where the consultant usually does all of this work for the client.

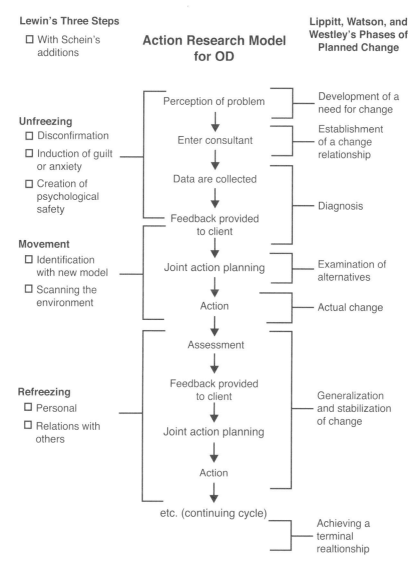

Figure 4.2 Comparison of the Four Models of Change

Even though we have labeled this section "the generic model," it may not be. Organization change is sufficiently complex that no generic model may yet exist. In any case, it is quite appropriate to refer to another model that has been given the label of generic. The difference is that what we have called generic encompasses diagnosis and intervention whereas the one we are now referring to is labeled by its authors as a "generic model of intervention" (Bushe & Shani, 1991).

Building on the earlier work of Howard Carlson at General Motors (Miller, 1978) and Zand (1974), Bushe and Shani make the argument, with case examples to support their points, that (1) bureaucracy remains as powerful and influential as ever as a primary way for organizational functioning (or nonfunctioning as the case may be), and therefore (2) parallel structures are required for innovation and change in large, complex bureaucracies. Galbraith (1982), using similar arguments, has also suggested alternative structures for innovation. These parallel learning structures, as Bushe and Shani refer to them, are used typically temporarily to overcome the limitations of bureaucracy. Bushe and Shani describe eight phases, which are similar to those of Kolb and Frohman (1970) and to the phases described later in this chapter.

While focusing primarily on the intervention aspect of change, these ideas of Bushe and Shani are sufficiently broad and applicable to be worthy of the label *generic.*

Now we shall consider a case that should help to understand how these models of action research—including principles applied by Bushe and Shani, and Lewin's three stages incorporating the elaborations of Schein and Lippitt et al.—are applied in an actual OD consulting example.

Practicing OD: A Case History

The action research model and the phases of planned change provide the framework for OD practice. We shall consider in more specificity these practice phases, but first let us consider an actual case of OD consultation that should help our later understanding of the phases of OD practice.

I (Burke) was contacted initially by Carol, the manager of human resources for a regional division of a large, international financial corporation. She reported directly to Ron, the regional manager. Carol called me because I had previously consulted with other divisions of the corporation and was therefore familiar with their business. She also told me that she had sought advice from others in the corporation and that I had been recommended. She explained that Ron was new in his position as regional manager and was anxious to make some changes. He was considering an off-site meeting with his senior management group and believed that an outside consultant might be helpful, Carol then asked if I would be interested and, if so, if we could have lunch together soon to explore the matter.

Exploration

At the lunch meeting a few days later, Carol and I asked each other many questions. She was interested in what I had done before, how I liked to work, what I might do or suggest if such and such were to happen, what I knew about her company's business, and whether I would be interested in continuing to consult with them if the initial effort went well. I asked her such questions as why the business had lost money four years in a row; what Ron's predecessor was like; what Ron was like—his managerial style; his previous job history; how people in the region, especially the senior management group, felt about him, and whether any of the others thought they should have become the new regional manager instead of Ron; how the senior management group worked together—if off-site meetings were common occurrences; and so forth. Toward the end of our exploratory discussion, Carol explained that she needed to talk further with Ron and that she would be in touch with me again soon.

Meeting with Ron

The following week, Carol called to schedule a meeting for me with Ron. In my meeting with Ron, it was soon clear to me that he trusted Carol a great deal. He was essentially sold on me, and all we needed to do was to discuss details. He explained that, although he had been in the region for more than three years as head of consumer services, he had only been regional manager for a month. He felt pressure from higher management to make the region profitable, and he reasoned that he must have his senior management group solidly with him in order to "turn the region around." He further stated that he wanted to have an off-site meeting with his senior management group to establish two-year profit goals, to develop an overall regional business strategy, and to begin the process of building a senior management *team.*

I explained that I would like to conduct individual interviews with the members of his senior management group, including himself, determine if they thought an off-site meeting was appropriate, summarize and analyze the information from the interviews, meet with him again to go over the data, plan the meeting (if warranted), and clarify our respective roles—that he would lead the meeting and I would help. In OD language, my role would be a facilitating one.

Agreement

We reached agreement concerning what Ron wanted and how I wanted to proceed. This verbal agreement was followed a few days later with an exchange of letters to confirm our agreement in writing.

Interviews

Over a one-week period, I conducted one-hour interviews with each member of the senior management group. This group is depicted in the chart shown in Figure 4.3. I explained to each manager that the interview would be confidential and that only a summary of the interviews in aggregate form would become public.

Although I asked many questions in each interview, I asked four general questions of everyone:

1. What are the strengths of the region?
2. What are the weaknesses of the region?
3. Are you in favor of the off-site meeting?
4. What should be the objective of the off-site meeting?

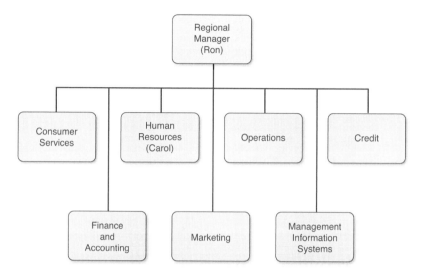

Figure 4.3 Organization Chart for Regional Division of International Financial Corporation

The interviews went well. All the managers were cooperative and expressed themselves openly and candidly, and I took many notes.

Summary and Analysis of Interviews

Although some of the managers thought the off-site meeting was somewhat premature because Ron had only been in his position for one month, others believed that the timing was right. Regardless of the timing, however, all thought an off-site meeting was a good idea. Thus, the summary of my interviews was categorized according to the three other questions—strengths and weaknesses of the region and objectives of the off-site meeting. Table 4.1 provides a partial listing of some of the major points of the interviews. As is typical for such an activity, the weaknesses listed outnumbered the strengths. People, especially managers, tend to focus more on problems than on what is going well or is positive for the organization.

Table 4.1 Partial Summary of Eight Interviews Conducted with a Regional Senior Management Group

Strengths of the Region

1. Senior management group is highly experienced in the business (7)

2. Commitment of work force; community spirit (5)

3. Considerable opportunity; natural market area (3)

4. Good people throughout (3)

5. Last four years we have experienced success in many areas (3)

6. Have become more of a marketing organization (3)

7. We are technologically superior and a market leader as compared with our competitors (3)

8. Creativity (2)

9. Managers think entrepreneurially (2)

Weaknesses

1. Our marketing and services system (6)

2. Try to do too many things at once; do not establish priorities (3)

3. Region priorities are always secondary to individual manager's (3)

4. Lack of management depth (3)

5. Little planning (3)

6. Structure (2)

7. High costs (2)

8. Overly change-oriented (2)

9. Poor reward system (2)

10. Low morale (2)

11. Internal competition (2)

12. High degree of mistrust (2)

Objectives of Off-Site Meeting

1. Agree on the regional structure (7)

2. Set financial objectives for next two years (6)

3. List of things we need to do and stop doing (4)

4. Must hear from Ron about his team notions, ideas, expectations (4)

5. Some ventilation of feelings needed (3)

6. Must come together more as a top management team (3)

7. Establish standards for performance (3)

8. Increase mutual respect (2)

Note: The number in parentheses after each item indicates the number of respondents who specifically mentioned that point.

Some general problems in the region became clear to me as a result of the interviews. Although the group believed that they were highly knowledgeable and experienced in their business, they recognized that remaining unprofitable was not going to get them to where they wanted to go, especially in their individual careers. There was also a conflict over whether theirs was a marketing and sales organization or a consumer services organization. Actually, it had to be both, but, from the standpoint of strategy and with respect to individuals' roles and responsibilities in lower levels of management, there was considerable ambiguity. This ambiguity contributed to problems of priorities, numbers 2 and 3 in the list of weaknesses. The emphasis on structure and financial objectives was therefore appropriate in the major objectives for the off-site meeting.

Planning for the Off-Site Meeting

Ron and I met before the off-site meeting to go over my summary and analysis of the interview information and to plan the meeting. I gave him the summary and analysis of the interviews just as I would later give it to the entire group. Thus, Ron received the same information but received it earlier. The purposes of this advance notice were (1) to use the information as a basis for planning an agenda for the meeting and (2) to allow Ron to have time to understand and react to the information before the meeting. Ron would then have an opportunity to discuss his reactions to the information, particularly his feelings so that if he felt defensive, for example, he could talk about it with me and not be as defensive during the meeting. In such situations, especially if it is the first time, bosses frequently receive more criticism for problems than any other member of the group. Even if interview comments are not specifically directed at the bosses, they may feel responsible and accountable for the problems because of their positions, regardless of where the actual causes may lie. In Ron's case, he was not angry and he was not particularly defensive. He didn't think he had contributed to the weaknesses and problems any more than anyone else had. If he had been regional manager longer than a month, of course, his feelings may have been different. Ron was pleased with his group's openness and accuracy regarding the issues, and he was enthusiastic about the upcoming meeting.

Our plan for the meeting was simple and straightforward. We wanted as little interference and distraction as possible, so we would hold the meeting at a hotel-resort that was fairly remote yet comfortable. The site was less than two hours away from the region's headquarters by automobile, and it met our criteria. Regarding the agenda, we planned to begin at 4:00 p.m. on Wednesday. Ron would open the meeting with a statement of his goals and expectations regarding the meeting, and I would follow with a summary of the interviews. The group would then have a chance to react to and discuss the interview summary. Before dinner, Ron would present some financial data that would show clearly how the region compared with the other regions (they were close to the bottom), and after some discussion we would eat dinner together as a group. Thursday morning would be devoted to setting a two-year profit goal and to establishing priorities among the many objectives. Thursday afternoon we would discuss potential obstacles to reaching the profit goal and to realizing some of the more specific objectives of the region, such as clarifying their objectives regarding the balance of marketing versus service. Friday morning we would discuss an overall strategy that would incorporate the profit goal and these objectives, and Friday afternoon would be devoted to a summary of the meeting, to members' reactions to and critique of the meeting, and to a discussion of the specific plans for follow-up.

The Off-Site Meeting

The meeting proceeded essentially as planned. We took a two-hour break for lunch and some physical recreation in the middle of the day on Thursday and then worked from 2:00 p.m. to about 7:00 p.m. On Friday, we had a quick lunch and continued to work until about 3:00 p.m., when we adjourned. This was somewhat short for such a meeting, but adequate. During the summary and critique of the meeting, I also participated, giving my observations of them as a group and making suggestions about how they could improve their work together as a team. Everyone considered the meeting to have been worthwhile and useful, and Ron was particularly pleased. He believed that the formation of a team, as opposed to an administrative aggregate of senior managers, had begun, and I agreed.

After the Off-Site Meeting

A few weeks after the meeting, Ron and I met again and agreed on a plan for my continued consultation. Some of the changes I helped to make were (1) installation of a planning function reporting directly to Ron; (2) reorganization of the consumer services area, particularly regarding the functions of marketing and sales as they related to service (an off-site meeting with the head of consumer services and his management group was part of the planning for these changes); (3) modifications in the reward and performance-appraisal processes of the region (I worked with Carol in this area); and (4) development of the senior management group into more of a team. Eventually, though certainly not overnight, the profit picture for the region began to change, and they did indeed move from the red to the black.

Now that we have the case as an illustration of OD consultation, let us reconsider the steps I took so that we can translate the activities into OD language and understand more thoroughly the concepts and principles of this kind of consultation.

Phases of OD Practice

Based on the Lewinian concepts of unfreezing, changing, and refreezing and on Lippitt, Watson, and Westley's (1958) phases of planned change, as well as Schein's (1987), but oriented more specifically to current OD practice, Kolb and Frohman (1970) give seven phases to be followed in an OD consultation: scouting, entry, diagnosis, planning, action, evaluation, and termination. I have modified their list by putting scouting and entry together, separating contracting and feedback into distinct phases, using intervention instead of action, and eliminating termination. What Kolb and Frohman call *scouting*, I call *entry*, and I consider *contracting* a more appropriate term for what they label as *entry*. Our differences are simply in labels and emphasis; the overall process is the same, except for termination, which I will explain later. Thus, my seven phases are as follows:

1. Entry
2. Contracting
3. Diagnosis

4. Feedback

5. Planning change

6. Intervention

7. Evaluation

We shall consider each of these phases in turn, using the case to illustrate the characteristics of OD consultation.

Entry

Contact between the consultant and client is what initiates the entry phase. This contact may result from either the client's calling the consultant for an exploratory discussion about the possibility of an OD effort, as in the case example, or from the consultant's suggesting to the client that such an effort might be worthwhile. For an external consultant, the contact is likely to result from the client's initiative. For an internal consultant, either mode could occur. Internal consultants, being employees, typically feel some commitment to their organizations, or it may be part of their job descriptions to call on managers in the organization and suggest preliminary steps that might lead to an OD effort. Internal consultants also may have experienced success with organization development in one subsystem and may wish to spread this effect further within the organization. Initiating contacts with clients therefore comes naturally for internal OD practitioners, and there is certainly more opportunity for informal contacts to occur—at lunch, at committee meetings, and so forth—when questions can be asked and suggestions explored.

After the contact, the consultant and the client begin the process of *exploring* with one another the possibilities of a working relationship. The client is usually assessing whether he or she can relate well with the consultant, whether the consultant's previous experience is applicable to the present situation, and whether the consultant is competent and can be trusted.

My lunch meeting with Carol served as the beginning of the exploration process. I repeated the process with Ron, the regional manager, but this second round was rapid because it had already been facilitated by Carol's previous meeting with and assessment of me.

During the exploration process, the consultant is assessing (1) the probability of relating well with the client, (2) the motivation and values of the client, (3) the client's readiness for change, (4) the extent of resources for supporting a change effort, and (5) potential leverage points for change—whether the client has the power to make decisions that will lead to change or whether higher authority must be sought. In my conversation with Ron, I became satisfied that he was motivated and ready for change, that he had the resources, and that he had the leverage—enough autonomy to take considerable action without getting approval from higher management.

There are additional criteria and ways of determining a client's readiness for change. Pfeiffer and Jones (1978), for example, have developed a useful 15-item checklist for such a determination. They urge the consultant to check, among others, such things as flexibility of top management, possible labor contract limitations (which could be crucial if job enrichment, for example, were a potential intervention), any previous experience the organization may have had with OD (or what some may have called OD, regardless of what the activities were), structural flexibility with respect to the organization's design, and the interpersonal skills of those who would be involved.

Contracting

Assuming that the mutual explorations of the consultant and the client in the entry phase progress satisfactorily, the next phase in the process is negotiating a contract. If the entry process has gone smoothly, the contracting phase is likely to be brief. The contract is essentially a statement of agreement that succinctly clarifies what the consultant agrees to do. If it is done thoroughly, the contract will also state what the client intends to do. The contract may be nothing more than a verbal agreement, with a handshake, perhaps, or it may be a formal document, with notarized signatures. Most often, the contract is considerably more informal than the latter extreme, typically involving an exchange of letters between the two parties.

Unlike other types of contracts, the OD contract states more about process than about content. According to Weisbord (1973), it is an explicit exchange of expectations...which clarifies for consultant and client three critical areas:

1. What each expects to get from the relationship;
2. How much time each will invest, when, and at what cost;
3. The ground rules under which the parties will operate (p. 1).

My contract with Ron was fairly straightforward. The letters we exchanged simply confirmed in writing what we had agreed to in our meeting. The letters summarized what I would do and some of what he planned to do. The case as I described it was indeed the implementation of our contract.

When we met after the off-site meeting, Ron and I agreed on a further contract, which was also confirmed in an exchange of letters.

It is a good practice in OD consultation to renew or renegotiate the contract periodically. In my consultation with Ron, the second contract was essentially an extension of the first, occurring about three months after the earlier one. The timing of the renewal or renegotiation is not as important as seeing that this phase is periodically repeated. It is also a good practice to have the agreement in writing. Although an exchange of letters may not necessarily constitute a legal document, the written word usually helps to avoid misunderstandings.

Diagnosis

There are two steps within the diagnostic phase: gathering information and analyzing it. Diagnosis has usually begun even at the entry phase—if the consultant is alert. How the client reacts to the possibility of change at the outset may tell a great deal not only about the client as an individual, but also about the part of the organization's culture that he or she represents. Initially, therefore, information gathering is accomplished through the consultant's observations, intuitions, and feelings. Later, more systematic methods are used, such as structured interviews, questionnaires, and summaries of such organizational documents as performance records and task force reports. Once the data are collected, the consultant must then put all the varieties of information together, summarize all the information without losing critical pieces, and finally organize the information so that the client can easily understand it and be able to work with it so that appropriate action can be taken.

As we shall see in the next chapter, there are several models to help the consultant with both steps of the diagnostic phase: knowing *what* information to seek and knowing *how* to analyze and interpret the information.

In my initial work with Ron and his management group, I relied on three methods of data gathering: interviews, my observations, and my reading of two documents—one concerning Ron's thinking about long-range planning and another that summarized the issues regarding the problem of marketing versus service orientation.

My diagnosis consisted of (1) summarizing the data according to the categories of the interview questions (see Table 4.1) and elaborating on what the interviewees had said and (2) drawing certain conclusions from the combination of my observations and some relationships I perceived in the interview results.

Feedback

How effectively the consultant has summarized and analyzed the diagnostic information will determine the success of the feedback phase to a significant extent. This phase consists of holding meetings with the client system—usually first with the boss alone and then with the entire group from whom the data were collected. The size of the group would determine the number of feedback sessions to be held. If the client system consisted of a manager and his or her immediate subordinates only, then two sessions would be required, one with the manager alone and the second with the entire group, including the manager. If more than these two levels of the overall managerial hierarchy were included—for example, four levels of management, involving 30 or more people—then as many as four or five feedback sessions may be necessary. A feedback session should allow for ample discussion and debate, and a small group that does not involve multiple levels of management is best for such purposes.

A feedback session generally has three steps. First, the consultant provides a summary of the data collected and some preliminary analysis. Next, there is a general discussion in which questions of clarification are raised and answered. Finally, some time is devoted to interpretation. At this stage, some changes may be made in the consultant's analysis and interpretation. Thus, the consultant works collaboratively with the client group to arrive at a final diagnosis that accurately describes the current state of the system.

In my work with Ron and his management team, I followed essentially the steps I've just outlined. The feedback phase consisted, first, of our discussion of the interview results early in the off-site meeting. Toward the end of the meeting, I provided additional feedback, which was a combination of my observations of the group as they worked together for two days and my further analysis of the interview data. I told them, for example, that I had observed that their competition with one another, a weakness some of them had identified, conformed to a particular norm. The norm seemed to be: "Let's see who among us can best identify and analyze our problems and weaknesses as a region." Everyone tackled every issue and problem, and it appeared that winning the game of "best analysis" was critical to all. My diagnosis, with which they agreed, was based in a social-psychological frame of reference and was particularly related to the concept of norm.

Planning Change

The planning phase sometimes becomes the second half of the feedback session, as happened with Ron and his team. Once the diagnosis was understood and deemed accurate, action steps were planned immediately. It has been noted that a good diagnosis determines the intervention. The only required planning may be the implementation steps—what to do. The more complex the diagnosis or the larger the client system, however, the more likely it is that the planning phase becomes a later event, following the feedback sessions. It may be best generally to allow some time to pass between feedback and planning—a few days, perhaps, but probably no more than a week. This passage of time might allow the feedback to sink in and would create an opportunity for more thought to be given to the planning process.

The purposes of this planning phase are to generate alternative steps for responding correctively to the problems identified in the diagnosis, and to decide on the step or order of steps to take. The OD practitioner again works collaboratively with the client system during this phase, primarily by helping to generate and explore the consequences of alternative action steps. The final decision of what steps to take is the client's, not the consultant's.

Intervention

The intervention phase consists of the action taken. The possibilities are numerous, and the selected interventions should be a direct reflection of and response to the diagnosis. Some examples of interventions at the individual level are job redesign and enrichment, training and management development, changes in the quality of working life, management by objectives, and career development. At the group level, interventions might include team building, the installation of autonomous work groups or quality control circles. Resolving intergroup conflict might be an intervention, as might changing such structural dimensions of the organization as reporting relationships, moving toward or away from decentralization of authority, modifying physical settings, or creating informal structures in the organization.

The interventions used in Ron's region were team building, process consultation, some minor structural changes, career development, and a change in the region's reward system by installation of a bonus plan for managers.

Whatever the intervention might be, the OD practitioner continues to work with the client system to help make the intervention successful. As Kolb and Frohman (1970) point out: "the failure of most plans lies in the unanticipated consequences of the change effort" (p. 60). The OD consultant's job is to help the client anticipate and plan for the unanticipated consequences.

Evaluation

It is usually best for someone other than the consultant to conduct an evaluation of any OD effort. The consultant cannot be totally objective, and it is difficult to concentrate on what needs changing and on evaluating its success at the same time (Lewicki & Alderfer, 1973).

The mode of evaluation may range from clients saying that they are pleased with the outcome to a systematic research effort employing controls and multiple data analyses. A more objective and systematic evaluation is obviously better, at least for determining cause and effect. It is difficult to do a highly scientific evaluation of OD efforts. The main problem, of course, is control; it is almost impossible to have a proper control group for comparison. Furthermore, the client is usually more interested in taking action that will pay off than in objectively determining whether the action results were attributable to the OD intervention. What is important to the client is whether the action taken was successful according to the organization's usual standards—profits, reduction of costs, or higher performance in general; what *caused* the success is less important. This was essentially the case with Ron and his region, and so no formal evaluation was conducted. Evaluation did occur, however, as I periodically checked and asked for feedback, and the profit results, although they did not necessarily prove a cause-effect relationship, were sufficient evaluation in this case.

Regardless of its form or index, evaluation is very important because the process usually reinforces the change effort, and it is a primary way to learn about the consequences of our actions.

In Chapters 8 and 9, "Understanding Organizations: Covert Processes" and "Planning and Managing Change," respectively, we shall consider evaluation again. It should be clear that some form of evaluation is a critical part in the OD process. Although the evaluative effort does not have to meet all the standards of rigorous research and the scientific method, it must at least provide adequate data for making reasonable decisions regarding further changes.

Termination of the OD Effort

The foregoing seven phases constitute what I consider the primary, sequential actions a practitioner takes in an organization development effort. My list differs slightly in emphasis and labels from the earlier list of Kolb and Frohman (1970), but the phases are essentially the same, with one exception: Kolb and Frohman's termination phase. They argue that "the consultant-client relationship is by definition temporary" (1970, p. 61), that the effort either succeeds or fails. If it fails, termination is abrupt; if it is successful and the goals are reached, the consultant may not leave so abruptly, but the relationship terminates because there is no further need for consultative help. It should be noted that Kolb and Frohman's seventh step is consistent with the phases of planned change delineated earlier by Lippitt, Watson, and Westley (1958).

I do not include termination in my list of phases for three reasons. First, termination is not an applicable phase for internal OD practitioners. Although they may conclude specific programs and projects with their clients, they should not terminate the relationship. A primary role of internal practitioners is to serve as guardians of the new culture. They help to regulate the social change that has become a new routine in organizational life (Hornstein et al., 1971). This regulation may take a variety of forms, ranging from periodic checks with client managers regarding the continuing effectiveness of changes to more systematic follow-up activities, such as conducting annual surveys, attending a manager's staff meetings as a process consultant, or helping to design and conduct off-site planning or diagnostic meetings for departments or divisions.

The second reason concerns external OD consultants. A termination phase is and should be more common for external consultants than for internal ones, but it is not necessarily a requirement for effective consultation. A major goal of an external OD consultant is to see that internal resources are established for the kind of help he or she is providing. As soon as possible, internal practitioners should begin to take over the work the external consultant initiates. Thus, although the external consultant's activities with the client organization may decrease, they do not necessarily have to be terminated. Kolb and Frohman's argument for termination is to prevent the client from becoming dependent on the consultant. As an external consultant, I have had long-standing relationships with some clients, but I have never felt them to be too dependent on me. Although dependency may occur as a problem in personal therapy, it rarely becomes an issue in consultation with organizations. I know of consultant-client relationships that have continued for more than a decade, and I consider them healthy and useful for both parties. An organization has a constant need for periodic, objective diagnostic checkups by external consultants—a need that exists, incidentally, whether or not the organization's managers see it.

Finally, I do not think a termination phase is appropriate because when OD practitioners follow the action research model, they naturally generate new data for further diagnosis and action. The process is cyclical (French, 1969), and because an organization is both dynamic and naturally follows the entropic process, there is always a great deal of consultative work to be done. For further elaboration of these three reasons, see Van Eron and Burke (1992).

Phases, Not Steps

Phases is a more appropriate term than *steps* for describing the flow of events in OD work. *Steps* implies discrete actions, whereas *phases* better connotes the reality of OD practice—a cycle of changes. Although it is useful for our understanding of OD practice to conceive of distinct phases, in actual practice they blend, overlap, and do not always follow one from the other. Diagnosis, for example, comes early in the OD process and intervention later, but when one is collecting information from the organization for diagnostic purposes, an intervention is occurring simultaneously; when the OD practitioner begins to ask questions about the organization and its members, he or she is intervening.

Phases is an appropriate term also because of the cyclical nature of the OD process. As the process continues, new or undisclosed data are discovered. These data affect organization members, and the members react, creating additional information for diagnosis. Further action is then planned as a consequence of the new, perhaps more refined diagnosis.

Another implication of the cyclical nature of OD relates to the characteristics of open social systems, as delineated by Katz and Kahn (1978). Two of these characteristics are relevant—the notion that organizations proceed through cycles of events over time and the notion that systems seek equilibrium. The first characteristic, that organizational life runs in cycles, is precisely the reason that OD is cyclical. Because organizations are cyclical, OD must also be in order to respond in an appropriate and timely manner. Major events in organizations—planning, budgeting, quarterly reports—are repeated over time; as these events are repeated, new data are likely to be generated each time. Two quarterly reports are rarely the same, and plans and budgets change continuously. Consequently, the diagnosis of an organization in December will be at least somewhat different from the diagnosis conducted the previous June—significantly different if a significant intervention has occurred during the intervening six months. If things in the organization are significantly different six months later, and if these differences are disturbing to organization members, they will seek equilibrium—back to the former state. Organization development involves change. When change occurs in one of the organization's components or subsystems, other subsystems act to restore the balance. Pressure is brought to bear on organizational behavior that is different from the norm of the organization's culture as it has evolved. Thus, in OD practice, for change to last, recurring diagnoses must be undertaken to determine the state of earlier interventions, and further actions (interventions) are usually needed to reinforce the new behaviors. The long-run objective is to institutionalize the change so that possibilities of changing the OD change will be resisted within the normal pattern of open-system life—equilibrium seeking.

Conclusion

This chapter considered the four background models for any OD effort and the seven primary phases of OD consultation using a case to illustrate the phases. Although it is instructive to consider these phases—entry, contracting, diagnosis, feedback, planning change, intervention, and evaluation—as discrete steps, and although the consultative flow of events essentially follows the order of the seven phases, in practice the phases are not discrete; they blend together and overlap. When the consultant enters the client organization to collect information (by interviews, questionnaires, or observations), the intervention phase, sixth in the ordered group of seven, has already begun, and although evaluation is listed as last, it begins at the entry stage as far as the client is concerned.

These phases are therefore guides for OD consultation. They are highly useful for planning and for ordering sequences of activities and events, but they should not be considered as discrete, rigid steps to follow or as the only phases of consultation in organization development.

Finally, it should be remembered that these guides help to accomplish primary objectives of any OD effort. That is, as OD practitioners, we are concerned with (1) providing people with choices, so that their feelings of freedom will not be unduly curtailed and thus their resistance will be minimized and (2) involving people at some level of participative decision making and communication regarding the direction of organizational change, so that commitment to change implementation will be enhanced. Although we have used slightly different language with this closing statement, we are meaning the same as Argyris (1970) when he describes his criteria for an effective intervention.

Endnote

1. Lippitt et al.'s model is an elaboration of Lewin's three steps. Schein (1987) has provided a more recent elaboration. We shall cover his version as well.

5

Defining the Client:
A Different Perspective

Over the many years of my work in organization development (OD), I (Burke) have overheard or taken part in numerous discussions about "Who is the client?" Is the client the head person, the boss, a particular unit or group, or the total system? In these discussions, OD practitioners have identified at least one of the above.

Let me be concrete by using an actual case, a consulting project of mine a few years ago, with a small, highly technical company, a subsidiary of a large corporation. I was introduced to the president by an employee relations person to explore the possibility of working with the company. Contracting with the president and later with his top group went fairly smoothly. After some interviewing and observing, I was soon able to provide them with some preliminary feedback. Although the employee relations person did not accompany me during this early stage, at my request he became my internal counterpart as I began to move downward through the organization.

I looked forward to this consulting project because I had rarely worked with an organization so small—about 90 employees—and so interesting scientifically and technically. (The firm was developing commercial lasers.) In short, this was an organization of a size that I believed I could "get my arms around" and one that seemed to be on the verge of exciting technical advances.

The top management group was relatively small, consisting of five persons, including the president (see Figure 5.1). Most of the staff was located in operations, which consisted of both manufacturing and marketing/sales. At least a third of my consulting effort was within this unit of the company.

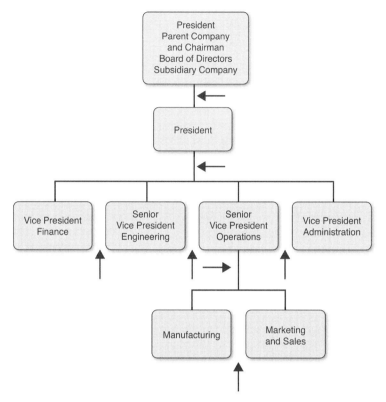

Figure 5.1 Partial Organizational Chart of Client Firm

Now to the central question: Who is my client? Answer by responding to the following multiple-choice question:

The client is which of the following?

a. Company president
b. Top management group
c. Employee relations person
d. Total company
e. Parent corporation
f. All of the above
g. None of the above

To be *au courant*, you would choose either (d) or (f). After all, OD is a total system approach to planned change that starts from the top. My contracting, however, was done first with the president and next with his immediate reports as a group. Perhaps a better answer is (a) or maybe (b). But what about the employee relations person? My coming in was originally his idea and he paved the way. Also, he later was very much involved in my efforts. Alternative (c) may be the best answer. But what about the parent company? Was I not really serving them? The president of the parent company was chairman of the board of the subsidiary. Although he was not the subsidiary's CEO, he was nevertheless clearly in a position of authority. Maybe (e) is the best reply. These answers all seem reasonable. Thus, the safest alternative should be (f).

Consider the title I chose for this chapter and now, perhaps reacting to the way I presented the multiple-choice question, you already conclude that my answer is (g). The purpose of this chapter, therefore, is to provide a rationale for that answer.

But, first, one other viewpoint should be considered. Schein's (1987) definition of the client is valuable because it is practical and multiple. He states that we must think in terms of client *categories:*

- *Contact clients* approach the consultant initially (the employee relations person in my example).
- *Intermediate clients* get involved with the consultant in the early stages of the OD effort (the top management group in my example).
- *Primary clients* own a problem for which help is requested (the operations group in my example).
- *Ultimate clients* may or may not be directly involved with the OD practitioner "but their welfare and interest must be considered in planning further interventions" (Schein, 1987, p. 118). (In the case I described, this could be the parent company.)

The value of Schein's categories is the fact that he addresses the reality of consulting. We often do not end up where we started in the consultant-client relationship.

Relations and Interfaces

Now back to my selection of (g) "none of the above." I chose it because I believe that our client in OD consultation is never one individual, regardless of position or role, or any particular group, team, or subsystem of the organization, or any combination thereof. Even though I generally subscribe to the idea of OD being a "total system," I often wonder if changing a whole system is even possible. Besides, I have trouble defining what the total system is because each one resides within yet a larger "total system."

The truth is that I have come to think of my client as the relationship and/or interface between individuals and units within and related to the system. Thus, the arrows in Figure 5.1 depict my view of the true client. This in-between-ness is the main subject of my consulting.

From the perspective of the consultant role, my notion of client is not new. In his 1970 book, Argyris avoided terms such as consultant, change agent, or practitioner, favoring instead *intervenor* and *interventionist*. These terms were, of course, an extension of his definition of a consultant intervention:

> To intervene is to enter into an ongoing system of relationships, to come between or among persons, groups, or objects for the purpose of helping them. There is an important implicit assumption in the definition that should be made explicit; the system exists independently of the intervenor (Argyris, 1970, p. 15).

For Argyris, then, to consult is to intervene.

Margulies (1978) characterized the role of the OD consultant as a marginal one (see Chapter 8, "Understanding Organizations: Covert Processes"). He argued that the degree to which the consultant is effective is a function of how capable he or she is at maintaining a certain social distance between self and other individuals in the client organization and at operating on the boundaries of units rather than exclusively within them. In these ways, the consultant can more readily maintain an objective stance *in between* persons and units in conflict rather than by being *with* one or the other.

Although I agree with both Argyris and Margulies regarding the consultant role, the focus here is on the other side, the client, and on the perspective of defining the client as relationships and interfaces rather than individuals and units, singular entities within the organization. To pursue this perspective, we first consider theory and then practice—the why and then the where and how.

Theory

Both general systems theory and the theory that underlies Gestalt therapy have furnished me with useful conceptual frameworks for understanding OD practice (Burke, 1980). Notions of entropy, input-throughput-output, and equilibrium from the former and the ideas of energy, existentialism, and polarities from the latter have been particularly helpful in understanding some mistakes I have made in consultation; that is, why some efforts turned out other than as I had expected. To explain in more depth the ideas touched on in Chapter 2, "Organization Development Then and Now," I find the theoretical thinking of Capra (1977, 1983) in high-energy physics and Prigogine (Nicolis and Prigogine, 1977) and Jantsch (1980) in chemistry and evolution, respectively, particularly stimulating because their ideas both confirm and challenge general systems and related theory.

Capra stimulated me to consider organizational diagnosis in quite new ways. Like most OD practitioners, I have depended on models to help me make sense of all the data I collect from interviews, documents, observations, and the occasional questionnaire. I have relied on Weisbord's six boxes at certain times and on other models with clients (see Chapter 6, "Understanding Organizations: The Process of Diagnosis"). Although they have been invaluable, they have not been the *sine qua non* of diagnosis. The boxes and connecting lines direct me where to look and how to interpret certain information, yet when I concentrate exclusively on the components of these models I find that I overlook other important data—the nuances, certain reappearing yet inconsistent patterns of behavior, hidden agendas, and collusions. Yes, I know it is imperative that the client organization declare its purpose and mission, clarify its strategy, design an appropriate, workable structure, provide for its members reasonable and attractive rewards, and so on (see Chapter 7, "The Burke-Litwin Model of Organizational Performance and Change"). But focusing entirely on these dimensions obscures other data that should enter the consultant's field of vision. It may be that what happens out of the ordinary is just as important, if not more so, than what happens routinely. It may be that repercussions in one or more of the boxes brought about by events in another box in the model are more important for diagnosis than what happens in the changed box itself. For example, a change of leadership may have stronger implications for organizational purpose than for the organization's leadership per se.

Let us now consider some of Capra's thoughts more directly. According to Capra and other physicists, matter at the subatomic level does not exist in terms of *things* but as *probability waves.* They only *tend* to exist. Those terms that we learned in high school, *protons* and *neutrons,* the subparts of an atom, are not parts, particles, or tangible things as we normally think of them. They may be conceived of as entities but only as a convenience. Capra's own words may help:

> Depending on how we look at them, they appear sometimes as particles, sometimes as waves....

> The apparent contradiction was finally resolved in a completely unexpected way that dealt a blow to the very foundation of the mechanistic world view—the concept that matter is real. At the subatomic level, it was found, matter does not exist with certainty at definite pinpointable places but rather shows "tendencies to exist."

> At the atomic level, then, the solid-material objects of classical physics dissolve into wavelike patterns of probabilities. These patterns, furthermore, do not represent probabilities of things, but rather probabilities of interconnections (Capra, 1977, p. 22).

Capra is therefore discussing *relations* of abstract particles. These relations constitute a unified whole. This kind of thinking suggested to me that I should consider more directly and diligently the web (to use Capra's term) of relations in organizations. It is this web, the interactions, the interfaces, that make up or at least define the total system more clearly than the units and individuals that form the connecting points. For me, this way of conceiving and diagnosing a system depicts the reality of organizational behavior more closely than other models.

Jantsch, basing much of his theorizing on the prior work of Prigogine, states that to understand the evolution of living things, one must concentrate more on disequilibrium than on equilibrium. The former, he contends, is far more natural, affirmative, and central to growth and change. To achieve equilibrium is to gain comfort, yet this victory may bring us closer to stagnation and death than to vibrancy and life. Jantsch also holds that evolution is accelerating just as the overall process of change appears to be.

His theory has been heralded by some as a paradigmatic shift comparable to Einstein's move away from Newton. Just as Einstein's theory of relativity wrested the physical sciences away from Newton's static ideas of gravity, Jantsch's ideas challenge us to view movement, relativity, and change in living systems as *constant.* He argues that all living things are always coevolving, yet maintaining a "relativity" to one another. Both Jantsch and Prigogine believe that the disequilibrium and perturbation that are from time to time in living things are actually a kind of molting, a shedding of the old within organisms as they strive to attain a higher level of existence. These perturbations, activities of disequilibrium, are signs of positive change that lead to self-organization rather than to decline. Thus, out-of-the-ordinary events may be more significant for organizational understanding than ordinary ones.

A related principle from general systems theory is the idea of the steady state and dynamic homeostasis (see Goodwin Watson's 1966 article for an analysis of resistance to change within this theoretical context). According to this principle, open systems to survive must maintain a steady state. However, a steady state is not motionless or a true equilibrium. As Katz and Kahn (1978) characterize this principle for organizations, "There is a continuous inflow of energy from the external environment and a continuous export of the products of the system, the ratio of the energy exchanges and the relations between parts, remains the same." Even though their theory contends that the steady state is not motionless, Katz and Kahn do note that "relations between parts remain the same" and they conclude that "The basic principle is the preservation of the character of the system." Perhaps their interpretation of general systems theory and Jantsch's thinking are not that different. Perhaps it is a matter of emphasis.

But it may be that practitioners of OD would have overly emphasized the client's achievement of a steady state and equilibrium. Yes, OD is at heart identified with change, yet one of our major interventions, team building, is more often than not a striving toward greater equilibrium. ("Let's learn to work better together; let's learn to trust; let's build a more cohesive unit"; etc.) These equilibrating goals are worthy, but if OD practitioners spend all their consulting time in this manner and in resolving conflicts, they may be helping to squash needed perturbations and disequilibrium.

Life cycle theory of organizations is pertinent to this last point (see, for example, Greiner, 1972). Usually for an organization to move successfully from one state of the cycle to another, wrenching changes have to be made even to the point of modifying the basic character of the organization.

To summarize, theory from sources other than the ones I usually turn to has challenged my way of understanding and diagnosing organizations. These ideas about matter and living things have stimulated me to concentrate more on the relationships between people and units rather than necessarily the individuals and units per se, and on unusual events rather than on routine operations.

Let me now call attention to some findings and different emphases from the world of practice that have influenced my outlook.

Practice

Some studies in management have further influenced my thinking about the importance of relationships and interfaces. We consider these studies in four different domains of relationships: the manager's relationships downward with subordinates, upward with his or her boss, lateral relationships, and the manager's unit's relationships with other individuals and units.

Managing Subordinate Relationships

There is mounting evidence that, used appropriately, a participative management approach pays off. For example, some recent research reveals that managers who move rapidly up the hierarchy tend to involve their subordinates in decision making more than do managers who move up less rapidly. These faster-rising managers were rated by themselves and their subordinates as having a participative style, whereas less-successful managers were rated as having a persuasive, "selling" style or one that we might characterize as laissez-faire (Hall, 1976).

In a study of executive competence in a large federal agency, those executives who were widely considered the most competent tended to manage more collaboratively, communicate more openly, solicit information from subordinates more frequently, more often establish mutual trust and respect with subordinates, provide more opportunities for subordinates to express openly their objections and disagreements with their superior's proposed actions or decisions, and manage work group meetings in ways to ensure that a frank and open exchange of ideas occurred (Burke & Myers, 1982). There were at least 16 other significant differences between the most competent executives and those who were less so. The six I have cited sound to me like a partial role description of a participative manager. In any case, the other behaviors were related to and supportive of the six above.

Blake and Mouton (1982) have also provided further theoretical support for their advocacy of participative management (see Chapter 6) as well as some indirect empirical evidence.

Moreover, as pointed out in a *Fortune* magazine article (Saparito, 1986), it seems quite clear now that participative management works (also, see Huselid, 1995; Kizilos, Cummings, & Strickstein, 1994; and Sashkin, 1984); what prevents this form of management becoming more pervasive in spite of the evidence, according to the magazine reporter, is managers' reluctance to share power. As one senior executive put it, "It's no fun if you *can't* make the right decisions" (p. 60).

Although I believe that the overall pattern of evidence respecting executive competence leans more and more toward participative management, my point here is not to debate the issue of management style. I *do* wish to emphasize that management is becoming more and more a reciprocal process and less and less a top-down, boss-to-subordinate, one-way street. If reciprocal relationships are a crucial ingredient of management competence, then my job as a consultant is to facilitate reciprocity, to mediate a two-way street, in other words, to work in *between.*

Managing Up

We have some findings about the importance of learning how to influence one's boss. Failure to "manage up," to relate in an active rather than passive way with one's superior, can readily lead to grave problems in the organization if not outright dismissal of a subordinate. Gabarro and Kotter (1980) advise that one should learn quickly the boss's personal and organizational goals, strengths and limitations, work habits and preferences, as well as one's own patterns and style and how they fit with the boss's. The more one knows about these subjects, the more influential one is likely to be.

In the aforementioned study of federal executives, we found that three competencies in this domain are critical: (1) the executive going to bat for subordinates with his or her superiors, (2) the executive's ability to present bad news to superiors in a constructive way, and (3) the executive establishing good relations with upper-level executives.

OD consultants can help subordinates sharpen their abilities to influence those above them in the hierarchy. Helping subordinates to disclose threatening news, for example, will ensure that a boss is never surprised (a sin). Likewise, knowing how to deflect one's boss from his or her preferred path is no small feat, yet it is often critical to organizational effectiveness. The point, once again, is to work in between.

Managing Lateral Relationships

Another set of competencies important to federal executives is skill at managing relationships with outside contractors and with other units within their organization. Moreover, a recent intensive study of successful general managers in the private sector found that the ability and energy to maintain contact with many people (in the hundreds) in their organization was key to their effectiveness (Kotter, 1982). Successful managers knew an amazing number of people throughout the organization on a first-name basis, and they made frequent use of these relationships to be effective in their work. Maintaining a network is therefore highly significant to the success of a general manager just as it is to the politician. Note that Chapter 10, "Understanding and Changing Loosely Coupled Systems," covers loosely coupled systems with a network as the prime example. This coverage helps to explain the importance of networks now and in the future.

What struck me about these findings is, of course, the importance of multiple relationships, of establishing as well as maintaining them. In the federal agency study, we labeled one set of the competencies (about a sixth of the total) *influence management* because they were all concerned with the executive's ability to influence others by means other than formal authority. It is perhaps in this domain of management in particular, and organizational functioning in general, that Capra's "web of relations" becomes more salient. The consultant being able to perceive this web in all its intricacy is central to a good diagnosis and vital to constructive intervention.

Managing Unit Interfaces

In an important paper about the dilemmas of managing by participation, Kanter (1982) treats the matter of linking teams with their environment. This linkage consists of six dilemmas:

1. *Problems of turnover ("You had to be there").* A major outcome of good team building is an increase in member participation accompanied by a lift in team spirit. This same spirit becomes a problem when new members join the team, especially if a newcomer happens to be a new boss. The boss can undercut the group's work and/or lead the team in unwanted directions. If the team is to remain effective, these new and changing relationships must be managed.

2. *The fixed decision problem.* When a group first begins to operate participatively so that a new team starts to emerge, certain ground rules, norms, and policies gradually become decisions. Later, when membership changes, the new members do not necessarily feel bound by these decisions because they took no part in framing them. Moreover, because all team members

should have influence, prior decisions should not be viewed as immutable, the new members might argue. The dilemma, then, is how to continue the process of participation yet not to be obliged continually to renegotiate the team's earlier decisions.

3. *Suboptimization: too much team spirit.* A team can become so preoccupied with itself that its members lose sight of the team's role and function within the larger organization.

4. *Stepping on toes and territories: the problem of power.* There may be other constituencies within the overall organization who believe that they have a stake in the problem or issue that the team holds as its exclusive domain. The team feels that it has worked so well together on this problem or issue that no one else is qualified to understand it as well, much less to deal with it effectively. With this knowledge and spirit comes a feeling of power that may be difficult to share when it is clear that others outside the team need to be involved.

5. *Not invented here (NIH): the problem of* ownership *and* transfer. It is commonplace that individuals and organizational units want to do things in their own way. And the greater the team spirit, the more reluctant members may be to adopt someone else's ideas, especially another team's. This reluctance, however, may lead to the waste of "reinventing the wheel" and of not cooperating, say, in the sharing of information. Diffusion of innovation is one of the most difficult problems of organizations.

6. *"A time to live and a time to die."* Although the evidence is not yet conclusive, there is some indication that participation needs regular renewal. Members of intensive participation groups, such as quality circles and semiautonomous work teams, have experienced burnout after 18 months of activity. Periods of interpersonal intensity should alternate with periods of distance. This suggests that some old teams need to die; new ones will form in their place. With other kinds of groups and teams, such as task forces, boards, councils, and so on, perhaps it is best to rotate membership rather than kill off old teams and start anew. Kanter's point is that it is necessary for management to find ways to sustain continuity of participation as members of groups and as units come and go.

Kanter covers other dilemmas of management participation, especially within teams themselves and in leader-member relationships. Her dilemmas concerning a team's linkage with its environment are particularly pertinent to areas of relationships and interfaces that OD practitioners may overlook. Flushed with the success of a team-building effort, the consultant may be blind to the greater need of helping the team with new members, a new leader perhaps, other units that may have a stake in some of the outcomes of the team's work, and its own team members over time because the need for renewal will emerge sooner than one might expect.

Kanter's dilemmas of managing participation, particularly those dealing with a team and its environment, represent fertile ground for OD consultation and further illustrate that the ground for consultation largely comprises relationships and interfaces.

Conclusion

Although I have usually been clear about the person in the client organization with whom I should contract for OD consultation, I have not always been clear that my *ultimate* client was the same person, or his or her boss, or a specific organizational unit such as the top management group, or the total system. It seems to me that other OD consultants are likewise somewhat perplexed about the identity of the ultimate client. As I read works about living systems and reflect on OD practice, I conclude that my ultimate client is that *behavior* in organizations represented by *interactions*, by relationships and interfaces. These interactions represent the basic reality of organizational life and therefore my consultation should concentrate on them. Furthermore, I should pay special attention to nonroutine events of organizational life because these occurrences generate energy among members to return the system to a steady state, to achieve homeostasis and equilibrium. It is this use of energy and its direction that will tell me more about how the organization really operates than the energy that the members of the organization expend to maintain normal, daily operations. Just as Kurt Lewin observed that the best way to diagnose an organization is to attempt to change it, we may also state that it is easier to understand an organization when it is disturbed by atypical events than when it is operating as usual.

It is not my contention that one should entirely ignore everyday routine, the organizational structure with its boxes and lines, individuals, work units, the president, and the board of directors. It is more a matter of emphasis for me to focus especially on the in-between. I also believe that relationships and interfaces in organizations will grow even more important in the future because of the changing nature of authority, insofar as authority becomes more of a function of expertise and knowledge rather than position, and of the increasing degrees of complexity in managing organizations. It is virtually impossible for a single individual to know a considerable amount, much less everything, about running an organization or even a part of it. This is especially true of high-technology organizations, public or private. Thus, mutual dependency is more the rule than the exception.

Because OD practitioners are knowledgeable about interpersonal process and are skillful in dealing with relationships, there will be plenty of opportunity for constructive work, changing cultures, and applying OD in new ways. We simply must become clearer about the true subject (in my term, *client*) of that work.

6

Understanding Organizations: The Process of Diagnosis

Without a framework for understanding, the data an organization development (OD) practitioner collects about a client organization may remain nothing more than an array of personal comments of the who-said-what-about-whom variety. For the information to become useful, it must be treated in organizational terms. Because OD represents a systematic approach to change, and the data for diagnosis are largely in systems language, the categories for diagnosis are systems labels.

This chapter covers selected models of and theories about organizations that are useful in the diagnostic phase of OD consultation because they help to organize and systematize the potentially confusing masses of data. Among the models and theories from which the OD practitioner may choose, some are merely descriptive while others emphasize dimensions for diagnosis, thereby providing direction for change. The purpose of this chapter is to provide the practitioner with some criteria and bases for making choices.

The models and theories that have been chosen to consider in this chapter are all behavior-oriented. Although some other frameworks emphasize technological, financial, or informational aspects of organizations, behavior-oriented models are more valuable for OD practice because the role of the OD practitioner is to understand what *people* do or do not do in organizations. Social media and other kinds of technology, for example, are of interest to OD practitioners, but only in terms of what it means for how people work, not for the technological wizardry involved (Bush & McCord, 2010; Kaplan, 2005).

The various models we explore are all based on the open-system notion of input-throughput-output and all recognize that an organization exists in an environmental context and is a sociotechnical system. All recognize the same fundamentals—an open system that exists in an environment and consists of people and technology.

Organizational Models

We first examine four models that are largely descriptive: a model of simplicity with structure, two models of complexity with structure, and a develop-your-own model.

Weisbord's Six-Box Model

A model is useful when it helps us visualize reality, and Weisbord's (1976, 1978) model meets this criterion very well. Weisbord depicts his model as a radar screen, with "blips" that tell us about organizational highlights and issues good and bad. Just as air traffic controllers use their radar, we too must focus primarily on the screen as a whole, not on individual blips (see Figure 6.1).

Every organization is situated within an environment and, as the arrows in the figure indicate, is influenced by and influences various elements of that environment. In Weisbord's model, the organization is represented by six boxes: purposes, structure, rewards, helpful mechanisms, relationships, and leadership. Weisbord believes that, for each box, the client organization should be diagnosed in terms of both its formal and its informal systems. A key aspect of any organizational diagnosis is the gap between the formal dimensions of an organization, such as the organization chart (the structure box), and its informal policies, such as how authority is actually exercised. The larger this gap is, the more likely it is that the organization is functioning ineffectively.

Weisbord provides key diagnostic questions for each of the six boxes. For the *purposes* box, the two most important factors are goal clarity, the extent to which organization members are clear about the organization's mission and purpose, and goal agreements, people's support of the organization's purpose. For *structure*, the primary question is whether there is an adequate fit between the purpose and the internal structure that is supposed to serve that purpose. With respect to *relationships,* Weisbord contends that three types are most important: between individuals, between units or departments that perform different tasks, and between the people and the nature and requirements of their jobs. He also states that the OD consultant should "diagnose first for required interdependence, then for *quality of relations,* and finally for modes of conflict management" (Weisbord, 1976, p. 440).

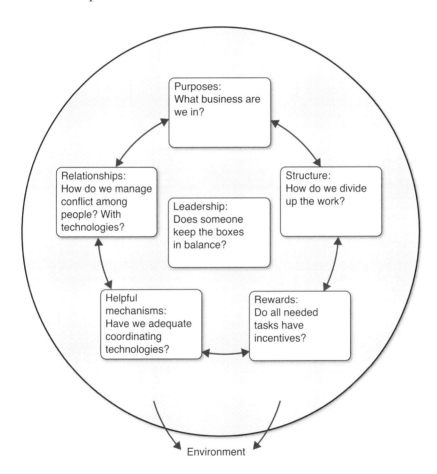

Figure 6.1 Weisbord's Six-Box Organizational Model

Source: Weisbord, M. R. (1976). Organizational diagnosis: Six places to look for trouble with or without a theory. *Group and Organization Studies,* 1, 430–47. Reprinted by permission.

In assessing blips for the *rewards* box, the consultant should diagnose the similarities and differences between the organization's formal rewards (the compensation package, incentive systems, and the like) and organization members' perceived rewards or punishments.

Weisbord makes the *leadership* box central because he believes that a primary job of the leader is to watch for blips among the other boxes and to maintain balance among them. To help the OD consultant in *diagnosing* the leadership box, Weisbord refers to an important book written by Selznick (1957) and published more than a half century ago yet remains highly relevant today. Citing the four most important leadership tasks, according to Selznick, the consultant should determine the extent to which organizations' leaders are (1) defining purposes, (2) embodying purposes in programs, (3) defending the organization's integrity, and (4) maintaining order with respect to internal conflict.

For the last box, *helpful mechanisms*, Weisbord refers analogously to "the cement that binds an organization together to make it more than a collection of individuals with separate needs" (Weisbord, 1976, p. 443). Thus, helpful mechanisms are the processes that every organization must attend to in order to survive: planning, control, budgeting, and other information systems that help organization members accomplish their respective jobs and meet organizational objectives. The OD consultant's task is to determine which mechanisms (or which aspects of them) help members accomplish organizational purposes and which seem to hinder more than they help. When a helpful mechanism becomes red tape, it probably is no longer helpful.

Table 6.1 gives a summary of the six-box model and the diagnostic questions to be asked.

In summary, Weisbord's model is particularly useful when the consultant does not have as much time as would be desirable for diagnosis, when a relatively uncomplicated organizational map is needed for quick service, or when the client is unaccustomed to thinking in systems terms. In the latter case, the model helps the client to visualize his or her organization as a systemic whole without the use of strange terminology. We have also found Weisbord's model useful in supervising and guiding students in their initial OD consultations.

Table 6.1 Weisbord's Matrix for Survey Design or Data Analysis

	Formal System (Work to Be Done)	Informal System (Process of Working)
1. Purposes	Goal clarity	Goal agreement
2. Structure	Functional, program, product or geography, or matrix?	How is work actually done or not done?
3. Relationships	Who should deal with whom on what?	How well do they do it? Quality of relations? Modes of conflict management?
4. Rewards (incentives)	Explicit system What is it?	Implicit, psychic rewards What do people *feel* about payoffs?
5. Leadership	What do top people manage?	How? Normative "style" of administration?
6. Helpful mechanisms	Budget system Management information (measures?) Planning Control	What are they actually used for? How do they function in practice? How are systems subverted?

Diagnostic questions may be asked on two levels:

1. How big a gap is there between formal and informal systems? (This speaks to the fit between individual and organization.)

2. How much discrepancy is there between "what is" and "what ought to be"? (This highlights the fit between organization and environment.)

Source: Weisbord, M. R. (1976). Organizational diagnosis: Six places to look for trouble with or without a theory. *Group and Organization Studies, 1,* 430–47. Reprinted by permission.

The Nadler-Tushman Congruence Model

For a more sophisticated client and when more time is available, a more complex model of organizations might be useful for OD diagnosis. In such instances, the Nadler and Tushman (1977) congruence model might serve the purpose.

Nadler and Tushman make the same assumptions as Weisbord—that an organization is an open system and therefore is influenced by its environment (inputs) and also shapes its environment to some extent by outputs. An organization thus is the transformation entity between inputs and outputs. Figure 6.2 represents the Nadler-Tushman congruence model.

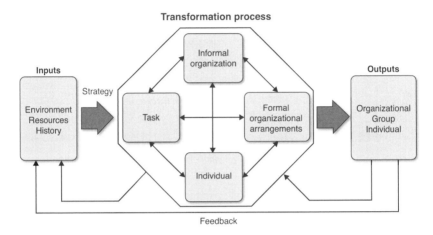

Figure 6.2 The Nadler-Tushman Congruence Model for Diagnosing Organizational Behavior

Source: Nadler, D. A., & Tushman, M. L. (1977). A diagnostic model for organization behavior. In J. R. Hackman, E. E. Lawler, & L. W. Porter (Eds.), *Perspectives on Behavior in Organizations* (p. 92). New York: McGraw-Hill. Reprinted by permission.

Inputs

Nadler and Tushman view inputs to the system as relatively fixed; the four they cite are the *environment,* the *resources* available to the organization, the organization's *history,* and the *strategies* that are developed and evolve over time. These inputs help define how people in the organization behave, and they serve as constraints on behavior as well as opportunities for action.

As we know from the works of Burns and Stalker (1961), and Lawrence and Lorsch (1967), the extent to which an organization's environment is relatively stable or dynamic significantly affects internal operations, structure, and policy. For many organizations, a very important aspect of environment is the parent system and its directives. Many organizations are subsidiaries or divisional profit centers of larger corporations, colleges within a university, or hospitals within a larger health-care delivery system. These subordinate organizations may operate relatively autonomously with respect to the outside world (having their own purchasing operations, for example) but because of corporate policy may be fairly restricted in how much money they can spend. Thus, for many organizations, we must think of their environments in at least two categories: the larger parent system and the rest of the outside world—government regulations, competitors, and the marketplace in general.

According to the Nadler-Tushman model, resources include capital (money, property, equipment, and so on), raw materials, technologies, people, and various intangibles, such as company name, which may have a high value in the company's market.

An organization's history is also input to the system. The history determines, for example, patterns of employee behavior, policy, the types of people the organization attracts and recruits, and even how decisions get made in a crisis.

Although strategies are categorized as an input in the model, Nadler and Tushman set it apart. Strategy is the process of determining how the organization's resources are best used within the environment for optimal organizational functioning. It is the act of identifying opportunities in the environment and determining whether the organization's resources are adequate for capitalizing on these opportunities. History plays a subtle but influential role in this strategic process.

Some organizations are very strategic; that is, they operate according to a plan. Other organizations simply react to changes in their environments or act opportunistically rather than according to a long-range plan that determines which opportunities will be seized and which will be allowed to pass. As Nadler and Tushman point out, however, organizations have strategies whether they are deliberate and formal or unintentional and informal.

Outputs

We move to the right side of the model to consider outputs before covering the transformation process. Thus, we examine the organization's environment from the standpoint of both how it influences the system and how the organization operates internally.

For diagnostic purposes, Nadler and Tushman present four key categories of outputs: system functioning, group behavior, intergroup relations, and individual behavior and effect. With respect to the effectiveness of the system's functioning as a whole, the following three questions should elicit the necessary information:

1. How well is the organization attaining its desired goals of production, service, return on investment, and so on?
2. How well is the organization utilizing its resources?
3. How well is the organization coping with changes in its environment over time?

The remaining three outputs are more directly behavioral: how well groups or units within the organization are performing; how effectively these units communicate with one another, resolve differences, and collaborate when necessary; and how individuals behave. For this last output, individual behavior, we are interested in such matters as turnover, absenteeism, and, of course, individual job performance and satisfaction.

The Transformation Process

The components of the transformation process and their interactions are what we normally think of when we consider an organization—the people, the various tasks and jobs, the organization's managerial structure (the organization chart), and all the relationships of individuals, groups, and subsystems. As Figure 6.2 shows, four interactive major components compose the transformation process that changes inputs into outputs.

The *task* component consists of the jobs to be done and the inherent characteristics of the work itself. The primary task dimensions are the extent and nature of the required interdependence between and among task performers, the level of skill needed, and the kinds of information required to perform the tasks adequately.

The *individual* component consists of all the differences and similarities among employees, particularly demographic data, skill and professional levels, and personality-attitudinal variables.

Organizational arrangements include the managerial and operational structure of the organization, workflow and design, reward system, management information systems, and the like. These arrangements are the formal mechanisms used by management to direct and control behavior and to organize and accomplish the work to be done.

The fourth component, *informal organization,* is the social structure within the organization, including the grapevine, the organization's internal politics, and the informal authority-information structure (whom you see for what).

Congruence: The Concept of Fit

As Nadler and Tushman point out, a mere listing and description of these system inputs, outputs, and components is insufficient for modeling an organization. An organization is dynamic, never static, and the model must represent this reality, as the arrows in Figure 6.2 do. Nadler and Tushman go beyond depicting relationships, however. Their term, *fit,* is a measure of the congruence between pairs of inputs and especially between the components of the transformation process. They contend that inconsistent fits between any pair will result in less-than-optimal organizational and individual performance. Nadler and Tushman's hypothesis, therefore, is that the better the fit, the more effective the organization will be.

Nadler and Tushman recommend three steps for diagnosis:

1. *Identify the system.* Is the system for diagnosis an autonomous organization, a subsidiary, a division, or a unit of some larger system? What are the boundaries of the system, its membership, its tasks, and—if it is part of a larger organization—its relationships with other units?
2. *Determine the nature of the key variables.* What are the dimensions of the inputs and components? What are the desired outputs?
3. *Diagnose the state of fits.* This is the most important step, involving two related activities: determining fits between components and diagnosing the link between the fits and the organization's outputs.

The OD consultant must concentrate on the degree to which the key components are congruent with one another. Questions such as the following should be asked:

- To what extent do the organizational arrangements fit with the requirements of the task?
- To what extent do individual skills and needs fit with task requirements, with organizational arrangements, and with the informal organization? Hackman and Oldham's (1975) job characteristics theory is a useful supplementary model for this part of the diagnosis, as is expectancy theory (Vroom, 1964; Lawler, 1973).
- To what extent do task requirements fit with both the formal and the informal organization? Information-processing models are useful supplements for this aspect of the diagnosis (Galbraith, 1977; Tushman & Nadler, 1978).

To diagnose the link between fits and outputs, the OD consultant must focus the outcome of the diagnoses of the various component fits and their behavioral consequences on the set of behaviors associated with systems outputs: goal attainment, resource utilization, and overall systems performance. Considering the component fits, or lack thereof, in light of system outputs helps identify critical problems of the organization. As these problems are addressed and changes are made, the system is then monitored through the feedback loop for purposes of evaluation.

In summary, the dimensions of the Nadler-Tushman model are quite comprehensive and have face validity. Moreover, their notion of congruence suggests certain cause-effect linkages. For example, little or no congruence between, say, strategy and structure in their model produces poor organizational performance. Also, a mismatch between what's going on in the organization's environment and strategy—for example, no plan for dealing with a recent change in government regulation—would imply a causal relationship to performance. Many other congruences or lack thereof could be mentioned. The number of possibilities is large. Nadler and Tushman, however, do not provide ideas or, say, a formula for determining which variables in their model are central. For example, they include under a single heading, organizational arrangements, quite a number of components, any one of which could easily be central. Finally, they do not suggest any means for knowing when congruence has occurred or what levels of congruence or incongruence produce desirable or undesirable effects.

To be fair, Nadler and Tushman (1989) had some second thoughts about their congruence position:

> While our model implies that congruence of organizational components is a desirable state it is, in fact, a double-edged sword. In the short term, congruence seems to be related to effectiveness and performance. A system with high congruence, however, can be resistant to change. It develops ways of insulating itself from outside influences and may be unable to respond to new situations (p. 195).

Tichy's TPC Framework

With his organizational framework, Tichy (1983) focuses explicitly on the management of change. He states that there are nine organizational change levers. They are the (1) external interface, or the organization's external environment; (2) mission; (3) strategy; (4) managing organizational mission/strategy processes, that is, realistically engaging the relevant interest groups; (5) task—change often requires new tasks; (6) prescribed *networks*—more or less, the formal organizational structure; (7) organizational processes—communicating, problem solving, and decision making; (8) people; and (9) emergent networks—more or less, the informal organization. Figure 6.3 shows how Tichy arranges these nine levers. He assumes that "organizational effectiveness (or output) is a function of the component of the model, as well as a function of how the components interrelate and align into a functioning system" (p. 72).

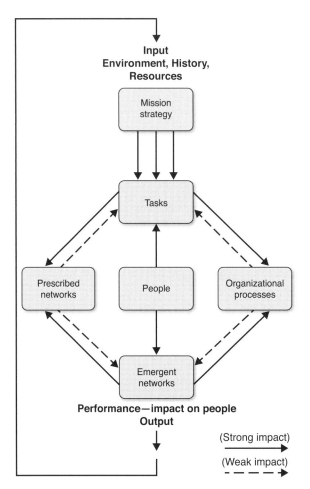

Figure 6.3 Tichy's Framework

Source: Noel M. Tichy, *Managing Strategic Change: Technical, Political, and Cultural Dynamics*, copyright © 1983 Wiley Interscience. Reprinted by permission of John Wiley & Sons, Inc.

Even more important in Tichy's thinking about organization change is his TPC framework. The model in Figure 6.3 is not unique. What makes Tichy's thinking unique is his overlay of the three systems—technical, political, and cultural—across the nine-lever model. He contends that there have been three dominant yet fairly distinct traditions guiding the practice of organization change. The *technical* view is rational, based on empiricism and the scientific method. The *political* view is based on the belief that organizations have dominant groups, and bargaining is the primary mode of change. The *cultural* view is the belief that shared symbols, values, and "cognitive schemes," as Tichy labels them, are what tie people together and form the organization's culture. Change occurs by altering norms and the cognitive schemes of organizational members. Taking only one or only two of these views for managing organizational change is dysfunctional. All three must be adjusted and realigned for successful change. The metaphor that Tichy uses to capture this thinking is a rope with three interrelated strands. The strands, or three views, can be understood separately but must be managed together for effective change.

For diagnostic purposes, Tichy uses a matrix like the one shown in Figure 6.4. This format summarizes what he calls "the analysis of alignments." Tichy describes the use of the matrix this way:

> Based on the diagnostic data collected, a judgment is made for each cell of the matrix regarding the amount of change needed to create alignment. Working across the matrix, the alignment is within a system: technical, political, or cultural. Working down the matrix, the alignment is between systems. The 0 (no change), 1 (moderate change) or 2 (great deal of change) ratings represent the amount of change needed to align that component (p. 164).

In summary, Tichy's model includes many, if not most, of the critical variables important to understanding organizations. His model is unique with respect to the strategic rope metaphor and is particularly relevant to OD work because the emphasis is on change. Moreover, Tichy is clear about what he considers to be the primary organizational levers that must be pushed or pulled to make change happen effectively. Instead of congruence, alignment is the operational term. And Tichy provides a way of analyzing the key alignments that are necessary according to his framework. Data are first collected and then categorized within his matrix (Figure 6.4).

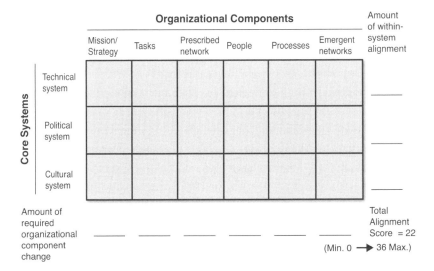

Figure 6.4 Tichy's TPC Matrix

Source: Noel M. Tichy, *Managing Strategic Change: Technical, Political, and Cultural Dynamics,* copyright © 1983 Wiley Interscience. Reprinted by permission of John Wiley & Sons, Inc.

There is a human component in Tichy's model, but for the most part his framework ignores issues at the individual level. He admits this omission at the end of his book by stating that he skimmed over the psychological aspects of change. The political and cultural strands are, of course, people concerns but much broader than, say, job-person match (or alignment) and local work unit activities such as teamwork. Finally, the criticism of too much congruence potentially working against change could also apply to Tichy's insistence on alignments.

Hornstein and Tichy's Emergent Pragmatic Model

The emergent pragmatic model of organizational diagnosis (Hornstein & Tichy, 1973; Tichy, Hornstein, & Nisberg, 1977) is based on the premise that most managers and consultants "carry around in their heads" implicit theories or models about organizational behavior and about how human systems actually operate. These notions are usually intuitive, ill-formed, and difficult to articulate. Because they are largely intuitive, different observers and members of organizations have different theories, which gives rise to conflicts among consultants or between consultants and clients about what is really wrong with the organization and how to fix it.

Hornstein and Tichy have developed a procedure for helping managers articulate and conceptualize their implicit models. The procedure has managers represent the information they would seek in diagnosing an organization by selecting labels from among 22 samples or creating their own from 28 blank labels provided. The labels include such items as informal groupings, fiscal characteristics, turnover, goals, and satisfaction of members with their jobs.

Hornstein and Tichy's approach to organizational diagnosis is shared between consultant and client and among members of the client organization. The approach is called an emergent-pragmatic theory because "the model *emerges* from an exploration of both the consultant's and client's assumptions about behavior and organizations...and draws on both the consultant's and client's organizational *experiences* as well as on empirical and theoretical work in the field" (Tichy, Hornstein, & Nisberg, 1977, p. 367; emphasis added).

Another of Hornstein and Tichy's premises is that, consciously or not, organizational consultants tend to impose their theories and models of human systems on their clients. These impositions often do not fit with the client members' perceptions and beliefs or do not jibe with the client organization's underlying values. To improve congruence, Hornstein and Tichy advocate a highly collaborative approach between consultants and clients, one that results in an emergent model representing different perspectives and experiences.

There are five phases to the emergent-pragmatic approach. The consultant guides the client group through these phases:

1. Exploring and developing a diagnostic model
2. Developing change strategies
3. Developing change techniques
4. Assessing the necessary conditions for assuring success
5. Evaluating the change strategies

To summarize, the emergent-pragmatic approach to organizational diagnosis is based on the assumption that most managers and consultants have intuitive theories about how organizations function, rather than well-formed conceptual frameworks, and the assumption that many consultants impose their models and theories on client organizations, regardless of how appropriate they may be for the particular client. Hornstein and Tichy advocate a collaborative model of diagnosis to avoid the potential negative consequences of operating on the basis of these two assumptions.

The three models described earlier—Weisbord's six-box model, the Nadler-Tushman congruence model, and Tichy's TPC framework—are generic frameworks and do not fall prey to the problems of Hornstein and Tichy's two premises. When the consultant and the client do not find the Weisbord, Nadler-Tushman, or other formal models to their liking, however, the emergent-pragmatic approach offers a clear alternative. It is a do-it-yourself model and, if both consultant and client are willing to spend the time required to do it right, a mutually satisfying and appropriate model for the client organization is likely to result.

The four models described may all be categorized as *contingency* models. They do not specify directions for change prior to diagnosis; rather, what needs to be changed emanates from the diagnosis. None of the models advocates a particular design for an organization's internal structure, a certain style of behavior, or a specific approach to management. The inventors of these models do have biases, however. Weisbord says the boxes should be in balance, Nadler and Tushman argue that the various dimensions of their model should fit with one another, as does Tichy, and Hornstein and Tichy state that the consultant and client should collaborate toward the emergence of a model that is appropriate for the given organization. These biases have more to do with the best way to diagnose than with the most important dimension to change.

We now shift from organizational frameworks to more theoretical ways of describing, understanding, and changing organizations.

Lawrence and Lorsch's Contingency Theory

Lawrence and Lorsch, early contingency theorists, specify neither a best way to diagnose nor a particular direction for change. They do emphasize structure and intergroup relationships.

Lawrence and Lorsch hypothesize a cause-and-effect relationship between how well an organization's internal structure matches environmental demands and how well the organization performs (accomplishes its goals and objectives). Their research in the 1960s provided support for their argument (Lawrence & Lorsch, 1967).

To understand the use of Lawrence and Lorsch's contingency theory for diagnosis, keep in mind that its primary concepts are differentiation and integration. These two concepts represent the paradox of any organization design—that labor must simultaneously be divided and coordinated or integrated. Within the Lawrence and Lorsch framework and for diagnostic purposes, therefore, we want to examine our client organization along the dimensions they consider to be important. The methodological appendix of their book provides considerable detail concerning these dimensions and the questions to ask for obtaining the relevant information (Lawrence & Lorsch, 1967). The following lists summarize these dimensions and some of the related questions:

Environmental Demands

1. On what basis does a customer evaluate and choose between competing suppliers in this industry (price, quality, delivery, service, and so forth)?

2. What are the major problems an organization encounters when competing in this industry?

3. Have there been significant changes in the market or technical conditions in this industry in recent years?

Differentiation

1. Regarding structure, what is the average span of control? How important is it to have formal rules for routing procedures and operations?

2. Regarding the timespan of feedback, how long does it take for employees to see the results of their performance? (In sales, for example, the time lag is typically short, whereas in research and development [R & D], it may take years.)

3. Regarding interpersonal relationships, how important are they, and how much interaction is necessary?

4. Regarding goal certainty, how clear-cut are the goals? How are they measured?

Integration

1. How interdependent are any two units: high (each depends on the other for survival), medium (each needs some things from the other), or low (each functions fairly autonomously)?
2. What is the quality of relations between units?

Conflict Management

1. What mode of conflict resolution is used: forcing (top-down edicts), smoothing (being kind and avoiding), or confronting (exposing differences and solving problems)?
2. How much influence do employees have on the hierarchy for solving problems and making decisions?

Employee-Management Contract

1. To what extent do employees feel that what is expected of them is appropriate?
2. To what extent do employees feel that they are compensated and rewarded fairly for their performance?

In summary, these five dimensions represent the organizational domains that Lawrence and Lorsch believe most important for effective diagnosis. Based on their research findings, the organizational diagnostician would be looking for the degree of match between environmental demands and complexities and the internal organizational structure. The greater the environmental complexity, the more complex the internal design should be. If the organization's markets change rapidly and are difficult to predict and forecast, and if the environment in general fluctuates considerably, the organization's internal structure should be relatively decentralized so that many employees can be in touch with the environment and can act quickly as changes occur. Under these conditions, differentiation may still be high, but a premium is placed on integration. There must be sufficient integrating mechanisms so that communication flows adequately across and among the many subunits and so that superiors in the hierarchy are kept well informed. The plastics industry represented this type of organization in the Lawrence and Lorsch research study. When the environment is relatively stable and not particularly complex (the container industry in their study), a fairly simple and straightforward internal structure may be best, with functional division of labor and centralized authority.

The issue is not whether one organization should be highly differentiated and another highly integrated but that they should be highly differentiated *and* integrated. High integration seems to be important regardless of environment, and differentiation may be lower for organizations with stable environments. The paradox remains in any case: Both are needed, but they are antagonistic—the more the organization is differentiated, the more integration is required.

The organizational diagnostician should also seek the mode of conflict resolution. Lawrence and Lorsch found that the more organization members and units confront their differences and work to resolve them, rather than smoothing them over or squashing them with edicts from on high, the more effective the organization tended to be.

Finally, it is necessary to know the degree of employees' satisfaction with their psychological contract with the organization. There is apparently a positive relationship between clarity of employees' understanding of what is expected of them—their perceived satisfaction with the rewards they receive for performance—and overall organizational performance.

Although Lawrence and Lorsch are contingency theorists, particularly with respect to organization structure, they too have their biases. They stress interfaces—between the organization and its environment, between and among units within the organization, and between individual employees and the organization as represented by management.

Normative Theories

Unlike contingency theorists, normative theorists argue that, for organization development, there is one best way to implement change and one best direction for change. Major proponents of normative theory are Likert (1967) and Blake and Mouton (1968, 1978).

Likert's Profiles

Likert categorizes organizations, or systems in his terms, as one of four types:

- *System 1.* Autocratic, top-down, exploitive management
- *System 2.* Benevolent autocracy (still top-down but not as exploitive)
- *System 3.* Consultative (employees are consulted about problems and decisions but management still makes the final decisions)
- *System 4.* Participative management (key policy decisions are made in groups by consensus)

Likert's approach to organizational diagnosis is standardized. The mode used is a questionnaire, the "Profile of Organizational Characteristics," with six sections: leadership, motivation, communication, decisions, goals, and control. (The latest version is labeled the "Survey of Organizations.") Organization members answer questions in each of these sections by placing the letter N at the place on a 20-point scale that best represents their opinion now and a P at the place that indicates their previous opinion—how they experienced their organization one or two years ago. Sometimes the consultant asks organization members to use an I instead of a P, to indicate what they would consider ideal for each of the questions.

Organizational profiles typically fall into the System 2 or System 3 categories. If the ideal response is used, its profile will usually occur to the right of the now profile, toward or within System 4. In such cases, the direction for change is established, toward System 4.

When one declares that there is one best way, in this case System 4 management, others usually demand evidence. Is System 4 management a better way to run an organization than System 3 or 2 or 1? Contingency theorists, of course, would say no; it depends on the type of business, the nature of the environment, and the technology involved. Likert contends that, regardless of these contingencies, System 4 is best. Likert's (1967) own research supports his claim, and so does research by others. A longitudinal study of perhaps the most systematic change to System 4 management—conducted in the Harwood-Weldon Company, a manufacturer of sleepwear—is a noteworthy example (Marrow, Bowers, & Seashore, 1967). Changes were made in all dimensions of Likert's profile as well as in workflow and organizational structure. The durability of these changes was supported by a later study conducted by Seashore and Bowers (1970).

A System 4 approach was also used as the change goal for a General Motors assembly plant (Dowling, 1975). As a result of these deliberate change efforts toward System 4, significant improvements were accomplished on several indices, including operating efficiency, costs, and grievances.

In summary, Likert's approach to organizational diagnosis is structured and directional. It is structured by use of his questionnaire and later versions of his profile (Taylor & Bowers, 1972), and it is directional in that data collected are compared with System 4. The survey feedback method (see Chapter 3, "Where Did Organization Development Come From?," and Mann, 1957) is used as the main intervention; that is, the data from the questionnaire (survey) are reported back to organizational members in a set manner.

To use Likert's approach, the consultant should feel comfortable with the questionnaire method as the primary mode for data gathering and with System 4 management as the goal for change. Although participative management may feel comfortable as a change goal for many consultants and clients, the relatively limited diagnosis by profile characteristics only may not be so comfortable.

Blake and Mouton's Grid Organization Development

The other normative approach to OD is based on the managerial grid model developed by Blake and Mouton (1964, 1978). Like Likert's System 4 approach, the grid method of OD is structured and involves a high degree of packaging. Blake and Mouton also argue that there is one best way to manage an organization. Their label is 9,9, which also represents a participative style of management.

Blake and Mouton also depend on questionnaires, but grid OD (Blake & Mouton, 1968) goes far beyond an initial diagnosis with a questionnaire. Blake and Mouton start from an initial, general diagnosis. In a cross-cultural study of what managers consider the most common barriers to business effectiveness and corporate excellence,

Blake and Mouton (1968) found that communication topped the list often, and a lack of planning was second. These two barriers were selected by managers much more frequently than the remaining eight (74 percent noted communication and 62 percent mentioned planning); morale and coordination, for example, the next most frequently mentioned barriers, were noted by less than 50 percent. Blake and Mouton further pointed out that communication and planning were the top two mentioned regardless of country, company, or characteristics of the managers reporting. These two major barriers, and the other less-prevalent ones, are symptoms of organizational problems, not causes, according to Blake and Mouton. The causes lie deeper in the system. Faulty planning, for example, is a result of an organization's not having a strategy or having a strategy that is based on unsound rationale. Communication problems derive from the nature of the supervision practiced in the organization.

For addressing these underlying causes, Blake and Mouton have developed a six-phase approach to organization development that considers both the organization's strategic plan, or lack thereof, and the style or approach to supervision or management. They contend that, to achieve excellence, an organizational strategic model should be developed and the supervisory style should be changed in the direction of participative management. Organization members should first examine managerial behavior and style and then move on to develop and implement an ideal strategic organizational model. Before explaining the six phases of their OD approach in more detail, we should consider Blake and Mouton's managerial style model, the Managerial Grid®, because most of their normative rationale is based on this model.

Building on earlier research work on leadership, in which the dual functions of a leader were variously labeled as initiation of structure and consideration, task and maintenance and task and socioemotional behaviors, Blake and Mouton (1964) simplified the language by using terms closer to managers' understanding: *production* and *people*. They did more, however; the creative aspect of their work was to conceptualize each of the two leader functions on a continuum, one for the manager's degree of concern for production and one for his or her concern for people, and to put the two together in the form of a graph, a two-dimensional model.

Blake and Mouton (1981) contend that they have done more than merely simplify the language and create nine-point scales. They argue that the original dimensions—initiation of structure and consideration—and those that followed, especially Hersey and Blanchard's situational leadership model (Hersey & Blanchard, 1993), were conceptualized as independent dimensions. Blake and Mouton's dimensions—production and people—are interdependent, however, and represent attitudes more than behavior. They note that leadership is not possible without both task and people. We now consider Blake and Mouton's model in more detail.

Any manager will have some degree of concern for accomplishing the organization's purpose of producing products or services—that is, a concern for production, results, or profits. A manager will also have some degree of concern for the people who are involved in helping to accomplish the organization's purpose. Managers may differ in how concerned they are with each of these managerial functions, but how these two concerns mesh for a given manager determines his or her *style* or approach to management and defines that manager's use of power.

Blake and Mouton chose nine-point scales to depict their model and to rank the manager's degree of concern for production and people; 1 represents a low concern and 9 indicates a high concern. Although there are 81 possible combinations, Blake and Mouton realistically chose to consider only the four more or less extreme positions, represented in the four corners of the grid, and the middle-of-the-road style, position 5,5 in the middle of the grid. Figure 6.5 illustrates the managerial grid and defines each of the five primary styles.

As noted earlier, Blake and Mouton contend that communication problems in the organization stem from the nature of supervision. The predominant style in U.S. organizations today can be characterized as 5,5 (Blake & Mouton, 1978). A popular book at the time, *The Gamesman* (Maccoby, 1976), was a description of Blake and Mouton's 5,5 manager. In an unpublished study, a colleague, Barry Render, and Burke also found 5,5 to be the predominant style of middle managers in a large government agency ($N = 400$). This style, according to Blake and Mouton, is bureaucratic and mechanistic, thus less than effective, especially regarding communication. The three styles labeled 9,1, 1,9, and 1,1 are even poorer, causing similar, if not worse, communication problems. The 9,9 style, then, is best when practiced consistently and will assure significantly fewer problems of communication. Training managers to adopt a 9,9 style will therefore lead to significantly fewer barriers to organizational effectiveness.

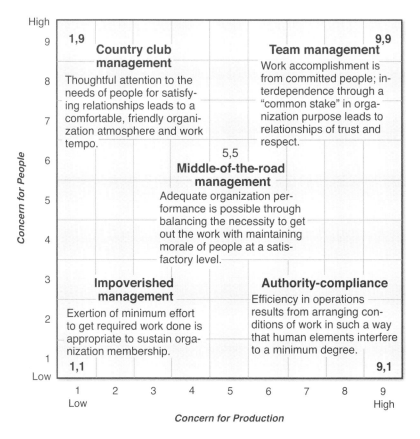

Figure 6.5 The Leadership Grid® Figure

Source: The Leadership Grid® Figure from *Leadership Dilemmas-Grid Solutions,* by Robert K. Blake and Anne Adams McCanse (formerly the Managerial Grid Figure by Robert R. Blake and Jane S. Mouton) Houston: Gulf Publishing Company, p. 29, Copyright © 1991, by Scientific Methods, Inc. Reproduced by permission of the owners.

The six phases of Grid Organization Development begin with a one-week seminar at which participants assess their present styles and learn the behaviors associated with the 9,9 style. Participants also receive feedback on their styles from their fellow group members.

Phase 2 of grid OD is teamwork development. Assessment again takes place, to identify the norms and working characteristics of all managerial teams in the organization, starting with the top team and moving downward in the hierarchy to include the others.

Phase 3 is intergroup development. The objective of this phase is to reduce win-lose patterns of behavior between groups in the organization.

Phase 4 is development of an ideal strategic corporate model. Essentially what is called corporate strategic planning, this phase begins with the development of an ideal strategic organization, usually done by the top management team.

Phase 5 is implementation of the ideal strategic model. This phase, similar to what Beckhard and Harris (1987) later called transition management, consists of moving toward the ideal model in a carefully managed, evolutionary manner while continuing to run the organization as before.

Phase 6 is systematic critique. During this final phase, the change effort is evaluated and so-called drag factors are identified. (*Drag* factors are specific barriers that still exist and must now be overcome.)

Phases 1–3 are thus designed to deal with communication barriers to organizational effectiveness, and Phases 4–6 deal with the planning barriers.

It is interesting that not until Phase 6 do Blake and Mouton begin to deal with an organization diagnostically in terms like those of the other diagnostic models we have considered. Blake and Mouton have evidently decided that all fairly large organizations that are not already involved in OD have serious communication and planning barriers to effectiveness. These two primary barriers must be reduced first, and grid OD will do the job. At Phase 6, we will see how effectively the first five phases have progressed and we will know, in particular and in detail, what barriers must now be tackled.

Blake and Mouton never state it, but they apparently assume that, unless an organization learns how to communicate more effectively (practice 9,9 management) and plan more logically and systematically (build an ideal strategic model and begin to implement it), its management will never be able to deal optimally with the specifics of running a business. Phase 6 in the grid OD sequence gets to the specifics.

Levinson's Clinical-Historical Approach

Levinson's theory of organization behavior is grounded in psychoanalytic theory and views organizations in familial dimensions: "An organization is composed of persons in authority and 'siblings' who relate to these authorities" (Levinson, 1972a, p. 23). Because it is so closely aligned with psychoanalytic theory, it is not surprising that Levinson's approach to organizational diagnosis (1972b) is very detailed, emphasizes history, and generally relies on clinical methods. Using this approach, the consultant does a workup on a client organization much as a physician would do with a patient and obtains as complete a history as possible, especially in terms of how the organization fits into its environment. In the search of information, Levinson suggests:

> Most newspapers have morgues, or files of clippings, filed by subject. Historical societies often have much information on file. Large organizations will frequently be the subject of articles in trade or professional magazines which may be located through libraries.... The sheer availability of various kinds of information is a datum of diagnostic value (1972a, p. 26).

Just as physicians "take a history," order a blood test, and thump the patient's body here and there, Levinson also stresses observation. He notes: "Since the consultant is his own most important instrument, he should begin [by using] his antennae for sensing subtleties" (1972a, p. 18). Levinson suggests that the consultant request a tour of as much of the organization as time and practicalities permit in order to form and record initial impressions. "The consultant will find it helpful to keep a diary of his experiences in the company, to record events and observations which will not likely be reported in interviews or questionnaires" (1972a, p. 19).

Levinson (1972a) relies on six categories of data for diagnosis:

1. *Consultant observations and feelings.* Notes on how the consultant experiences the organization, especially initial impressions, are recorded and become a set of information for later diagnosis.

2. *Factual data.* Recorded policies and procedures, historical data on file in the organization, annual reports, job descriptions, personnel statistics, and former consultant or task force reports are perused. Collecting this information is not enough, according to Levinson; analyzing how the data interrelate is important, as is the type of language used. The language will convey attitudes toward people and assumptions about what motivates employees.

3. *Outside information.* Information is collected, primarily through interviews, from the organization's suppliers and competitors, cooperating organizations, agents, professional associations, and the like. This information will help the consultant understand the organization's environment in general and the impact it has on the client.

4. *Pattern of organization.* The organization chart and the authority-responsibility structure of the organization are the primary indicators of patterns of organization. Levinson stresses a holistic approach rather than a view of the interaction of just one or two subsystems.

5. *Settings.* According to Levinson, "First overall organizational purposes and then how these purposes are subdivided into specific functions performed by definable groups within definable temporal and physical space.... The consultant must learn where and by whom essential functions of the organization are carried out" (1972a, p. 28). Levinson also notes in this context what Rice (1958) has called the time dimension: "temporal boundaries within which the setting's central purpose is accomplished...such as factory shift work...or...planning activities in a management group" (Levinson, 1972a, p. 29).

6. *Task patterns.* Group-level variables exist in each setting. Levinson cites four such patterns:

   • *Complementary activities.* Contributions of each work group member toward some common goal

   • *Parallel activities.* Group members performing essentially identical tasks

- *Sequential activities.* Group members performing some phase of the overall group task
- *Individualized activities.* Unique functions performed by each person

These patterns constitute a setting, and the consultant attempts to learn the setting boundaries by analyzing the task patterns.

It is important to note that, although Levinson's theoretical base is psychological and his method of diagnosis is patterned after the clinical model, he does not become absorbed in pieces of the system. His approach is systemic and holistic. Although he is biased toward a Freudian view, he does not lose himself in the analytics but rather looks for systemic issues and considers how the organization influences and is influenced by its environment, how subparts of the organization relate, and how work flows from one setting, activity, and function to another. Thus, being an organizational diagnostician of the Levinson school would require a thorough grounding in psychoanalytic theory, an understanding of the clinical method of diagnosis, and a systems view of organizations that highlights patterns of relationships and workflow.

Conclusion

In this chapter, we have considered the diagnostic phase of organization development consultation in some depth by examining certain models. These models—Weisbord's six-box model, Nadler and Tushman's congruence model, Tichy's TPC framework, Hornstein and Tichy's emergent-pragmatic model, Lawrence and Lorsch's contingency model, the normative models of Likert and Blake and Mouton, and Levinson's historical-clinical approach—are not the only ones available (see the next chapter, for example). For OD purposes, however, they are some of the most relevant ones and they demonstrate the diversity of the field. There is considerable choice for the OD practitioner-consultant.

Rarely does one have the time required for using Levinson's approach, although his thoroughness and the systemic-flow perspective are admirable. When time is short and the client is naive about systems, Weisbord's six-box model works well. Nadler and Tushman's model is appealing for some of the same reasons Levinson's is, but it is easier to work with and easier to communicate to a client. Tichy's framework is fairly easy to understand, yet somewhat complex in use. Hornstein and Tichy's approach is very useful for clients who are concerned that a consultant might impose something on them, and it is useful for setting the stage for in-depth diagnosis. Lawrence and Lorsch's contingency model is often the most popular one among OD practitioners, and with good reason. It emphasizes organizational structure, which was overlooked by OD people in the early days, and shows how the organization's environment has an internal impact. Likert's and Blake and Mouton's theories are appealing because they clearly show the way, but if their approaches are chosen, they must be followed completely; a partial application will not work. Their high degree of structure and their normative view turns away some OD practitioners. Under certain circumstances, however, both may be useful—Likert's profile for providing an outside, more objective questionnaire assessment of an organization, and Blake and Mouton's grid for providing a framework for examining managerial style in the organization.

An OD practitioner's choice from among these models should be based primarily on three considerations. First, it is difficult to use a model effectively if you do not understand it. Second, the practitioner should feel comfortable with the model and its approach. If the practitioner does not really believe in participative management, using Likert's or Blake and Mouton's approach is not likely to be successful, for example. Third, the model should match the level of sophistication of the client; that is, when working with a complex organization, the practitioner should choose a model that adequately represents its complexity.

As the following chapter shows, we have one more model to consider. As the chapter also shows, Litwin and Burke have tried to learn from many of the models and theories that have preceded their organizational performance and change framework.

7

The Burke-Litwin Model of Organizational Performance and Change[1]

In presenting this causal model (therefore a normative view, Burke & Litwin, 1992) we are attempting to provide yet another perspective, and at the same time demonstrate that this more recent framework captures some of the best qualities of previous models. As does Tichy in the technical political cultural (TPC) framework, this model takes certain positions about organization change and thus *predicts* behavior and performance consequences and therefore deals with cause (organizational conditions) and effect (resultant performance).

Important background regarding the development of the model (the concepts of organizational climate and culture) is presented first, followed by a description of the model. Finally, suggestions for ways to use the model as well as case examples are provided.

Background

Climate

The original thinking underlying the model came from George Litwin and others during the 1960s. In 1967, the Harvard Business School sponsored a conference on organizational climate. Results of this conference were subsequently published in two books (Litwin & Stringer, 1968; Tagiuri & Litwin, 1968). The concept of organizational climate that emerged from this series of studies and papers was that of a psychological state strongly affected by organizational conditions, such as systems, structure, and managerial behavior. In their

145

theory paper, Tagiuri and Litwin (1968) emphasized that there could be no universal set of dimensions or properties for organizational climate. They argued that one could describe climate along different dimensions, depending on the kind of organization being studied and the aspects of human behavior involved. They described climate as a molar, synthetic, or changeable construct. Further, the kind of climate construct they described was relatively malleable; it could be modified by managerial behavior and by systems and strongly influenced by more enduring group norms and values.

This early research and theory development regarding organizational climate clearly linked psychological and organizational variables in a cause-effect model that was empirically testable. Using the model, Litwin and Stringer (1968) were able to predict and to control the motivational and performance consequences of various organizational climates established in their research experiment.

Culture

The concept of organizational culture is drawn from anthropology and is used to describe the relatively enduring set of values and norms that underlie a social system. These may not be entirely conscious. (Elaboration on this point is the theme of Chapter 8, "Understanding Organizations: Covert Processes.") Rather, they constitute a "meaning system" that allows members of a social system to attribute meaning and value to the variety of external and internal events they experience. Such underlying values and meaning systems change only as continued culture is applied to generations of individuals in that social system.

The distinction between climate and culture must be very explicit because this model attempts to describe both climate and culture in terms of their interactions with other organizational variables. Thus, this model builds on earlier research and theory with regard to predicting motivation and performance effects.

In addition, the variables that influence and are influenced by climate need to be distinguished from those influenced by culture. Thus, there are two distinct sets of organizational dynamics. One set primarily is associated with the transactional level of human behavior or the everyday interactions and exchanges that create the climate. The second set of dynamics is concerned with processes of human transformation; that is, sudden "leaps" in behavior. These transformational processes are required for genuine change in the culture of an organization. Efforts to distinguish transactional and transformational dynamics in organizations have been influenced by the writings of James McGregor Burns (1978) and by consultants' efforts to change organizations.

The Model

The Burke-Litwin model has been refined through a series of studies directed by Burke (Bernstein & Burke, 1989; Fox, 1990; Michela et al., 1988). Later collaboration led to the current form of this model, which attempts to:

1. Specify the interrelationships of organizational variables
2. Distinguish transformational and transactional dynamics in organizational behavior and change

Figure 7.1 summarizes the model.

In accordance with accepted thinking about organizations from general systems theory (Katz & Kahn, 1978), the external environment box represents the input and the individual and organizational performance box represents the output. Feedback loops go in both directions. The remaining boxes of the model represent the throughput aspect of general systems theory.

The model is complex, as is the rich intricacy of organizational phenomena. However, this model, exhibited two-dimensionally, is still an oversimplification; a hologram would be a better representation.

Arrows in both directions convey the open-systems principle that change in one factor will eventually have an impact on the others. Moreover, if the model could be diagrammed so that the arrows were circular (as they would be in a hologram), reality could be represented more accurately. Yet this is a *causal* model. For example, although culture and systems affect one another, culture has a stronger influence on systems than vice versa.

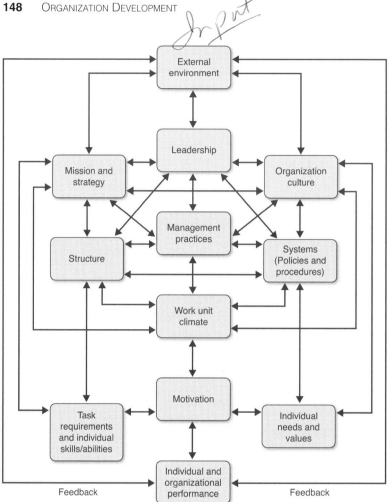

Figure 7.1 The Burke-Litwin Model of Organizational Performance and Change

Source: The Burke-Litwin Model of Individual and Organizational Performance (Burke & Litwin, 1992).

The model could be displayed differently. External environment could be on the left and performance on the right, with all throughput boxes in between, as with the Nadler–Tushman model (see Chapter 6, "Understanding Organizations: The Process of Diagnosis"). However, displaying it as shown makes a statement about organizational change: Organizational change stems more from environmental impact than from any other factor. Moreover, with respect to organizational change, the variables of strategy, leadership, and culture have more "weight" than the variables of structure, management practices, and systems; that is, having leaders communicate the new strategy is not sufficient for effective change. Changing culture must be planned as well as aligned with strategy and leader behavior. How the model is displayed does not dictate where change could start; however, it does indicate the weighting of change dynamics. The reader can think of the model in terms of gravity, with the push toward performance being in the weighted order displayed in Figure 7.1.

In summary, the model, as shown in Figure 7.1, portrays the following:

- The primary variables that need to be considered in any attempt to predict and explain the total behavioral output of an organization
- The most important interactions among these variables
- The ways the variables affect change

Transformational and Transactional Dynamics

The concept of transformational change in organizations is suggested by such writers as Bass (1985), Burke (1986), Burns (1978), McClelland (1975), and Tichy and Devanna (1986). Figure 7.2 displays the transformational variables (the upper half of the model). *Transformational* refers to areas in which alteration is likely caused by interaction with environmental forces (both within and without) and which require entirely new behavior sets on the part of organizational members.

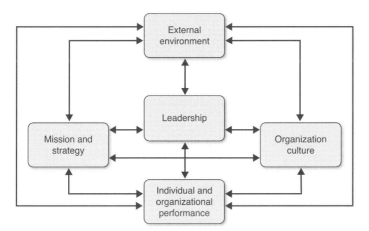

Figure 7.2 The Transformational Factors

Figure 7.3 shows the transactional variables (the lower half of the model). These variables are very similar to those originally isolated by Litwin and Stringer (1968) and later by Michela et al. (1988). They are *transactional* in that alteration occurs primarily via relatively short-term reciprocity among people and groups. In other words, "You do this for me, and I'll do that for you."

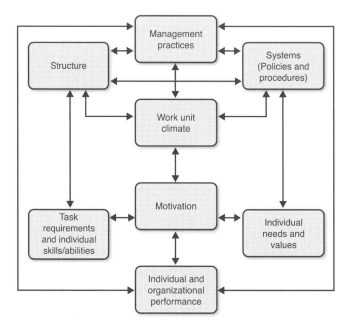

Figure 7.3 The Transactional Factors

Each category or box in the model can be described as follows:

- *External environment.* Any outside condition or situation that influences the performance of the organization. These conditions include such things as marketplaces, world financial conditions, political/governmental circumstances, and so on.

- *Mission and strategy.* What employees believe is the central purpose of the organization and how the organization intends to achieve that purpose over an extended time.

- *Leadership.* Executive behavior that provides direction and encourages others to take needed action. For purposes of data gathering, this box includes perceptions of executive practices and values.

- *Culture.* "The way we do things around here." Culture is the collection of overt and covert rules, values, and principles that guide organizational behavior and that have been strongly influenced by history, custom, and practice.

- *Structure.* The arrangement of functions and people into specific areas and levels of responsibility, decision-making authority, and relationships. Structure assures effective implementation of the organization's mission and strategy.

- *Management practices.* What managers do in the normal course of events to use the human and material resources at their disposal to carry out the organization's strategy.

- *Systems.* Standardized policies and mechanisms that are designed to facilitate work. Systems primarily manifest themselves in the organization's reward systems and in control systems, such as the organization's management information system, goal and budget development, and human resource allocation.

- *Climate.* The collective current impressions, expectations, and feelings of the members of local work units. These in turn affect members' relations with supervisors, with one another, and with other units.

- *Task requirements and individual skills/abilities.* The behavior required for task effectiveness, including specific skills and knowledge required for people to accomplish the work assigned and for which they feel directly responsible. This box concerns what is often referred to as job-person match.

- *Individual needs and values.* The specific psychological factors that provide desire and worth for individual actions or thoughts.

- *Motivation.* Aroused behavioral tendencies to move toward goals, take needed action, and persist until satisfaction is attained. This is the net resultant motivation; that is, the resultant net energy generated by the sum of achievement, power, affection, discovery, and other important human motives.

- *Individual and organizational performance.* The outcomes or results, with indicators of effort and achievement. Such indicators might include productivity, customer or staff satisfaction, profit, and service quality.

Climate Results from Transactions; Culture Change Requires Transformation

In the causal model, day-to-day climate is a result of transactions related to issues such as the following:

- *Sense of direction.* The effect of mission clarity, or lack thereof, on one's daily responsibilities
- *Role and responsibility.* The effect of structure, reinforced by managerial practice
- *Standards and commitment.* The effect of managerial practice, reinforced by culture
- *Fairness of rewards.* The effect of systems, reinforced by managerial practice
- *Focus on customer versus internal pressures or standards of excellence.* The effect of culture, reinforced by other variables

In contrast, the concept of organizational culture has to do with those underlying values and meaning systems that are difficult to manage, to alter, and even to be realized completely (Schein, 1992). Moreover, instant change in culture seems to be a contradiction in terms. By definition, those things that can be changed quickly are not the underlying reward systems but the behaviors that are attached to the meaning systems. It is relatively easy to alter superficial human behavior; it is undoubtedly quite difficult to alter something unconscious that is hidden in symbols and mythology and that functions as the fabric helping an organization to remain together, intact, and viable. To change something so deeply embedded in organizational life does indeed require transformational experiences and events.

Using the Model: Data Gathering and Analysis

Distinguishing transformational and transactional thinking about organizations has implications for planning organizational change. Unless one is conducting an overall organizational diagnosis, preliminary interviews will result in enough information to construct a fairly targeted survey. Survey targets would be determined from the interviews and, most likely, would be focused on either transformational or transactional issues. Transformational issues call for a survey that probes mission and strategy, leadership, culture, and performance. Transactional issues need a focus on structure, systems, management practices, climate, and performance. Other transactional probes might involve motivation, including task requirements (job-person match) and individual needs and values. For example, parts or all of "The Job Diagnostic Survey" (Hackman & Oldham, 1980) might be appropriate.

An organization development (OD) consultant helping to manage change would conduct preliminary interviews with, say, 15 to 30 representative individuals in the organization. If, on the other hand, the organization is a loosely coupled system (see Chapter 10, "Understanding and Changing Loosely Coupled Systems") such as a network, then all individuals need to be interviewed. If a summary of these interviews revealed that significant organizational change was needed, additional data would be collected related to the top or transformational part of Figure 7.1. Note that in major organizational change, transformational variables represent the primary levers, those areas in which change must be focused. The following examples represent transformational change (concentrated at the top of the model, as illustrated in Figure 7.2):

1. An acquisition in which the acquired organization's culture, leadership, and business strategy are dramatically different from those of the acquiring organization (even if both organizations are in the same industry), thereby necessitating a new, merged organization (for an example of how the model has been used to facilitate a merger, see Burke & Jackson, 1991).

2. A federal agency in which the mission has been modified and the structure and leadership changed significantly, yet the culture remains in the past.

3. A high-tech firm whose leadership has changed recently and is perceived negatively, whose strategy is unclear, and whose internal politics have moved from minimal (before) to predominant (after). The hue and cry here is "We have no direction from our leaders and no culture to guide our behavior in the meantime."

For an organization in which the presenting problem is more a fine-tuning or improving process, the second layer of the model (shown in Figure 7.3) serves as the point of concentration. Examples include changes in the organization's structure; modification of the reward system; management development (perhaps in the form of a program that concentrates on behavioral practices); or the administration of a climate survey to measure job stratification, job clarity, degree of teamwork, and so on.

It is also useful to consider the model in a vertical manner. For example, Bernstein and Burke (1989) examined the causal chain of culture, management practices, and climate in a large manufacturing organization. In this case, feedback to executives showed how and to what degree cultural variables influenced management practices and, in turn, work-unit climate (the dependent variable).

The change effort at British Airways (BA) is a good example of an organization in which practically all boxes of the Burke-Litwin model were eventually examined and changed. The model provided a framework for executives and managers in BA to understand the massive change they were attempting to manage. To understand the model in use a bit more as well as to consider a significant example of large system change, let us review the change in BA.

Change at British Airways

Prior to 1987 and practically since World War II (although two organizations for most of that time period), British Airways (BA) was a government organization, the product of a merger between British European Airways (BEA) and British Overseas Airways Corporation (BOAC) in the early 1970s. These two organizations had in turn been spawned from Britain's Royal Air Force. The BA of 1983, when Colin Marshall arrived as president and CEO, operated largely as a function of its history, rather like the military, and was draining the British treasury with financial losses year after year. Moreover, passengers referred to BA as "bloody awful." Prime Minister Margaret Thatcher had decided earlier that BA was to be privatized and had brought in Lord John King, a successful businessman, to be chairman. King recruited Marshall from Avis Rent-A-Car in 1983 and gave him the charge and the authority to change BA so that it could survive privatization.

In addition to the external environmental force on British Airways by Prime Minister Thatcher and her government administration, another key environmental change was the growing deregulation of international air traffic—many air fares were no longer set by governments but instead by the marketplace.

Internally, BA had to change its mission and strategy as well as its corporate culture. BA's mission was to serve with distinction as the United Kingdom's flagship airline and strategically to compete both domestically and internationally. The mission and strategy would need to change more toward the customer and BA would need to become much more competitive. The culture would need to be transformed from one described as bureaucratic and militaristic to one that was service oriented and market driven.

Let us now consider the changes that took place in BA's mission and strategy, leadership, and culture, in other words the transformational changes:

- *Mission and strategy.* To make BA more competitive and to reduce costs, the first step Marshall took was to reduce the size of the workforce from about 59,000 to 37,000. The downsizing was done with a certain amount of compassion via primarily early retirements with substantial financial settlements. Marshall's background was marketing in a service industry and he began to change BA's strategy accordingly. BA was to become "The World's Favourite Airline" with a strong emphasis on the customer by providing superior service.

- *Leadership.* Of course the major change here was the hiring of Marshall. He in turn hired Nicholas Georgiades, a psychologist and former professor and consultant, as head of human resources (HR). Georgiades developed the specific tactics and programs required to bring about the culture change. Gordon Dunlop led the way financially via his position as chief financial officer. He was indispensable in transforming the accounting and financial functions from a government orientation to one that helped managers to understand competition and the marketplace.

- *Culture.* Led by Georgiades, a series of programs and activities were developed to shift the culture from too much bureaucracy to a real service orientation. The first program was called "Putting People First." "Aimed at helping line workers and managers understand the service nature of the airline industry, it was intended to challenge the prevailing wisdom about how things were to be done at BA" (Goodstein & Burke, 1991, p. 12).

The next steps were to focus even more intensely on the culture. Georgiades conceptualized the process metaphorically as a "three-legged stool." The seat was the new, desired culture (customer-service oriented) and the three legs were (1) the "Managing People First" (MPF) program, a five-day residential experience to help managers learn about how to manage their people in such a way (more participatively, for example) that they would be more service oriented; (2) a performance appraisal where half of a manager's evaluation was based on results and half on *how* the results were achieved, the how being an incorporation of the behaviors and practices emphasized in the MPF program; and (3) pay for performance, rewarding managers according to how they were rated in (2) above.

In addition to these interventions primarily targeted at management, a five-day residential training program was conducted for all human resource people in BA. This program concentrated on consultation skills to enhance the HR people's abilities to help line managers to apply what they had learned in the MPF program.

Part of the rationale for concentrating on managers in the early stages of the culture change was based on the research work of Ben Schneider. In a series of studies (Schneider, 1980, 1990; Schneider & Bowen, 1985), he has demonstrated that how frontline people in a service business (in his case, banks; therefore, tellers, loan officers) are treated by their respective supervisors has a differential effect on customer satisfaction. In bank branches where frontline employees were managed more participatively as opposed to bureaucratically—following procedures strictly, for example—customer satisfaction was significantly higher. With British Airways being a service business, we applied this same principle. You do not have to teach cabin crew members or ticket agents how to smile. Rather you need to teach managers about how to manage these frontline people so that smiles come naturally by their desire to treat customers with respect and enthusiasm. The MPF program was therefore designed and conducted to help managers to manage more participatively, openly, respectfully, enthusiastically, and with greater trust in their subordinates. Managers cannot manage the myriad of hour-by-hour contacts that employees who have direct contact with customers encounter every day, those 50,000 "moments of truth" as Jan Carlzon, another successful airline CEO, described in his popular book (Carlzon, 1987). Managers can, however, work with their subordinates in an involving manner that will in turn have a positive effect on customers.

In summary, because the BA change was clearly fundamental and transformational in nature, concentrating on the top three boxes of the Burke-Litwin model that were changed in response to external environment demands was the appropriate approach to take. Subsequently, efforts were concentrated on (1) the climate via team-building processes, (2) support systems by modifying, for example, rewards (pay for performance) and, as noted above, (3) training all human resource people in consulting skills to help managers apply what they had learned in the MPF program.

For a more detailed description of the history behind the BA change and a brief overview of the change effort, see the case by Leahey and Kotter (1990). Goodstein and Burke (1991) as well as Burke (2014b) have provided a more comprehensive analysis of the change process itself at BA.

That BA has changed is now a matter of record (Goodstein & Burke, 1991). It became one of the most profitable airlines in the world and its significantly improved service meant that passengers considered it "bloody awesome" rather than "bloody awful" (see the article by Power in *Business Week*, October 9, 1989; 97).

Considering the Burke-Litwin model from a vertical perspective entails hypothesizing causal effects and assuming that the "weight" of change is top-down; that is, the heaviest or most influential organizational dimensions for change are external environment, first and foremost, and then mission/strategy, leadership, and culture.

It is interesting to note that executives and managers typically concern themselves with the left side of the model illustrated in Figure 7.1: mission and strategy, structure, and task requirements and individual skills or abilities. In contrast, behavioral scientists are more likely to be concerned with the right side and middle of Figure 7.1: leadership, culture, systems (especially rewards), management practices, climate, individual needs and values, and motivation. For a fundamental, large system change effort, one should be concerned with the entire model and with a more effective integration of purpose and practice.

As with other models, the Burke-Litwin model has its limitations. For example, the model does not explicitly account for technology, the organization's technical strengths, those core competencies that make it competitive in the marketplace, or effective in accomplishing its mission. Because technology largely pervades the entire organization, displaying the Burke-Litwin model three-dimensionally with technology as the third dimension might improve its validity.

Conclusion

Provided we do not allow ourselves to be trapped by a particular model, and as a consequence "not see" certain, critical information about an organization, using a model for diagnosis is highly beneficial. A sufficiently comprehensive model can help us to organize data into useful categories and to see more easily and quickly domains in the organization that need attention. Choosing the model should depend on at least three criteria. First, the model should be one that you as a practitioner thoroughly understand and feel comfortable with as you work with organizational members. Second, the model you choose should fit the client organization as closely as possible—that is, be comprehensive enough to cover as many aspects of the organization as appropriate, yet be simple and clear enough for organizational members to grasp fairly quickly. Third, the model should be one sufficiently comprehensive to allow you to gather your data about the organization according to the model's parameters without missing key bits of information.

This chapter, along with Chapter 6, covered organizational diagnosis by examining models and theories that can help to summarize considerable data and point the way for important organization change. These models and theories have been largely rational, a deliberate and overt way of understanding an organization. Yet we know that the reality of organizational dynamics is not by any stretch of one's imagination exclusively rational. Much of an organization's culture is below the surface buried within the collective unconscious of organizational members. To be thorough and subsequently effective with our organizational diagnosis, we must therefore examine both the rational and irrational, overt and covert, and what is apparent and transparent and what is not obvious. In other words, we must understand what is below the surface, not discussed, and perhaps avoided. We now address this other perspective in the following chapter.

Endnote

1. This chapter is based in part on Burke and Litwin (1989).

8

Understanding Organizations: Covert Processes[1]

As a result of a failed organizational change initiative, my colleagues and I (Noumair, Winderman, & Burke, 2010) argued for combining group relations and organization development in the practice of organizational consultation. Although tension exists between these approaches, we nonetheless made the case for the importance of organizational consultation practice that combines more deeply these two theoretical perspectives. OD models and frameworks alone are not always sufficient to surface underlying forces that influence the behavior of individuals, groups, and entire systems. Although attending to covert processes has long been an aspect of OD work, the aim of this chapter is to present a conceptual framework in addition to the ones discussed in Chapters 6 and 7, "Understanding Organizations: The Process of Diagnosis" and "The Burke-Litwin Model of Organizational Performance and Change," respectively, that incorporates elements of group relations and OD, and to demonstrate through a case analysis what blending the two can look like in actual practice.

Having defined the client, presented selected OD models, and the Burke-Litwin model of organizational performance and change, the purpose of this chapter is to expand our understanding of diagnosis by including covert processes in organizational life. Thus, we introduce what we refer to as "Beneath the Surface of the Burke-Litwin Model" and show how attending to both sides of the model can contribute to a deeper understanding of an organization, and a way of practicing that allows clients the possibility of approaching, and discussing, what heretofore may have been out of awareness and considered "undiscussable."

Combining Group Relations and Organization Development

A conceptual framework for consulting to organizations that builds on group relations principles and practice consists of three components: psychodynamic theory, group-as-a-whole level of analysis, and social-structural concepts. We discuss each component separately and show how they are integrated into a coherent practice of organization consultation applied to a case study.

Psychodynamic theory (Gould, 2004; Hirschhorn, 1988; Obholzer & Roberts, 1994) is a lens for understanding covert aspects of organizational life. In addition to rational processes in organizational life, irrational and emotional forces are in operation and also influence the dynamics between the consultant and client. To make use of psychodynamic theory, one must consider that social systems have unconscious dynamics that can shape behavior but that are beyond the awareness of individuals as well as a group or system as a whole. Attending to unconscious influences and irrational behavior requires a shift in mind-set regarding what counts as data when analyzing or consulting to a system. This broader definition of data includes elements beyond what can be observed, counted, and measured, including what is invisible and intangible, what is not said, as well as what is said, and what is felt and experienced in the relationship between organizational client and consultant.

By employing psychodynamic theory in organizational consultation, systems can be viewed as having greater capacity for complexity and behavior determined by multiple factors, some conscious and rational, some unconscious and irrational. A psychodynamic analysis of an organization entails the study of its choice of defense mechanisms. Hirschhorn (1988) provides an in-depth discussion of the use of defense mechanisms in organizational life, identifying three forms of social defense: the basic assumption, the covert coalition, and the organizational ritual. Identifying these three forms of social defense can provide relevant information for the consultant, and ultimately, for the organization in its effort to understand itself.

A group-as-a-whole level of analysis (Wells, 1995) is one way to uncover social defenses as it answers the question of why individuals can act differently as members of groups and organizations than they do when acting solely on their own behalf. It provides a framework for understanding how individuals, subgroups, and entire organizations participate in maintaining an organizational "problem." Unconscious group processes provide evidence for collusion among group members and connect individual and group behavior (Wells, 1995). When a consultant takes a group-as-a-whole perspective, she considers behavior at multiple levels and as such may uncover a problem's root. Although she may not make her discovery explicit, she uses the information to develop interventions aimed at addressing the unconscious collusion among group members.

In addition, a group-as-a-whole level of analysis offers the idea that individuals can serve as "containers" for various parts of the group or organization's emotional life—"serviceable others" (Morrison, 1992), compartments for painful, unwanted feelings, such as incompetence, in order for others in the organization to be viewed as competent or "stars." Processes of splitting and projection, and in particular projective identification, when occurring at the group level, create what is known as *role lock* whereby individuals are used to "contain" various components of the group's emotional life (Wells, 1995).

Individuals enter groups with valency (Bion, 1961), a predisposition based on background, personality, and social identities to carry certain emotions and attitudes. Recipients of projections must have valency to receive those particular projections. One useful metaphor for understanding valency is *Velcro*. When one has a predisposition for specific attributes or feelings, we say that the person has Velcro for those projections and therefore the projections "stick" more easily. When one does not have a predisposition for specific projections, we say the person has *Teflon*—the projections "slide" off. The metaphors of Velcro and Teflon enable individuals and groups to understand how *role lock* can occur as such unconscious processes are not readily observable and measurable and therefore are challenging to comprehend in organizational settings.

Although we use psychodynamic theory and a group-as-a-whole level of analysis to uncover what is below the surface of organizational life, our approach also borrows from open systems theory (Miller & Rice, 1967), Gould's (2004) Systems Psychodynamic organizational consultation, Schein's work on organizational culture (2004) and process consultation (1988, 1999), and Marshak's (2006) model for addressing hidden dimensions of organizational change, all directed toward removing impediments to healthy and effective organizational life. This approach and these concepts are especially useful when responding to resistance and ambivalence related to organization change as they equip the consultant with effective tools to address underlying concerns that might not be immediately manifest (Gould, 2004; Hirschhorn, 1988; Krantz, 2001). My (Noumair) work with the case study presented in this chapter reflects an integration of these approaches all aimed at employing group dynamics and group relations concepts in service of more effective practice in organizational consultation.

To identify and confront unconscious group processes in organizational life, our approach to consultation begins with social-structural concepts known collectively as BART (Boundary, Authority, Role, and Task) (Green & Molenkamp, 2005). Boundaries can be defined as physical or psychological discontinuities separating a system from its environment; they must be strong enough to maintain the integrity of what is inside but permeable enough to allow transactions between inside and outside. Authority is understood as the right to do work in service of the task and can be both formal and informal. Authority is related to role in that organizational authority accompanies formal, rational work roles; that is, authority is delegated to individuals to carry out the responsibilities of formal work roles of the organization. Authority for informal roles, in contrast, can be assumed by individuals, based on personality or valency ("Velcro"), to contain anxiety on the part of others in the organization. Task is the primary reason a group exists and while there are different kinds of tasks, clarity about the purpose of the group is essential to understanding it as a social system. Using BART as a diagnostic tool enables organizational members to consider emotional and other sub rosa factors that may affect, distort, or obscure rational structural features of an organization. Besides its diagnostic benefits, BART can also serve as an antidote to irrational dynamics in groups and assist in the management of projective processes in organizations.

A framework known collectively as GRPI (Goals, Roles, Processes, Interpersonal relationships) (Beckhard, 1972; Burke, 1988, 1994) is another useful tool for intervention and is similar to BART in that its components are usually more familiar to organizational members than are psychodynamic concepts. Lack of clarity about goals, roles and responsibilities, and processes and procedures often contributes to increased anxiety, which can produce difficulties in interpersonal relationships.

Often organization consultation is sought because of poor relations among its members as well as the quality of relatedness across subsystems—both of which interfere with an organization's capacity to produce high-quality work. Employing the GRPI framework (Beckhard, 1972; Burke, 1988, 1994), a consultant would not begin by addressing interpersonal relationships, however, because these difficulties in relationships would be viewed as symptoms and not as root causes. Rather, a consultant would employ GRPI in a hierarchical fashion initially assessing whether everyone was clear about organizational goals and purposes. Once alignment among organization members regarding the organizational mission was apparent, a consultant would work on clarifying roles and responsibilities, followed by helping the group to establish processes and procedures for collaboration. Usually once goals, roles, and processes are clarified, interpersonal tensions decrease in importance, or even disappear.

Organization members respond similarly to the frameworks of GRPI and BART, as both provide a way of understanding group and organization dynamics that are more recognizable and customary than a discussion of unconscious processes and irrationality in group and organizational life.

Employing this model, comprised of psychodynamic theory, a group-as-a-whole level of analysis, and social-structural concepts, allows consultants to take up an "interpretive stance" (Shapiro & Carr, 1991), searching for understanding without being judgmental either of their clients or of themselves. Second, sensitivity to group process in addition to content (Schein, 1988, 1999) enables early diagnosis of those group dynamics that may impede group functioning. This approach sets the stage for considering links between often unconscious emotional processes, group development, and organizational behavior.

Although psychodynamic theory, a group-as-a-whole level of analysis, and social-structural concepts represent the main components of this approach, other conceptual frameworks, theories, tools, and even language are necessary for intervention with organizations. We have learned of the need to transform psychodynamic conceptualizations into "client-friendly" language. One cannot discuss unconscious and irrational processes without—at least initially—linking the ideas to more familiar concepts. When trying to influence a client at the beginning of an engagement, it is not wise to use language related to the unconscious as it conjures up negative and fearful images of psychoanalysis, psychotherapy, and irrationality and a journey into the realm of deep emotionality. As a result, this approach should only rarely be used alone; it is best utilized in conjunction with other organizational models and frameworks. However, despite these cautions, it is an approach that tends to gradually appeal to clients once they have had the opportunity to experience its impact. Although at first organization members may feel the approach is off point, eventually they come to understand how the conscious and unconscious, rational and irrational, overt and covert are inextricably linked to the more prosaic problems they are experiencing.

Beneath the Surface of the Burke-Litwin Model

As discussed in Chapter 7, a well-established organization development model whose content is more familiar to organization members is the Burke-Litwin model of organizational performance and change (1992). The model—a well-suited companion to the psychodynamic approach—represents a more rational, linear way to think about organizations and, as such, organization clients are less threatened by it. The model serves as a point of departure for organization development as it allows clients to visualize the ways in which various components of organizations are connected and interact.

As shown in Figure 8.1, the top portion of the model contains transformational boxes (external environment, mission and strategy, leadership, and organization culture) and the bottom portion of the model contains transactional boxes (management practices, structure, systems, work unit climate, motivation, individual needs and values, individual skills and abilities, and individual and organizational performance). Organizations accomplish macro-organization change by focusing on the transformational (top) boxes of the model and micro-organization change is achieved by focusing on the transactional (bottom) boxes of the model. Based on open systems theory, the arrows between boxes depict how change in one part of the organization can affect change in another part of the organization.

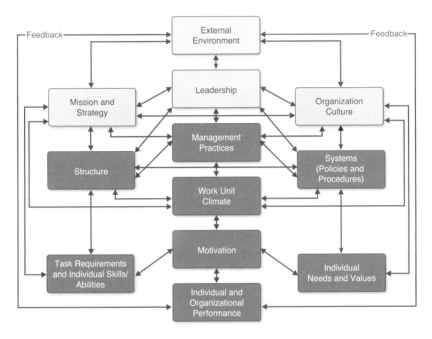

Figure 8.1 The Burke-Litwin Model—Organizational Performance and Change

Interestingly, although the Burke-Litwin model also serves as a guide for intervention in an organization change process, it does not always provide a lens for examining why 70 percent of change efforts fail (Burke, 2011a). Understanding such failures requires consideration of the challenges encountered in sustaining change (Burke, 2014b) and various forms of resistance that can arise in organizations (Piderit, 2000). An approach informed by the combination of psychodynamic theory, group-as-a-whole level of analysis, and social-structural concepts provides a particularly probing model for doing so. In effect, one can imagine that obscuring the Burke-Litwin model's boxes and arrows are veils, which must be removed in order to reveal, diagnose, and respond to covert processes that may be interfering with an organization's change efforts.

As depicted in Figure 8.2, beneath the surface of the Burke-Litwin model lie what may be unconscious and irrational aspects of an organization. For example, an overt conflict between two individuals may appear rational on the surface but might also be evidence of competitive dynamics related to leadership succession; that is, power and authority issues and unspoken conflict beneath the surface. Or, a team may act less competent than it actually is on the surface as evidence of performance anxiety and fear of making a mistake under the surface. When considering what lies beneath the Burke-Litwin model, as was the case in Chapter 7, it is important to visualize the model as a hologram, a three-dimensional illustration in which it is possible to see what is on top of and underneath the model simultaneously.

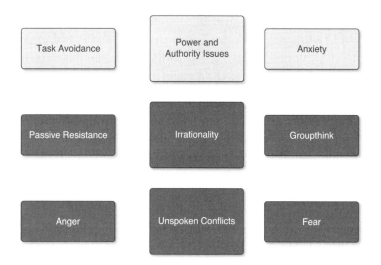

Figure 8.2 Beneath the Surface of the Burke-Litwin Model

A Case: Beyond the Presenting Problem— A Veiled Succession

The following case study provides an example of how utilizing a conceptual framework for organizational consultation informed by psychodynamic theory, a group-as-a-whole level of analysis, and social-structural concepts in combination with the use of the Burke-Litwin model of organization performance and change and beneath the surface of the Burke-Litwin model contributed to organizational culture change and facilitated leadership succession—an example of how removing the veils allowed the consultant and the client system to access covert processes that lie beneath the surface.

Initial Phase

The head of the Luminary Institute (a pseudonym for a think tank) had called me (Noumair), seeking consultation because of concern about two managers on his leadership team. He wanted to discuss the possibility of my providing coaching for them, although he was worried about singling them out because the organization was relatively small and "everyone knew everything."

Beyond hearing this presenting symptom, I noted to myself how defensive, withholding, and anxious the executive seemed during the conversation. Each suggestion I made was met with "no" for an answer. Although he said that he wanted consultation, he was emphatic that the "problem" to be addressed was at the individual level and distinct from any organizational-level phenomenon. The initial conversation ended with my feeling discouraged and trapped. How could I take the case given that it was clear from this initial contact that I would never please him? What help could I provide?

The next meeting I had was with the head of the institute and his deputy and it was similar to my phone conversation. He said no to all of the solutions I suggested, including coaching the managers individually and working with the two of them as a pair. Finally, toward the end of the meeting, I offered a system intervention, saying that often individuals carry symptoms on behalf of the organization and that what was going on with these two managers might be symptomatic of larger systemic issues. I asked them to tell me about the functioning of the leadership team. They were intrigued with this interpretation and we came to an agreement that I would work with the leadership team, composed of the heads of each of the institute's functional departments, rather than with the two "symptomatic" individuals.

Based on individual interviews with everyone on the leadership team, I discovered that the primary organizational concern was actually a high turnover rate rather than, or possibly in addition to, the functioning of the two individual managers initially discussed. It then made more sense to me why the request had been about coaching as high organizational turnover is often linked to leadership and culture (Follett, 1996). Further, I sensed that the institute was a challenging place to work as perfectionism at any cost was the standard by which individuals were measured—providing additional data for my developing hypothesis that the organization culture was problematic.

Using psychodynamic theory, a group-as-a-whole level of analysis, and social-structural concepts in conjunction with the Burke-Litwin model, I developed a working hypothesis that linked data from various sources. The organization had changed its mission and strategy from focusing solely on research to also including advocacy, and its structure from working individually to working in teams. This story framed the organizational concerns (i.e., high turnover, conflict among two members of the leadership team, and aspects of the culture) as consequences of the change in the organization's mission and strategy. Applying the top of the Burke-Litwin model, I suggested that the consultation could best focus on the leadership team because this model links leadership with both mission and strategy and with culture (Burke & Litwin, 1992) and proposed that it was the leadership team's responsibility to align mission and strategy with culture. As we set out on the consultancy, the Burke-Litwin model served as a comfortable conversation starter—a road map reminding participants that although they might feel lost along the way, they were actually on a particular track.

We often introduce personality assessments when working with an organization for several reasons: First, they provide individual information that might not otherwise be accessible and the assessment data invite a conversation about an individual's role in the organization and the reciprocal influences of the individual and the organization on each other. Second, they provide individuals with data for their own development apart from their specific work roles and therefore can motivate them to engage more fully. Third, the results can be used to compile a group profile; that is, a picture of the organization that serves as another way for the client group to understand itself as a collective entity. This additional snapshot allows for more candid conversation about the group's strengths and challenges as it is informed by assessment data rather than by what any one person reports in an individual interview and therefore is viewed as more objective. Using personality assessments to connect individual and group behavior to inform organization development work is a well-established data-based intervention (Burke & Noumair, 2002; Hogan, 2006). Given this rationale, I invited all members of the leadership team to take the Myers Briggs Type Indicator, Step II (MBTI) (www.ConsultingPsychologistsPress.com) and the Hogan Development Survey (assessment of leadership derailers) (www.HoganAssessments.com; Hogan, 2006).

The assessment results helped me deepen my working hypothesis about the leadership team. I viewed the two members of the leadership team who were depicted as the initial presenting problem as "containers" of a split in the organization. Their assessment profiles suggested that the two of them were more comfortable than others to serve as fight leaders. Whenever there were opposing sides to an issue, the leadership team could depend on the two of them to locate themselves in opposition to one another as they each had "Velcro" for such projections. When they did so, everyone else was off the hook; no one else had to enter the fray. Thus, the team's collusion in unwittingly allowing these two conflict-prone individuals to fight served them as everyone else on the team appeared affable and cooperative. I tucked away this idea until I had further data to support it and enough evidence to share it with the entire leadership team.

First Retreat

At the first retreat held for the leadership team, I first reported group profiles from the two personality assessments and then offered my thematic analysis and my working hypothesis about the organization.

This is a common practice, as presenting individual and group assessment profiles first can serve as a warm-up of sorts, providing an opportunity for the team to interact with each other and learn about themselves, individually and collectively. However, when I presented the MBTI group profile, the two fight leaders were immediately, and relentlessly, critical of my presentation, complaining that I did not present the data accurately and suggesting other ways of doing it. This reaction surprised me, and given that the rest of the leadership team, including the leader, remained silent during this attack, I viewed the two members who had Velcro for conflict, as speaking on behalf of the team as a whole. It was *as if* the leadership team unconsciously put them forward to challenge me.

When a group acts *as if* it is working on a task other than the task it has formally been assigned, it is often as a method of defending against the anxiety that is triggered by the real work (Bion, 1961; Gustafson & Cooper, 1992). What is challenging diagnostically is that often groups take up the *as if* task, in Bion's terms, basic assumption mode (Bion, 1961), with as much vigor as they would if they were working on the formally assigned task. Therefore, the consultant is easily seduced into believing the group is doing real work rather than obstructing progress.

After responding to a few iterations of their criticism in a straightforward, non-defensive manner, I began to understand the *as if* quality to what was going on. I said as much, deciding to use self-as-instrument (Berg & Smith, 1985, 1988; Burke, 1982, 1994; Cheung-Judge, 2001; Gillette, 1995; Levinson, 1972a; McCormick & White, 2000; Smith, 1995). I said that I had a pit in my stomach. I was filled with dread at the idea of working with them over the next day and a half during which I was to give three more presentations. Given this fight process, I understood why the turnover rate in the organization was so high.

There was a collective gasp in the room and a look of astonishment on their faces. They seemed horrified that I, or any consultant, would say such a thing to *them*. Their self-image was of a very smart, very buttoned-up, polite, and proper group of people. This was not a group characterized by candor.

Suddenly, one member of the team spoke up, "That pit in your stomach, I know that pit in your stomach—it is the same pit I have in my stomach every time I enter a leadership team meeting." Another added, "We hired you to shine a flashlight on what we do so we can better understand why we have the reputation that we do, and you have done that—whether we like what we see when the light is shone or not."

It was a critical moment in the consultation. I viewed the conversation that followed my "self-as-instrument" moment as the first evidence of real work among the team, and I labeled the person who identified with my "pit in the stomach" as the first work leader to emerge, other than the formal leader of the organization. The work leader's role was integral to what transpired as it symbolized the responsibility having shifted from the consultant to a member of the team, and soon after, to the other members of the team who had chimed in. By drawing the parallel between my experience in the retreat and her experience in leadership team meetings, she led the team to take ownership of their work in the retreat, gave legitimacy to the consultation, and credibility to me as its architect, reflecting an example of the use of parallel process in organizational consultation (Sullivan, 2002).

What then became clear was that the two members of the team who were the initial presenting problem, the two with "Velcro" for fight and conflict, represented the two separate components of the organization's mission, research, and advocacy. Although there certainly were interpersonal issues between these two team members, refocusing on the conflict inherent in having two primary tasks, which they symbolized, seemed to free up the team to work on those issues. What also became clear was that other members of the organization split these two parts of the overall mission, some aligning with research behind the researcher "spokesperson" and others more aligned with advocacy behind the head of advocacy, the "advocacy spokesperson." Once group members were able to own their individual contributions to the split, the antagonism between the two primary actors lessened in intensity and they too began to work together in a manner that appeared creative and free flowing.

To understand what happened next at the retreat, it is important to describe an interaction that occurred in preparation for it. I had gone to lunch with the leader and shared with him themes from the individual interviews I had conducted with leadership team members and said that I was concerned that at the retreat candor would be stifled and team members inhibited by his presence. Leadership team members perceived the leader as "the smartest person in the room" and they feared being shamed for not measuring up. He said that if that happened, I should "call him on it"—that I should make his behavior as well as its impact on his team explicit in the moment that it occurred. I responded, "Right then and there, in public?" And he said, "Yes, call me on it." Although I could not believe what I was hearing, at the same time, I thought to myself, "I now have a contract for work."

Having made this agreement with the leader, I felt confident that I did not have to collude with the organization. Had I not shared with him in advance what I had learned in my interviews about his staff's perception of him, I would have been mimicking his staff's behavior. I would have acted as if he were too scary to be talked to directly—that one should not speak truth to power. The effect of withholding that information would also have worked in the other direction; I would have been acting as if his staff's perceptions of him were "true" and therefore that I would be at risk in the same way in which they felt they were at risk. This preparation eventually allowed me to make what was covert, overt, and model for the staff how to have an authentic conversation with the leader.

Establishing a "contract for work" with the head of the organization allowed me to address at the retreat what I imagined would be necessary; that is, to confront the leader and his team about their authority relations with each other. For the first time, the leader acknowledged that he was part of the problem, that he was in part responsible for the high rate of turnover, a symptom of the organization's rough culture. Tears accompanied his revelation, which was quite upsetting to some members of his team, and also signified a second critical event in the consultation. It became clear that the leadership team was invested in protecting the leader and maintaining the status quo. One member said that my first responsibility was to do no harm and as far as he was concerned, I had done harm, as I should not be creating conditions in which the leader cried in public. His rebuke, followed by an elaborate argument that I should preserve the perceived invulnerability of the leader, brought to mind Lewin's maxim that the best way to understand an organization is to try and change it (Lewin, 1951).

My understanding of this reaction was that as long as the leader was seen as "the problem," no one on the leadership team had to take responsibility for it. If they instead engaged the interpretation that the issues related to high turnover were systemic, not personal, and that they had collective responsibility, each person could then be held accountable for his or her own behavior. Rather than going a level deeper and owning up to their contributions, some members of the leadership team preferred to remain invested in the more emotionally convenient arrangement. Further, it would later be revealed that the leadership team's lack of ownership of the organization's culture at the initial retreat was a warning sign that they were unable, or perhaps unwilling, to work without the leader. Although obvious in retrospect, competition among team members to be chosen as successor may have contributed to their investment in maintaining the illusion that only the leader was responsible for the organizational culture. Moreover, the leader's wish to remain solely in control of the organization and protect the legacy of its founder prevented him from more aggressively confronting the leadership team. At various points in the consultation, I thought about framing the organization as a family business given the ironclad adherence to roles displayed by the members. However, given that the institute did not initially sign up for changing the culture and the question of succession, though fundamental, had not yet been broached, pursuing these questions at this stage did not seem appropriate.

After the First Retreat

To build on the learning from the first retreat, I developed a plan to address the split in relating to the two organizational missions as well as to improve authority relations. It was necessary to address these issues at multiple levels. First, it was important to alert the entire organization that the leadership team was considering the application of group relations concepts to the organization's challenges as doing so meant that they were taking a systemic, rather than personal, view of the institute and *everyone* would be expected to participate in addressing the challenges. We decided that I would make a presentation at a staff meeting on group dynamics and team development to introduce the group relations perspective to the organization as a whole.

At the presentation, I introduced the ideas presented at the outset of this chapter, including psychodynamic theory (Gould, 2004; Hirschhorn, 1988; Obholzer & Roberts, 1994), a group-as-a-whole level of analysis (Rutan, Stone, & Shay, 2007; Wells, 1995), and BART (Green & Molenkamp, 2005) as a framework for analyzing groups in an organizational context. Doing so was an opportunity for me as the consultant to act as educator, providing the organization with a new way of thinking about organizational life. The staff was clearly relieved that I was analyzing the organization as a whole rather than the individuals within it. At the same time, it seemed like the beginning of interrupting a culture of blame; it was now at least theoretically possible to consider that the organization, collectively, was responsible for what had been created.

On the day I was to give the presentation, I arrived wearing a large necklace with three circular silver plates, positioned vertically one on top of the other so that the necklace hung from my neck to my waist. In an illustration of the extent to which the consultation had begun to have an effect on the organization, a member of the leadership team looked at my necklace and asked, "What is that, a bulletproof vest?" I responded in kind, "Yes, I figured that since I would be shot at once again I would protect myself this time." Although we both acknowledged the humor in our exchange, we were also acknowledging that we now had a familiar way of talking about the organization, about the culture, and about our work together. Once again, an organization member had made the covert overt.

Next, we introduced a plan to collect multi-rater feedback for the entire leadership team. Multi-rater or 360 feedback is a report of the perceptions of an employee's entire circle of work colleagues— manager, peers, direct reports, and sometimes even customers and clients (Bracken, Timmreck, & Church, 2001). Before beginning this feedback process, I met with those staff members who would be interviewed as direct reports of the leadership team in advance and explained the entire process and the rules of engagement, that is, confidentiality and anonymity.

This meeting, too, was an important turning point in the consultation as it was now becoming much clearer that the organizational culture required change, that the problem was not one of individuals but instead one of "how we do things around here" (Deal & Kennedy, 1982). Like the leadership team before them, it was now the staff's turn to resist. They did not think multi-rater feedback was the correct solution to the problem. In their minds, the problem was not any one of the individual leadership team members but the collective leadership team, and the organization's culture as a whole that they felt the leadership team had produced. Some went so far as to say that the problem was the leader of the organization as they were versed in leadership theory that suggests that the leader is responsible for driving the culture (Schein, 2004). They viewed multi-rater feedback as off target, misplaced, and a waste of resources. Concerned about retaliation for their comments in the interviews, they warned me about the lack of candor I could expect from them. The harmony of their voices was quite compelling and helped to make the case that organizational culture needed to be addressed.

As a consequence of this conversation, I kept a log of all comments related to the organizational culture that surfaced during the feedback interviews and agreed to report only those themes endorsed by more than one person to ensure that controversial issues could not be linked or traced back to any one individual. Not surprisingly, the environment was perceived as controlled, perfectionist, and risk-averse; overthinking and an inability to prioritize prevailed. In addition, there was a perceived lack of differentiation in task and responsibilities, and hierarchy ruled. If this was truly "the way we do things around here," one could see why there was a high turnover rate at this organization.

The final stage of the feedback process required that I interview the board of directors of the institute about the leader as they collectively held managerial authority over him. These discussions provided a window into the problem of succession as I learned that board members were concerned that there was no internal candidate who could serve as successor and therefore the long-term sustainability of the institute was at risk. The most pressing issue for board members was developing the leadership team's capacity to work without the leader at the same time as enabling them to follow the direction of a successor from outside the institute. When I shared the board members' feedback with the leader, I discovered that he, too, had concerns about the future of the institute and readily engaged the charge from the board that he prepare his staff to work without him. While focusing on culture change at the institute was the overt task the organization was working on at this point, the leader was working on a covert task; that is, developing his team in order to set the stage for his retirement while actively keeping his time frame for retirement a secret. I learned that the leader was concerned that if he made his plan to retire public he would become a lame duck leader and have to relinquish control; while wanting to step down on one hand, he was also concerned that the institute was not ready for leadership succession. The board's feedback enabled him to understand at a deeper level that his job as leader was to replace himself and that his leadership would be judged by the effectiveness of his leadership team after he was gone (Kaiser, Hogan, & Craig, 2008; Hogan, Curphy, & Hogan, 1994). The discourse on leadership succession became a central theme in parallel discussions I held with the leader and the board.

Second Retreat

Viewing the presentation of the culture data that had been collected during the multi-rater feedback interviews was very difficult for the leadership team: They were devastated. They found all sorts of reasons to deny what I had reported. Eventually, however, they realized that they were accountable for the processes that had been put in place to conduct the work and they had to acknowledge the unintentional consequences of those processes. Once again, the leadership team had to bend from its original idea about what the organizational consultation was about to discover the truth as perceived by those at lower levels in the organization. The task was not fixing individuals, but changing the way they as leaders worked together and with their staff and the way the organization as a whole did business. The organization, and specifically the leadership team, finally began to take responsibility for the culture it had created.

After the Second Retreat

As a result of the cultural revelations, every meeting agenda now included time for "bitching" at the outset—an acknowledgment of the importance of one's emotional state at work. Leaders and staff alike were now able to say what was usually left unspoken, denied, or even shoved aside. Although this might not seem like an important change, it represented the beginning of a shift in the culture, from controlled to expressive, solely cerebral to also emotional, and allowing room for play as well as work.

Team Retreats

As the leadership team focused on clarifying the organizational structure and roles and responsibilities, we decided to conduct individual team retreats for each functional department of the institute. At each retreat, we provided individual and group assessment profiles, reported on collective themes from individual interviews, and worked to create conditions in which difficult issues could be voiced, and the covert could be made overt.

With the completion of these retreats, a noticeable difference began to emerge in the ways individuals and teams interacted with each other. It was clear that work on creating a culture of candor was under way. There was also a significant change in the behavior of the organization's leader. He modeled open communication and expressed more vulnerability, which went a long way toward developing a more positive perception of his leadership as well as accelerating culture change.

The Final Veil

The next phase of the consultation involved working at multiple levels simultaneously. The leadership team focused on effective management by learning how to have difficult conversations, conducting more effective performance appraisals, modeling better meeting management, and increasing delegation of authority. Importantly, the organization as a whole began working on becoming more reflective and instituted mechanisms for individual and collective self-monitoring that allowed for the generating of insights that might facilitate further change. This was in sharp contrast to the organization that I initially encountered in which learning was equated with not having adequately prepared, and learning in public was equated with humiliation.

At this point, the organization had progressed enough that the leadership team saw fit to have conducted a formal survey on its culture; findings regarding trust, fairness, and psychological safety, not surprisingly, corroborated the findings from the consultation already under way. This "objective" data challenged the leadership team's previous defense that the data I had collected earlier were somehow not valid.

With no place to hide, the organization steeled itself to engage more broadly in the work necessary to change its reputation as a challenging place to work. We established a new ground rule in our work, namely that an organization member could not talk unless he acknowledged how he contributed to the problems in the current culture. The idea behind this was that dynamics related to trust, fairness, and psychological safety are co-created by all members of an organization even though differential responsibility and accountability are aligned with positional authority. At first, no one could speak, as all were invested in blaming others, and more specifically, in blaming up. Eventually, however, each person began to own his or her contribution to the dysfunction, providing evidence for the effectiveness of the group-as-a-whole level intervention.

Once the entire organization had digested the culture survey results, taken responsibility, individually and collectively, and worked on implementing action plans, we were ostensibly finished with the consultation. Now it was a matter of ongoing monitoring and making adjustments as needed. At last, the most important veil fell away: The leader decided to make public his plan for retirement.

After the Consultation

Monthly meetings between the consultant and the leader continued for eight months and then ceased during the search for the leader's successor. Once the search process was complete, meetings between the consultant and the leader continued until the leader retired from the organization. The engagement extended for five years in total, beginning with the initial phone call and ending with the completion of a search for the leader's successor.

Discussion

In hindsight, and with the psychodynamic veils removed and beneath the surface of the Burke-Litwin model revealed, the issues at this organization were rather straightforward. The real but underlying need of the organization was to find a way to survive without its leader. When the board first raised this issue, its members declared the leader could not retire until the organization could work without him. The challenge of meeting that condition had effectively brought the organization's progress to a halt and the organization had found refuge in obfuscation and fight—focusing on the two feuding principals, blaming the leader, and finally blaming the consultant. By pulling away the psychodynamic veils one by one, it became clear that in order to move forward, the entire organization needed to focus on repairing a culture dominated by perfectionism and hyperrationality as defenses against the covert processes. Only then could the organization become autonomous enough that the leader could step down.

Organizations are like individuals in that no two are alike. And while the integrative model of consultation illustrated here seems widely, if not universally applicable, its specific application needs to be adapted to the unique culture of a client organization.

To make the most effective use of this approach, consultants need to engage in reflective practice (discussed in Chapter 12, "The Organization Development Consultant"), action-reflection/reflection-action processes (Schön, 1983), double loop learning (Argyris & Schön, 1978), using self as instrument (Berg & Smith, 1985, 1988; Burke, 1982, 1994; Cheung-Judge, 2001; Gillette, 1995; Levinson, 1972a; McCormick & White, 2000; Smith, 1995), and "getting on the balcony" (Heifetz, 1994). They need to take the unfamiliar-to-the-world-of-business approach of honoring psychological experience and offer a model of how to do this for their clients.

This requires understanding the organization's resistance to thinking psychologically, making a compelling case for reflection, reframing individual behavior as symptomatic of systemic issues, and co-creating conditions that allow for the exploration of emotional and irrational, as well as rational, forces in organizational life.

Consulting to an organization, using this framework, requires a core capacity to reflect on one's emotional experience, interrogate that experience, make meaning of it, inquire about the emotional experience of others, and trust that emotional experience constitutes valid data (Argyris, 1965). The issues a consultant faces at the outset of a consultation may not make immediate rational sense, but will always make psychological sense. Once the consultant experiences the underlying reasons she was hired in the first place, her experience becomes perhaps the first useful data point in the discovery process.

That moment—like the moment when the leadership team member affirmed the pit in my stomach—will feel like a great relief because the consultant will know she is finally moving forward, but paradoxically, that is when caution is most necessary. Removing veils allows an organization's defense mechanisms to be revealed, providing important diagnostic information on where and what the underlying pain and anxiety are (Halton, 1994; Hirschhorn, 1988), but consultants must understand that some organizational defenses must be respected and left in place, for example, defending against the pain of having lost a beloved organizational member or leader.

The final chapter of any successful consultancy of this nature involves allowing an organization to reconstitute, enabling a more self-aware and self-monitoring organization that is able to use its defenses to confront adversity while at the same time maintaining a vibrant and healthy culture that supports its mission.

Conclusion

In addition to the models and frameworks covered in Chapters 6 and 7, we presented a conceptual framework for organizational consultation that incorporates group relations and organization development. As components of a group relations perspective, we introduced the utility of psychodynamic theory, a group-as-a-whole level of analysis, and social-structural concepts. Psychodynamic theory provides a lens for understanding covert aspects of group and organizational life. Focusing on the group as the level of analysis, a group-as-a-whole perspective allows for greater understanding of the root causes of behavior; provides an understanding of how individuals, subgroups, and entire organizations participate in maintaining a "problem"; and presents evidence for collusion among group members thereby linking individual and group behavior. Social-structural concepts, BART (Boundary, Authority, Role, and Task) (Green & Molenkamp, 2005), is a framework for understanding the extent to which groups and organizations are interdependent and structurally organized to do work. GRPI (Goals, Roles, Processes, and Interpersonal relationships) (Beckhard, 1972; Burke, 1988, 1994) is a diagnostic tool to be utilized hierarchically; that is, first determine the extent to which there is alignment about goals; once achieved, clarify roles and responsibilities followed by processes for collaboration. Both BART and GRPI use concepts and language that are familiar to organization members and therefore may be less threatening than tools that purport to uncover covert processes.

In addition to the Burke-Litwin model (Burke & Litwin, 1992) discussed in depth in Chapter 7, we introduced the Burke-Litwin model beneath the surface and as was the case earlier, we invited the reader to imagine a hologram, a three-dimensional image in which it is possible to simultaneously see what is on the surface and what is beneath the surface of the model. To bring to life this conceptual framework that expands the Burke-Litwin model to include the unconscious and irrational aspects of organizations, we presented a case analysis. The case included the use of assessments (multi-rater feedback and personality inventories) for individuals and teams, and the use of self-as-instrument and reflective practice.

Although detecting covert processes can contribute to a more robust organization diagnosis, employing both perspectives, group relations and organization development, allows the client system to work with what is on the surface, and probably more accessible, as well as what lies beneath the surface, and initially, out of awareness.

The conceptual framework presented in this chapter serves as a tool for shining a light on organizational dynamics.

Endnote

1. This chapter is a modification of the article published in *The International Journal of Group Psychotherapy* (Noumair, 2013).

9

Planning and Managing Change

It is easy to write, if not to assume, that diagnosis is one activity and intervention (that is, planning and implementing change) is quite another. In practice, however, this is simply not true. As Schein (1969) pointed out, merely entering a human system to conduct a diagnosis is an intervention.

It is helpful to our understanding, nevertheless, to consider the phases of planning and managing change as following diagnosis and feedback. Thus, once a diagnosis has been made and feedback has been provided to the client, it is time to plan the appropriate steps to take so that problems identified in the diagnostic phase are addressed and a more ideal future state for the organization can be determined. Guiding this planning phase should be a set of coherent and interrelated concepts—a theory, a model, a conceptual frame of reference.

This chapter first defines intervention and then covers the planning and management of change phase in more detail. Finally, we consider ways to determine if progress is being made in a change effort.

According to Argyris (1970), collecting data from an organization is intervening, which supports Schein's contention and our earlier claim that the phases of organization development (OD) are not discrete. For this phase of organization development, however, we think in terms of some specified activity, some event or planned sequence of events that occurs as a result of diagnosis and feedback. The process of moving from a functional way of organizing to a project form, for example, regardless of how long it takes (and it might take months) could constitute an OD intervention. Another example of a possible OD intervention would be a singular event and would take a comparatively short period of time. Either type of activity could serve as an OD intervention, provided the event responds to an actual and felt need for change on the part of the client, involves the client in the planning and implementing of the change (intervention), and leads to change in the organization's culture.

Criteria for Effective Intervention

Argyris (1970) has specified similar criteria for what he considers the primary tasks of an interventionist (OD practitioner). His three criteria are (1) valid and useful information, (2) free choice, and (3) internal commitment. By *valid and useful information,* he means "that which describes the factors plus their interrelationships, that create the problem for the client system" (p. 17). According to Argyris, the information the OD practitioner has collected from and about the client accurately reflects what people in the organization perceive and feel, what they consider to be their primary concerns and issues, what they experience as complexities and perhaps accompanying frustrations of living within and being a part of the client system, and what they would like to see changed. Argyris goes on to specify that, if several independent diagnoses lead to the same intervention, the data the practitioner has gathered are valid.

For all practical purposes, this first task of an interventionist, obtaining valid and useful information, is similar to our first criterion for intervention, responding to an actual and felt need for change on the part of the client. If valid information is obtained by the practitioner, it will reflect a need. If the practitioner responds to that need, he or she will have done so by providing valid and useful information.

By *free choice,* Argyris means that "the locus of decision making [is] in the client system" (p. 19) and that the client is provided alternatives for action. No particular or specified action is automatic, preordained, or imposed.

By *internal commitment,* Argyris means that the client owns the choice made and feels responsible for implementing it. Organization members act on their choice because it responds to needs, both individual and on behalf of the organization.

The primary tasks of choice and internal commitment will be accomplished if the practitioner involves the client in planning and implementing the intervention. Argyris does not specify cultural change, our third criterion. He implies that, if the practitioner accomplishes the three primary tasks, the organization's culture will be changed. This is only an implication, however; he does not specify it.

Although there are similarities between Argyris's criteria and ours, the primary difference is that we are expressing processes or means while he is stating end states or outcomes. Either way of expressing these criteria makes sense.

Planning the Intervention or Change

Readers may or may not agree on the fine points concerning a definition of and the criteria for an effective intervention. Unless there is some readiness for change within the client organization, definitions and criteria are no more than an academic exercise. Richard Beckhard expressed it one way and Harry Levinson another, but both essentially said, when it comes to organization (or individual for that matter) change: "No pain, no change." Unless enough key people in the organization feel a real need for change, none is likely to occur, at least none that is planned and managed.

The initiation of change, it should be noted, is typically in response to changes in the organization's external environment, as was Prime Minister Thatcher's decision to privatize British Airways. In other words, it is rarely true that top management comes together and states "Why don't we change the organization?" More likely, top management in initiating change is doing so as a reaction to changes in the organization's marketplace, to changes in technology, to changes in government regulations, to stronger competition, and so forth.

Readiness for Change

Sometimes determining readiness is quite obvious and straightforward. The company's sales have fallen dramatically, costs have risen so sharply that profit doesn't exist anymore, turnover and absenteeism are significantly out of line when compared with others in the same industry, morale has never been lower or the market strategy doesn't seem to work anymore—these are some obvious and rather straightforward examples of a need for change. Under any of these circumstances, it is not difficult to determine a readiness. As was the case for British Airways (Chapter 7, "The Burke-Litwin Model of Organizational Performance and Change"), the need for change was extremely clear. The degree of readiness varied among BA employees, but the need was obvious. In other instances, or even in the instances listed above, everyone may not see or understand a need for change. In this situation, the need must be generated. This may be done in either of two ways. One way is to gather information, the facts, about the current situation and contrast this information with where the organization was supposed to have been by this time. In other words, it is a matter of comparing actual achievements with what was desired, the organization's goals or mission.

Assuming that organizational members identified with these goals (no minor assumption, to be sure) and they then see a significant difference between actual and desired, they will experience a need to reduce the difference or gap between actual and what is desired. In this case, the desired state is known; not known is how far off the mark the organization's actual performance is from that which is desired. Contrasting actual with desired creates the required motivation for change.

Another way to generate a need for change is to develop a more desirable future state. Organizational members may be satisfied with the status quo and experience no need for change unless and until they are presented with a possibility of something better, more desirable. It might mean a lot of hard work and a considerable modification in the way that work is done, but the new mission and differences in how work would be accomplished may be sufficiently attractive that a motivational pull toward this more desirable future state would be generated. This, of course, requires leadership.

Even though generating a need for change may be accomplished in either of these two different ways, the principle is the same. Presenting people with a discrepancy between what is and what is desired will create tension, and the motivation will be in the direction of reducing that tension; that is, to move toward the more desired state. This principle of human behavior is based on sound theory and research; see, for example, Lewin (1936) or Duvall and Wicklund (1972).

Preparing the client for change, what we have labeled readiness, is what Lewin called the unfreezing stage (see Chapter 4, "Organization Development as a Process of Change"). Unfreezing is creating conditions whereby the client is shaken loose (unfrozen) from the status quo. The client's mental and emotional set has been broken and the client is therefore more amenable to consider, if not accept, change. For more elaboration on this stage, as well as additions to our understanding of Lewin's next two stages, changing and refreezing, see Schein (1980) and Chapter 4. And for more specificity regarding a conceptual model for understanding and creating readiness for change, see Armenakis, Harris, and Mossholder (1993) and for a scale to assess readiness, see Armenakis, Bernerth, Pitts, and Walker (2007) and Holt, Armenakis, Feild, and Harris (2007).

We have also used the terms *actual* and *desired* state. This is the language of Beckhard and Harris (1987). Developing a new mission, a new vision, a fresh image of the future is the process of creating a desired state, a way of being, of working that is more desirable than the present state. Planning any change effort involves this kind of development—that is, creating an image of the more desired future state. This creative process is not easy to do. Even more difficult, however, is moving the organization to that desired future. Beckhard and Harris (1987), based on the earlier thinking of Lewin, view the change process in three states:

Present State ➔ Transition State ➔ Future State

Although determining the future state is obviously critical, Beckhard and Harris concern themselves far more with the transition state, managing the change process, the more difficult phase.

Hanna (1988) has added to the Beckhard and Harris transition state by emphasizing in his coverage of managing change the importance of:

- Developing a true commitment to the change
- Training in the requisite skills
- Dedicating sufficient resources

- Overcoming old habits
- Managing the environment

Power and Leadership

In addition to determining readiness and preparing the client organization for change by contrasting actual with desired, other planning activities need to occur. It is a leadership function to see to it that the future state is developed. Leaders in the organization need to be far more concerned with determining the future than specifying how to get there. Gaining commitment from organizational members to the future state, a plan, is critical; gaining commitment to implementing the plan, as Hanna has emphasized, is even more critical. More will be stated on this latter point in the next section.

A leadership function, therefore, is to make certain that a plan for the future is in place, that the plan is adequately communicated, and then to generate energy within the organization to support the transition.

In any sizable organization, formal as well as informal leaders exist. Often overlooked in a change effort is the latter group. It is obvious that senior management needs to be on board. If unionized, leaders within the union(s) need to be involved and supportive. All of the key managers who head the various boxes on the organization chart need to be on board. Not so obvious, however, are those who informally, from time to time, influence people's opinions. In an organization such as the National Aeronautics and Space Administration, for example, informal leadership comes from scientists and engineers who are not line, operational administrators but who are, as individuals, highly respected. Their opinions about matters are sought and they are influential. If these highly respected, listened-to, powerful individuals are not supportive of the change effort, resistance among organizational members will be greater than would otherwise be the case. It is wise, therefore, early in the planning process, to engage these informal leaders in discussing what change is needed and what is more desirable for the future.

Also informal and powerful indeed is the political process, a process that is typically subterranean, below the surface, not discussed openly much less in formal meetings within the organization (see our Chapter 8, "Understanding Organizations: Covert Processes," for coverage of these covert processes and see Tichy's TPC framework in Chapter 6, "Understanding Organizations: The Process of Diagnosis"). By *political* we mean those activities and processes in an organization that emanate from one's self-interest, or the particular interest of a group, that may not be in the overall interest of the organization. Typically when faced with the possibility of organizational change, organizational members rarely at the outset ask the question, "What is the plan for the future?" but instead, whether openly or not, they ask "How will the change affect me?"

It is not a matter of right versus wrong. It is more a simple matter of human nature. Thus, during the planning phase, it is imperative to address these political concerns, motivated by self-interest. That is, it is imperative to respond to the tacit question, "What's in it for me?" Some examples of the advantages to be provided by the future state might be these:

- A mission and purpose that is more meaningful and inspiring
- A set of goals and objectives that are not only clearer but more sensible in potential for attainment as well
- A more participative, pleasant place to work
- A reward system that is more flexible and responsive to individual differences
- A more decentralized structure that supports greater worker autonomy as well as responsiveness to the customer
- A management information system that handles relevant, current, and therefore, useful data
- A set of management practices that engender trust

With such examples, a statement of the future could begin to be responsive to individuals' personal concerns. More specificity regarding such statements would be required, of course.

To summarize, in planning change, the first phase is unfreezing the organization. This means creating awareness of the need for change. This is best done by contrasting an actual with a more desired state. Also critical to this initial planning phase is leadership, in this case, leadership capable of establishing conditions whereby the desired future state can be determined. And, finally, for adequate planning, the political and power dynamics within the organization must be addressed. Addressing these organizational dynamics means involving informal leaders in the planning and making certain that the way the future state is described is responsive to organizational members' inevitable question, "What's in it for me?"

Managing the Change Process

The toughest job is to *manage* the change process. In writing about this management process, we can be logical, rational, and perhaps convey that dealing with organizational change is indeed subject to management. In reality, however, managing change is sloppy— people never do exactly as we plan. And it follows Murphy's Law— if anything can go wrong, it will. Moreover, organizational politics is always present and change, after all, affects us all emotionally.

Even with these qualifications and the perspective that managing change is not always manageable, it is useful to consider certain principles and guidelines. The more a process may seem unmanageable, the more we should stick closely to those activities that have been demonstrated to be helpful. The following principles and guidelines meet the criterion of demonstrated helpfulness.

Disengagement from the Past

Once it has been decided that change will happen and the planning has occurred, or is in process, time and energy need to be devoted to disengaging from the past, that is, from certain ways of working; from a program, project, or product; from a geographical location; or from a group of people with whom one previously worked. Disengagement may take a variety of forms. An event can be held to recognize in a formal way the contribution of a certain program that will no longer be implemented, and of the people who were involved. The event can be celebratory in nature despite conclusion of the program.

In an organization with which we are familiar, a particular program was to be phased out to make way for a new and different one.

The program had involved research and development on a rocket used by NASA and the U.S. Air Force that became obsolete. Yet R&D was conducted with the rocket program all along the way as if it would always exist and be constantly improved. After almost twenty years with this program, the engineers and technicians involved were to be reassigned or encouraged to retire early. Change came surely and swiftly for these rocket professionals. Before taking on a new program and having to acquire some new knowledge and learn new skills, senior management conducted a brief ceremony. On the front lawn in front of the administration building, a table draped in black cloth was the focal point. Underneath the cloth was a small replica of the old rocket. After the table was uncovered, certain senior managers made very brief speeches extolling the former program and the people who had contributed to it over the years. All drank a toast, and the rocket was then covered again, symbolically buried. The head of the organization then gave a short explanation of the new program (solar energy for propulsion in space) that was replacing the old. The entire event took less than 30 minutes. Accomplished with this event were two important outcomes: First, an unequivocal symbolic act demonstrated the end of the program, and, second, affirmative recognition was provided for those who had been involved.

Although one may not need to conduct a funeral or demonstrate an ending quite as dramatically, two critical principles of managing change should be considered, both tied directly to human emotion. One is the principle of "unfinished business" and the other concerns appealing to rather than ignoring people's feelings of pride.

Unfinished Business

When something is incomplete, we humans tend to attempt some form of completion. A simple example from introductory psychology is when viewing a figure such as the following, we psychologically close the gap and complete mentally what we believe to be a circle. Less simple, but based on the same principle, is the situation when we have an argument with someone that soon stops for one reason or another yet remains unresolved; one tends to continue the argument mentally even though the other party is no longer present. We spend mental and emotional energy in an attempt to finish, to resolve, to complete the argument. So it is with organizational change. When newness is thrust on organizational members replacing, say, former ways of doing things with no time to disengage and "finish the business" of the former way, they will spend energy trying to deal with the incompleteness. This energy may take the form of continuing simply to talk about the former ways, or criticizing the new ways as clearly imperfect, or even more resistantly, sabotaging the new ways. What is referred to as "resistance to change" often reflects energy devoted to closure attempts. Providing some way for organizational members to disengage, to finish, at least to some extent, the past helps them to focus on the change and the future.

We are not the first to relate this important human principle to organizational change. Nadler (1981), building on the theoretical writings of Lewin and the work of Beckhard and Harris (1987), discusses this disengagement process in his integration of a number of managing change principles. He categorizes managing change into three broad needs or challenges: (1) the need to motivate change (including disengagement), (2) the need to manage the transition, where he elaborates on Beckhard and Harris, and (3) the need to shape the political dynamics of change. Our treatment of this managing change section reflects Nadler's thinking as well as others', for example, Tichy (1983) and Tichy and Devanna (1986).

Pride

Even though pride is among the seven deadly sins, it can be appealed to in a positive way. People who have worked in a particular job over a period of years typically build feelings of personal pride in what they do. Sometimes when change comes and people are told they must now do things differently, not their old jobs anymore, an implied message may be that what they used to do is now wrong and no longer worthwhile. Often the tendency on the part of management is to want to "get on with it" and quickly forget the past. We no longer need to manufacture that product, provide that service, and so on.

The point is that when change takes place and no time is given to recognize that even though an era had ended, what organizational members had been doing was worthwhile, they will tend to feel less worthwhile themselves. The stronger this feeling, the more organizational members' energy will be focused on dealing with their wounded pride. Usually a simple yet formal recognition that people had worked on important products or services for the organization and that significant contributions were made will be sufficient. This kind of act again helps organizational members to deal with potentially strong human emotions, to achieve some degree of closure, and gradually to disengage from the past.

Communication

It is difficult to communicate too much during a major change effort. It is possible, of course. It is possible to communicate so much that the messages begin to raise people's expectations unduly. Just as important as the quantity of communicating is, of course, the content. Moreover, communicating what will remain the same is as important as communicating what will be different. Wisdom from the world of counseling and clinical psychology is relevant here.

To help individuals cope with and manage change in their lives, the wisdom is that of keeping something stable in life while changing other aspects. It is not wise to change a career, quit a job, and get a divorce all at the same time. Holding on to something that is *not* changing in life—having an anchor, as it were—helps people significantly to deal with the complexity of change in other parts.

The same is true at an organizational level. People can more adequately deal with and manage what may be considerable chaos and complexity with respect to an organizational change effort if they know that some aspects of the organization will remain stable—at least for the time being. We can more easily handle, say, a major overhaul of the organization's structure and even accompanying changes in our jobs if we can at the same time be assured that, for example, our compensation will not change; that is, the organization's reward system will remain intact.

Managing the Transition

As Beckhard and Harris (1987) emphasize, creating a transition management team can be very important and useful to the change process. The larger and more complex the change effort, the more systematic, concentrated attention needs to be paid to the management process. An occasional committee or task force meeting may not do the job. It may be wise to appoint a person to manage the transition full-time with others assigned on a part-time basis. Large, complex change will not manage itself; that's the point. For a later version of this kind of thinking, see Beckhard and Pritchard (1992). Other important factors to manage in the change process, as Nadler (1981) had highlighted, are discussed in the following sections.

Involvement

As noted before, a principle of behavior that is central to effective management, in general, and managing change, in particular, is "Involvement leads to commitment." Stated a bit more elaborately, the degree to which people will be committed to an act is a function of the degree to which they have been involved in determining what that act will be.

For organizational change to occur effectively, it is imperative to involve certain key individuals (opinion leaders), perhaps on a singular, one-on-one basis. But, in general, it is more effective to direct change at the group level than at the individual level.

If one attempts to change an attitude or the behavior of an individual without attempting to change the same behavior or attitude in the group to which the individual belongs, then the individual will be a deviate and either will come under pressure from the group to get back into line or will be rejected entirely. Thus, the major leverage point for change is at the group level, for example, by modifying a group norm or standards. Recall from Chapter 3, "Where Did Organization Development Come From?," a key aspect from Kurt Lewin's theory:

> As long as group standards are unchanged, the individual will resist change more strongly the farther he is to depart from group standards. If the group standard itself is changed, the

resistance which is due to the relation between individuals and group standard is eliminated (Lewin, 1958, p. 120).

For a much later and well-documented rationale for involving people in organizational life, in general, and particularly, in change efforts, see Lawler (1992).

Continuing with this involvement theme, let us now further consider the importance of including people in the implementation of goals.

For any given change goal, there will likely be multiple paths to that goal. Some of these paths may be more efficient than others, but most, if not all, paths that people can think of will lead to goal accomplishment. Because of circumstances, leaders and managers of change may not always involve organizational members to any significant degree in establishing the primary goals. For purposes of gaining commitment, involving organizational members in the planning of *how to reach* those goals is critical, however.

To repeat, there are usually different ways to reach a singular goal and no one way is always clearly superior. Thus, delegating decisions of implementation—that is, allowing organization members who must carry out the plans for reaching the goal to determine for themselves the steps for getting there—will increase overall commitment to the change effort.

To gain their commitment, it is beneficial to involve people in decisions that will directly affect them. At times, however, only a few executives will have the requisite information or relevant experience for optimizing the effectiveness of decisions regarding goals. Under these conditions, executives can carefully explain to organizational members the logic underlying a change decision and they will typically accept the change goal. To proceed with telling them in detail about how to reach the goal is to risk resistance. The point is that executives can more easily win acceptance for a predetermined goal, provided the goal is viewed as challenging yet reasonable, than they can have a predetermined implementation plan accepted. Commitment, therefore, can be gained by involving organizational members in the transition planning and process.

Multiple Leverage

Often managers of change rely too heavily on a singular system lever to move the organization toward the desired change. The lever most often chosen is structure. "Changing the organizational chart will do the job" is a frequent assumption. But in a study of successful versus unsuccessful OD efforts, Burke, Clark, and Koopman (1984) found that the intervention most associated with lack of success was a change in the structure and that intervention was the only change made.

In large, complex organizations composed of many subsystems, when one of these subsystems is changed, eventually all other subsystems will be affected. This principle is based on sound, general system theory (Katz & Kahn, 1978). Therefore, when managing change, multiple systems, or levers, must be considered. At the top of the list is mission and strategy. A change in strategy best precedes structural change (Chandler, 1962). Moreover, when a structural change is made, changes in the management information system are likely to be required. Because it is also likely that different management practices will be needed, changes in the reward system to reinforce these new practices will help to ensure the overall success of the change effort. These points follow from the discussion of the Burke-Litwin model and the British Airways example in Chapter 7.

The general idea to keep in mind, then, is the fact that organizations are dynamic, open systems. Changing an organization successfully requires that attention be paid to its multiplicity of subsystems, or levers, in tandem and in mutual support of the overall effort.

Feedback

In the face of ambiguity about how things are going, people more often than not assume the worst. "I knew this change wouldn't work!" To keep momentum, positive energy directed toward the change goal(s), providing feedback to organizational members about progress, regardless of how minor the progress may be, will likely help. Periodic progress reports, additional information incorporated within the management information system, and conducting brief celebratory events when a change milestone is reached are examples of how to monitor progress and, more important, are ways to provide organizational members with relevant feedback.

Symbols and Language

To keep organizational members focused and oriented, it is beneficial to have some symbol, acronym, or slogan to represent the change goal(s). The marketing department can be helpful with this process.

It is not always possible to state change goals in clear, simple statements. Although a new organizational strategy or mission may be clear in the minds of senior management because they have discussed and debated it for months and months, when put in writing, the new strategy may come across to the majority of people in the organization as vague, quite general, and abstract. Using a symbol may help not only to simplify and clarify the change goal, but also to capture organizational members' imagination and enthusiasm as well. A change in strategy from a technology-driven organization to a customer-driven one might, for example, be symbolized by a question inscribed on, for example, a paperweight for each organizational member's desk or work area, which asks "Have you talked with a customer today?"

An actual example from the change effort at British Airways (see Chapter 7) may help. The example concerned a training of trainers program for selected line managers. They were trained to help conduct a one-week residential "Managing People First" (MPF) program for upper-middle and midlevel management, well over 1,000 managers in total. Although couched within a training of trainers objective, the large, broader objective was to indoctrinate 16 hand-picked, high-potential managers with the underlying rationale for the specific MPF program and for the overall BA cultural change effort. Their broader mandate called for them to be change agents, to model the new behaviors associated with the desired culture. They were referred to as *culture carriers.* They were to help leverage change. The symbol for them was a lever with a hand gripping it and the accompanying slogan was the Greek philosopher Archimedes' famous quote, to paraphrase in English, "Give me a fulcrum [lever] and a place to stand, and I will move the world."

Stabilizing the Change

Actually, a part of the stabilization process should begin during the disengagement stage. Just as important for organizational members to learn about what will be different is to be informed about what will *not* change. During times of significant change, when people are clear about what is not changing amid all that is, they have something stable to hold on to, an anchor. For example, even though an organization might be changing its strategy and structure, people could still be rewarded for their performance as before, for example, on merit. If they can count on their rewards being administered as before, this element of stability will help them cope with the uncertainties. As a close friend once said years ago, "Never try to change everything at once."

The reward system is central to stabilizing change once it is under way. As new practices begin to occur, as people begin to behave in ways that help to move the organization toward the change goal(s), and as milestones are reached, the reward system should be deployed to reinforce these new, "right" behaviors and directions. As Tom Peters has put it, "Catch people doing the right thing."

Formally and publicly recognizing people for having helped to move the organization in the change direction will not only serve to reinforce and stabilize the new behaviors, but will also send a clear signal as well to others in the organization as to what the "right" behaviors are.

A final process of stabilizing the change, and clearly not mutually exclusive from the above points regarding the reward system, is to arrange for certain organizational members to serve as "guardians" of the new way of doing things (Hornstein, Bunker, Burke, Gindes, & Lewicki, 1971). They serve primarily as role models, as *norm carriers* of the new culture. Provided these people are carefully selected and strategically placed in the organization—that is, they are seen as powerful leaders and representative of the future—they can help significantly to stabilize the change.

By way of summary, refer to Table 9.1. The model depicts the three broad phases of planning, managing, and stabilizing the change effort as well as the more specific activities recommended for each phase.

Table 9.1 A Model for Managing Change

Planning Phase	Managing Phase	Stabilizing Phase
Generate need	Disengage from past (and communicate what will not change)	Utilize reward system Deploy guardians of the new way
Determine future state		
Address organizational power and political dynamics	Organize transition management team(s)	
	Involve organizational members	
	Use multiple levers	
	Provide feedback	
	Create symbols and language	

Theory about Culture Change[1]

Consulting work on business strategy or implementing the vision is stronger today than ever. In fact, when speaking to groups about my consulting efforts, I (Burke) characterize myself as working in the "McKinsey aftermarket." (Substitute the name of any number of other so-called traditional management consulting firms, and my point would remain the same. I simply have followed McKinsey more than any other name brand.) In response to a firm's desire to change its strategy or structure, a team from one of these big-name consulting firms sweeps into the client organization and changes things. Approximately six months later, someone like me is called in to help make these changes work, the big names having left the scene. I ask questions about the organization's culture and typically find that it hasn't been touched. I then initiate a discussion about the possible alignment of the culture with the new strategy, if not new mission; the point is that unless key aspects of the culture are modified to fit the new mission or strategy, the latter will not work. Now to some fundamentals about culture change.

When I begin a discussion with an audience about culture change, I like to start by writing these three words on an easel pad or overhead projection:

- Values
- Attitudes
- Behavior

I then ask people to rank these terms according to degree of difficulty to change. Practically everyone agrees that the order presented is the proper ranking from most difficult, *values*, to least, *behavior*. Not that behavior change is simple to do, but comparatively speaking, among the three, behavior is the least difficult.

I then make the point that you do not change culture by directly attempting to change culture, that is, values, norms, deeply held beliefs and attitudes, long-standing historical precedence—the primary ingredients of an organization's culture. You begin instead with the least difficult aspect to change: behavior.

Of course, you begin by determining what you want the new culture to be (in the case of British Airways, it was to become more service-oriented and customer-focused), followed by an identification of the behaviors required to realize that new and different culture. You work on managers first by identifying as specifically as possible the kinds of behavioral practices that will be manifestations of the desired culture, such as, for example, "Communicating with others in an open and frank manner," or "Involving subordinates in decisions that directly affect their work." Next, you train managers in these behavioral practices primarily via feedback and role or skill practice. Then you include these new practices in managers' performance appraisals and incorporate pay for performance so that the more managers actually use the practices, the more incentive pay they receive. To summarize, first you announce the change regarding the culture. Second, you get managers' attention by training them in the practices. Third, you measure their degree of use of the practices. And, finally, you reward them when they employ the practices. These were steps followed in the British Airways change effort (see Chapter 7).

I have grossly oversimplified the complicated change process. So, let me ground this summary in a theory you may have heard in

Psychology 101—the James-Lange theory. In essence, the theory is stated as follows: "I am afraid because I run" is more accurate than "I run because I am afraid."

At first, this sounds illogical. Around the turn of this century, the two theorists, James and Lange, the former a psychologist and the latter a physiologist, stated essentially the same idea independent of each other—that we act first and then attribute to that act a reason or at least a label for the action. Many years later, Stan Schacter (1959) conducted a series of laboratory experiments with humans that provided considerable support for the James-Lange theory. I have been a fan of the theory for a long time and follow the reasoning when consulting about planning and managing change in an organization's culture.

We first get managers to move behaviorally in the direction of the desired culture. At British Airways, this was the "Managing People First" program. We provide certain labels for clusters of these behaviors. These labels are actually values. Again, in the case of British Airways, these cluster labels of values (a total of four) were *clarity and helpfulness, promoting achievement, influencing through personal excellence and teamwork,* and *care and trust.* As managers begin to move (behave) in the desired direction, they get rewarded for doing so. As they behave and get rewarded for it every time, they begin to believe that this new way of managing is actually a good thing. If they believe it is good, then a value has been affected, and values, in part, comprise culture.

Eventually, then, culture change has begun to occur—but you act first, then help with reasons, labels, and values. All this may and probably should be stated at the outset. "With the new, desired culture we are attempting to adhere to a revitalized mission with a different strategy that will be supported by those values (for example, to be number one in customer service)." Organizational members' reactions are likely to be "Sounds good, but we'll see..." or "I'll believe it when I see it." So, for the sake of actual change, you plunge ahead with the behaviors because if you delay by trying to explain and explain, the "we'll see" attitude will never be addressed.

Even grounded in some theory, you may still say that it is more complicated than that—and you would be correct. Beginning in the mid-1980s, and particularly with my work at British Airways, I felt a strong need for a larger organizational framework that would help to guide the change effort. This need led to George Litwin and my developing a broader organizational model of performance and change that we found to be very useful for planning and managing change in large, complex systems such as BA (Burke & Litwin, 1992; see Chapter 7). The point is that it is critical to conceptualize culture in a broader framework.

In summary, one does not change (or shape) organizational culture by trying to change organizational culture directly. Values, perhaps the essential ingredient of culture, are difficult to change. First, then, leaders must identify the critical values. Second, rather than announce the values and expect employees to adopt them (not unlike trying to shape or change culture by directly trying to change it), organizational leaders must provide ways for the values to be incorporated within people's behavior. Thus, after providing the direction, the value choice is clearly the first step, the next immediate step is behavioral. Remember that behavior is easier, in relative terms to be sure, to change and shape than values and attitudes.

Measuring Progress of the Change Effort

How can you tell if you are making any progress in a change effort? The general answer to this question is, "Not in the most obvious ways." There are at least four ways to tell:

1. The quantity of problems that organizational members must handle may not decrease. In the short run, it may even increase. A clear sign of progress, though, is that the nature of problems has changed. Organization members are dealing with new and different problems.

2. When organizational members express frustration about lack of progress regarding change, as paradoxical as it might seem such expression is a clear sign of progress. People are complaining about the right things. The following illustration should help to clarify this point.

During the early 1960s, Abraham Maslow spent a summer observing work in a high-tech company in Southern California. He kept a diary of his observations and later converted it into a book (Maslow, 1965). One of his observations stands out—his distinction between grumbles and meta-grumbles. Grumbles are complaints about relatively small matters: "We never seem to have enough copy machines that are in good operating condition." "Why can't someone arrange for better maintenance of this building?" In other words, the grumbles concern hygiene factors, to use Herzberg's term, those aspects of work life that contribute to one's level of dissatisfaction. Meta-grumbles, on the other hand, are complaints about such things as lack of clarity about goals, people needing to have more autonomy in carrying out their assignments, or expressing a desire for greater teamwork and collaboration. These complaints are about broader organizational concerns, usually beyond an individual matter. Maslow contended that managers should be happy to hear meta-grumbles, that underneath such complaining was motivation to be tapped and directed for the good of the overall organization. So it is in assessing progress toward change. Meta-grumbles should be music to management's ears.

3. When issues, concerns, and progress reports regarding the change effort routinely become a part of the agenda for regular managers and staff meetings, that is a sign of progress. This means that the change effort is being monitored and constantly attended to.

4. And, finally, indicative of progress are special events held from time to time that assess progress, reevaluate the direction, celebrate milestones achieved, and recognize individuals and groups for their accomplishments in helping with the change effort.

Conclusion

In this chapter, we have considered the planning and management of change. The overall process is what OD practitioners refer to as the intervention phase. According to Argyris (1970), an effective intervention is one that (1) provides *valid information* for the client organization, (2) allows for *choice* by the client regarding the specific steps to be taken, and (3) leads to *commitment* on the client's part to those action steps for change.

In planning change, it is important, first, to assure that a need for change is determined if not developed and, second, to address the power and political dynamics of the organization. Managing the change effort is essentially transition management and concerns disengaging from the past, communicating with people about the change, involving people in implementation planning, organizing a transition management team, using multiple leverages, providing feedback, and creating symbols and language to help focus the effort. The final phase, stabilizing the change, consists of utilizing the reward system to reinforce the new "ways of doing things" and putting into place key individuals to serve as "guardians" of the change goal(s).

Because we have stipulated that OD is a process of change in the organization's culture, it is imperative that we are grounded in theory about this kind of change and that we conceptualize our effort within some overall framework or model.

Four ways to assess progress toward the change were covered. The four—different problems, meta-grumbles, change concerns as a regular part of a meeting agenda, and progress review events—were described as not-so-obvious ways to determine progress.

Two Caveats

This chapter has been a description of how OD—planned change in the organization's culture—is often conducted. The explanations of planning and managing change have a history dating back to 1959. But as Chapter 2, "Organization Development Then and Now," spelled out, things have changed over this more than half a century— and they continue to change even more rapidly. Speed and agility are the orders of the day. Thus, the way we have learned to do OD might need to change. Imagine that! Two examples in the form of caveats follow:

1. Clients are not as patient as they once were. Just one example will illustrate the point. Conducting a thorough diagnosis to establish the basis (with data) for an appropriate intervention takes time—weeks not days. As the OD consultant, you want to be comprehensive and collect data from multiple sources via interviews, perhaps a survey (not to mention the time it takes to construct a relevant and tailored questionnaire in the first place), archival records, visiting a plant, and maybe observe several executive meetings. But executives today can rarely tolerate taking the amount of time a complete diagnosis would require. They know their own organization and don't need someone else to tell them. Besides there are too many pressing matters that need immediate attention. So, what is a despairing OD practitioner to do?

   Once again, Kurt Lewin's thinking can be helpful regarding this problem of "not enough time." In so many words, he once said something like, "If you want to understand an organization, try to change it." In other words, when an intervention, of practically any kind, is made in the organization, forces emerge to return the organization to its state of equilibrium. An intervention toward change disturbs and perturbs the system. Paying attention to the nature of these forces; that is, organizational members' *reactions* to the disturbance, often perceived as resistance, reveals for the OD consultant a picture or story about the true nature of the system particularly its culture. In other words, the data for diagnosis are people's behavioral reactions to the intrusion. It is analogous to the saying that you really never fully understand someone until you see him or her confronted with if not tested under trying circumstances. The point of this caveat, therefore, is to understand that an organization does not always have to follow all of the processes and phases covered in this chapter. Sometimes it is really okay to go with an intervention that you have doubts about simply to learn about the organization via the reactions. Equal in importance to the goal of change is to learn as much as possible along the way.

2. No two people—even identical twins—are exactly the same. So it is with organizations. We can differentiate organizations in many ways; profit-nonprofit, large-small, global-regional, government-nongovernment, for example, NGO, private-public, and so on. One very important distinction is how loose or tight the organization may be regarding its structure, mode of operation, leadership, and so on. This particular distinction is usually referred to as tightly coupled systems compared with loosely coupled systems. A paragon of the tight system is the U.S. Marine Corps; a network exemplifies the loose system.

The development and growth of OD has largely been based on work with tightly coupled systems, the goal being to "loosen them up." If the goal is to "tighten" a network, would the OD procedure be the same? The answer is, of course, "not exactly." This second caveat, then, is again a word of caution regarding the application of "regular" OD processes, which work well with tightly coupled systems but will need to be modified when working with a loosely coupled system. The purpose of our next chapter is to address this caveat.

Endnote

1. This section is taken in part from Burke (1993).

10

Understanding and Changing Loosely Coupled Systems[1]

Imagine for a moment a network of eight organizations spread across the United States from Los Angeles to New York City that operated quite autonomously yet were held together by a small head-quarters composed of a paid part-time administrator and ten elected professionals who served voluntarily as a board of directors with a president and various committee heads. The network had recently experienced a breach of policy and violation of norms by a small group of members. This jolt to the network system led to an emergency meeting of the board of directors to determine what happened, why the breach occurred, and what, if anything, should be done about it. Led by the president, the board decided to take action. A consultant was contracted to help with a fundamental change of the system.

Now imagine yourself as the hired consultant. You have consider-able experience, especially within the corporate world, and a solid reputation as an organization change expert. This expertise, however, is primarily with tightly coupled systems consisting of clearly defined hierarchies and strong interdependence of subsystems—think General Motors, for example—and this client is a network with only a modicum of hierarchy and practically no interdependence among its eight centers nor with headquarters. These differences are significant and should be treated as such—differently. Although written with a request to use one's imagination regarding a loosely coupled network and being a consultant to such a system, this opening gambit is not merely an imaginary exercise. Rather, the imagining is based on an actual case, an example of a short-term success as an organization change effort yet within the span of approximately two years resulting in a failure. With linkage to theory for help with understanding, the story is told by Noumair, Winderman, and Burke (2010). For a condensed version of the story, see Chapter 12 in the text by Burke (2014b).

The failure experience with attempting to change this network, a loosely coupled system, brings to the forefront of our thinking how much has changed since the *Journal of Applied Behavioral Science* (JABS) was launched 50 years ago. See Chapter 2, "Organization Development Then and Now," for brief descriptions of many of these changes. Interestingly, during that same time period 50 years ago, the Organization Development Network was formed, the Civil Rights law was enacted, two scientists at Bell Labs went public with their Big Bang theory, and for the first time a Ford Mustang rolled off the assembly line. In other words, 1964 was quite a year!

Back then, our focus was on large bureaucracies such as "MA Bell," the Red Cross, Sears, the military, and the Episcopal Church. The case described in Chapter 1, "What Is Organization Development?," is illustrative. We didn't have global banks, Walmart, NGOs, Silicon Valley, or even network organizations as we know them today. Our world has become tighter—that is, more interconnected and interdependent—and at the same time looser—less centrally controlled, with government being less able to influence its citizenry, and so forth. See Chapter 2 for additional examples. As we know, technology and especially social media has enabled a lot of this change, which makes true network organizations possible. So, *JABS* began with an emphasis on "loosening up" rather than "tightening up." At the risk of jumping ahead, we are now challenged to get out in front of what is happening in organizations today with innovative change methods instead of continuing and trying to perfect techniques of change that may not be as relevant as they once were. But not everything has changed. At the core of what we do in the realm of organization development and change, whether a bureaucracy or a network, are human relationships in organizations.

Staying with the perspective of "not everything has changed," let us address two additional and important precautions regarding either-or thinking before getting to the central theme of this chapter.

Two Precautions Regarding Either-Or Thinking

First, we organizational theorists and practitioners, at times, may have a tendency to think in either-or terms regarding organizations—profit versus nonprofit, small-to-medium sized versus large and more complex, loosely coupled versus tightly coupled, and so on. We know better, of course. We know, for example, that the so-called bottom line for profit and nonprofit organizations is not the same, but there are at the same time many similarities; for example, hierarchy, functional silos, and issues of communication and collaboration. Small organizations such as a boutique consulting firm are not as complicated to operate effectively as a global corporation of 50,000 people, yet issues of leadership and goal clarity exist in both. There are other either-or examples, but the focus for this chapter concerns one such example only—loosely coupled versus tightly coupled systems. As Karl Weick (2001) has pointed out, and as noted above, a tightly coupled system can be characterized by two primary qualities—hierarchy and interdependence, whereas a loosely coupled system may or may not have much of a hierarchy and parts of the system are rarely dependent on one another for purposes of accomplishing tasks. For the epitome of tight, think U.S. Marine Corps, and for loose, think network. These two organizations, military and network, do appear to be very different—and they are. Yet, again, similarities exist. In recent times, when thinking of a network, al-Qaida has come to mind, a system that appears to have little hierarchy and scant interdependence. An article, however, published by the Associated Press (Callimachi, 2013) provided evidence to show that even al-Qaida has its own bureaucracy. Documents found in an abandoned house during January of 2013 in Timbuktu, Mali, included more than 100 receipts for purchases made ranging from food, to supplies for autos, to guns and ammunition. Also discovered were workshop schedules, salary spreadsheets, job applications, and memos from the equivalent of a human resources division. Al-Qaida has a financial policy across all divisions accompanied with regular bookkeeping techniques. In other words, al-Qaida is not an unorganized, like-minded assemblage of individuals but, rather, an attempt to operate like a multinational corporation. Either-or thinking, therefore, is unwarranted. Even al-Qaida sees the value of at least some bureaucracy.

Apparently, executives running high-tech firms in Silicon Valley have not seen such value. The lead sentence for another article from the news media (*The New York Times*) stated "The dirtiest word in Silicon Valley is bureaucracy." The reporter, Claire C. Miller (Miller, 2014), noted that high-tech executives tend to equate bureaucracy with the human resource (HR) function. Her article is based on the Stanford Project on Emerging Companies, a longitudinal study of 200 Silicon Valley start-ups beginning with the initial dot-com boom (Baron & Hannan, 2002). The study showed that high-tech entrepreneurs paid little attention to HR. In fact, "Nearly half of the companies left it up to employees to shape the culture and perform traditional human resource tasks. Only 6.6 percent had the type of formal personnel management seen at typical companies" (Miller, 2014, p. B3). It may be that Google was among this 6.6 percent. In any case, it should be noted that Google has been dedicated to the people side of their business. And they have been innovative regarding HR. Maybe it is not whether you have HR but what kind of HR you have. Google's HR function is more about development and change and less about following a personnel manual. HR unfortunately has been a handmaiden of power, tightening up talent management, compensation and reward systems, and so on. But what is needed today is for HR to develop more innovative and agile cultures. Google may be leading the way here. Incidentally, one of the first actions that the new head of HR, Nick Georgiades, at British Airways took when a significant culture change was launched in the 1980s was to toss out all of the personnel manuals and start over—see Chapter 7, "The Burke-Litwin Model of Organizational Performance and Change," in this volume and Chapter 11 in Burke (2014b) for the story of change at British Airways.

A side benefit from the data underlying the study at Silicon Valley by Baron and Hannan (2002) was that for the few high-tech firms that did have an HR function, there were much better prospects for employment of women in technical roles. Moreover, when high-tech companies left HR responsibilities for organizational members, regardless of function, to perform such tasks as hiring new employees, diversification suffered because the workers selected those for employment who were like themselves, including "too much emphasis on new employees' fitting into the existing culture" (Miller, 2014,

p. B3). This executive naiveté can obviously lead to significant issues for high-tech firms such as discrimination and groupthink (Janis, 1972), which are the opposite of what executives say they want—nimbleness, agility, innovation, and creativity. Can there be too much looseness? Of course.

A *second* precaution concerns thinking in either-or terms regarding the change process. Change is change, after all, and one is not likely to go far astray when following the basics of organization change consulting; that is, entry, contracting, data gathering, diagnosis, feedback, and intervention planned and implemented according to (a) the data and (b) reactions of the client to the feedback of the data. Regardless of system type or category, then, following this process is appropriate. The difference is a matter of *where* to focus our efforts and *what* to seek to change. More about following the organization development (OD) sequence yet differently when working with a loosely coupled system is provided later in this chapter.

As we know, like individuals, no two organizations are the same. Although as change leaders and consultants, we need to follow principles of organization change that are based on sound theory and research; at the same time, we should pay considerable attention to the idiosyncrasies of how the organization at hand differs from all others.[2] As noted already, we can be undermined in our consulting work by either-or thinking, but understanding the differences between a profit-making corporation and a nonprofit organization can be helpful for where to focus the change effort. For example, with a corporation, we will need to place emphasis on the competitive marketplace, whereas with a nonprofit, we should concentrate, at least at the outset, on mission. There is overlap, of course, between profit and nonprofit organizations, yet understanding the differences is key to leading and contributing to a successful change effort. And there is overlap between loosely coupled and tightly coupled systems, but the purpose of this chapter is to concentrate on the former, not the latter. There are sufficient differences between the two types of systems that demand our attention if we are serious about changing a loosely coupled system. Thus, the purpose of this chapter is an attempt to enhance our understanding of how to change a loosely coupled system. Before moving on, let us quickly reinforce one final point of clarification that was previously noted: We will consider networks *writ large*; that is, there are networks that are stand-alone organizations such as the OD Network, the NTL Institute for Applied Behavioral Science, and the A.K. Rice Institute, and there are networks, primarily informal, that exist within large, bureaucratic organizations. The latter is often considered the informal organization that parallels the formal system.

The Change Problem

With the preceding comments and precautions serving as background and context, let us now continue with a statement of the problem—attempting to change a loosely coupled system, which is not the same as trying to change a tightly coupled system—followed by coverage of a primary intervention for doing so, social network analysis, and then address additional and important issues that we need to be more informed about as we move forward with our learning process regarding organization change. As mentioned earlier, the impetus for this exploration emerged from a consulting experience with a network that began successfully but ultimately became a failure. Part of the explanation for this failure was the consultant's use of standard and accepted organization development (OD) techniques, social technology that may not be appropriate for attempting to tighten a loosely coupled system. The social technology of OD was essentially derived in the late 1950s, early 1960s, from consulting experiences with tightly coupled systems; that is, attempts to loosen bureaucracy, to involve organizational members in the change process, and to follow Lewin's three-step process of unfreeze, change, refreeze. To return to the thinking of Weick (2001), this approach for changing a loosely coupled system may not be appropriate. In fact, he suggested approaches that were directly opposite to "normal" OD change efforts. Instead of a planned approach, he suggested improvisation; instead of a large system focus, he suggested working at local levels; and change should be considered as continuous not episodic. Table 10.1, taken from Burke (2011a), provides a summary of these contrasts.

Table 10.1 A Comparison of Changing a Loosely Coupled System (LCS) with a Tightly Coupled System (TCS)

Dimension for Comparison	Process for Changing an LCS	Process for Changing a TCS
Focus	Continuous	Episodic
Scale	Small	Large
Type of initiative	Improvisational	Planned
Consulting process	Accommodative	Constrained
Locus of change	Local	Cosmopolitan

Source: Weick (2001).

For those of us who "grew up" with social technology for changing tightly coupled systems, how do we now expand our consulting repertoire to deal more effectively with changing a loosely coupled system? Moreover, how do we focus more on continuous change on a smaller scale that may from time to time be improvisational and accommodative to the client at local levels? And what about those organizations that are hard to classify and therefore present a complicated challenge regarding change, organizations such as a university, a partnership, or even the Academy of Management and the Society for Industrial and Organizational Psychology?

One response to those questions is to bear in mind that organizations are both loose and tight. Again, rather than thinking in either-or terms, it is likely to be more productive to determine within a given organization what should be tightened and what should be loosened. Perhaps, for example, in a university, financial matters should be fairly tight whereas curriculum decisions should be loose and localized.

Yet the fact remains that at least for the world of OD, we know less about how to work with, if not change, loosely coupled systems. For example, it may be more useful to rely on an intervention such as social network analysis than, say, the Burke-Litwin model—a heretical thought. Maybe a better answer is to use both, a social network analysis superimposed on the Burke-Litwin model. For another example of combining two perspectives (overt and covert) using the Burke-Litwin model, see Chapter 8, "Understanding Organizations: Covert Processes." In any case, what we need to learn more about is what new, if not different, diagnostic and intervention tools have potential for improving our work with loosely coupled systems such as social network analysis, boundary spanning strategies and practices, large group interventions, and a consultant role that is more direct and serves as a "go-between" across independent units, which may need more active interaction such as convening a meeting rather than merely a role of facilitation. We also need to be clear about what OD interventions serve change well regardless of how much the organization is loose or tight, such as involvement techniques, creating a sense of need if not urgency, and developing a vision for change.

Loosely Coupled Systems and the Change Process: Social Network Analysis

One of my (Burke) early experiences with an informal social network was long ago in the late 1950s when I was serving two years of full-time, active duty in the U.S. Army. In those days, there was a military draft and every able-bodied young man had to serve a minimum of two years in the military. In college, I joined the Reserve Officer Training Corps (ROTC) in the hopes of making my two years more bearable as an officer instead of an enlisted man. After artillery school at Ft. Sill, Oklahoma, I was assigned to an armored artillery battery (company) in the Second Armored Division at Ft. Hood, Texas. Soon I was given a special assignment by one of the senior officers at the battalion level, Major Saldana. He wanted me to build for training purposes a miniature artillery range on some vacant land on the post. My deadline was one month. The practice range required digging long ditches, constructing a replica of a mountain range with the dirt, and setting up small air cannons that fired steel balls for up to several hundred yards. This meant reassigning, at least temporarily, soldiers from the battery, providing them with shovels, rakes, and other tools to construct the range. I didn't see how we could do it in a month. And besides the soldiers would complain and, if not ever so subtlety, rebel. I called my staff of sergeants (all grizzled and highly experienced) together to help me figure out what to do. They agreed that we had little time to accomplish this task. My most senior sergeant suddenly had an idea. He had a buddy over in engineering at the division level who was "sitting on a bulldozer with nothing to do." I asked the sergeant if we could get him to come over and do the digging, moving, the dirt, etc. He said "no problem." The bulldozer friend and several others came over and helped us to complete the job in less than a month. Major Saldana was very pleased. Within a few days, however, I was in trouble. The major called me into his office. I stood before him at attention and answered his questions nervously yet truthfully. I was then reprimanded for having violated the chain of command. I had not formally requisitioned the bulldozer and crew via division headquarters. Major Saldana knew that he had to reprimand me, yet at the same time, he was clearly pleased that he now had his prized practice range, and on time. I was later promoted to the rank of first lieutenant in spite of the previous reprimand. Achieving goals counts for a lot in any organization.

This tale from my Army days illustrates the simultaneous existence of formal and informal systems. My sergeant and his bulldozer buddy were "members" of an informal social network, which existed within a highly formal organization. It is no secret that in such systems informal relations can facilitate work getting done by "going around" the formalities. In fact, Army lore has it that World War II would not have been won without the Army's informal social networks.

As we know, most organizations have both a formal system and an informal one. Each is overlaid on the other. An interesting hypothesis in this regard is that the tighter the formal system, the more prevalent and active the informal system, the social network.

With respect to the term *network,* let us pause for a moment and attempt to be clear. There are two categories. One is the informal system within an organization, the U.S. Army example just described, and the other is the external or stand-alone category; that is, the organization itself. Al-Qaida, the A.K. Rice Institute, and the OD Network are examples of this second category. What the two forms of networks have in common is "looseness," with no formal hierarchy and little interdependence. It may be that an informal system within an organization is somewhat tighter than a free-standing network, but we are considering a degree of difference, not an either-or situation. What now follows is a description of a useful tool for assessing either category of network.

A *social network analysis* is a data-gathering tool for assessing or mapping the informal system; that is, networks in and of themselves or networks within a large formal system. Organizational members respond to a brief questionnaire asking them to identify the people with whom they interact within the organization. The interaction can be defined as information exchange, informal relationships, simply as those one works with most closely, and so on. As you might imagine, asking the right question(s) is very important. The typical outcome is a computer-generated "picture" or map with small circles or dots depicting organizational members and lines between the circles that show who relates with whom and perhaps how often.

Incidentally, an early and simple version of such a network was recently presented at the Museum of Modern Art in New York City. It showed the network of artists, broadly defined, in the early twentieth century (1910–1925) in terms of who was in the network and who interacted with whom. The circle in the center with the most connective lines was none other than Picasso. To remind us of the importance of loose systems, that network is now framed and hanging in our offices.

There is a considerable body of literature on social network analysis. See, for example, Freeman (2006), Kilduff and Tsai (2003), Knoke and Yang (2008), Wasserman and Faust (1994), and since 1979, there has been a journal devoted to the field: *Social Networks: An International Journal of Structural Analysis.*

Although smaller in scope, there is a growing interest in social network analysis and organization change. One rather complex study regarding organization change was conducted by Battilana and Casciaro (2012). They analyzed 68 organizational change initiatives that were conducted in the early 2000s in the National Health Service of the United Kingdom. These change initiatives were attempted by *change agents* operating within networks existing in the larger formal system. Many of the initiatives were attempts to shift decision making from physicians to nurses; for example, decisions regarding the dismissal of patients from the hospital. This decision example is one that Battilana and Casciaro considered to be quite divergent from the status quo and therefore consisted of contingencies that were complex. Change leaders (*agents* as these researchers referred to them) were therefore predominantly members of nurses' networks. These networks were classified by the researchers as either tight—a cohesive network of closely linked *social actors*—or loose, referred to as having a low degree of structural closure, which, according to Burt (2005), is considered to be full of "structural holes." Battilana and Casciaro hypothesized that the looser the network, the more likely the change leader would "initiate a change that diverges from the institutional status quo" (p. 383). But initiation of change is one thing and acceptance of the change is another. Thus, the researchers' second hypothesis was that the tighter the network to which the change leader belonged—tight or structured closure being a function of group pressure and redundancy of information; that is, the tighter the network, the more information is limited—the less likely a change that was divergent from the status quo would be adopted. In other words, a tight network will foster change that is less divergent but hinder a change that is more divergent. Resistance to the more divergent change comes from peer pressure and a deficiency of novel thinking. Battilana and Casciaro (2012) conclude their extensive research article with the following statements:

> Structural holes in change agents' networks increase the likelihood that these actors will initiate organizational changes with a higher degree of divergence from the institutional status quo. The effects of structural holes on a change agents' ability to persuade organizational constituencies to adopt a change, however, are strictly contingent on the change's degree of divergence from the institutional status quo. Structural holes in a change agent's network aid the adoption of changes that diverge from the institutional status quo, but they hinder the adoption of less divergent changes (p. 393).

The Battilana and Casciaro study helps us to understand more thoroughly how internal organizational networks, one version of the intraorganizational context, affect organization change. Should their contingency theory showing the difference between initiation and the adoption of change gain further empirical support, there are at least *three* primary implications for practice. *First*, we need to be clear about the fact that networks, while having common properties, for example, little if any hierarchy, are not the same. They differ particularly with respect to how tight (structured closure) or how loose (consisting of structural holes) they are. Tight networks may facilitate continuous improvement but hinder large-scale transformation.

A *second* implication for practice concerns how divergent from the status quo the proposed change may be. Novel and divergent ideas are more likely to come from loose networks but are difficult to get adopted. Adoption and implementation of change, to be successful, means that people must pull together, collaborate, and support one another. Tighter networks facilitate this kind of process, which, in turn, leads to the *third* implication for practice.

It is useful to think of different people taking on different roles in a change effort, in this case change initiators and change implementers. Because the former are more likely to emerge from a loose network and a successful implementer from a tight network, two different roles by two different people may work better than a single role/individual for both. In other words, different people have different skills. Thinking comparatively, consider Burke's (2014b) application of Gladwell's (2000) identification of people in organizations who have social power—salesmen, mavens, and connectors—from his book, *The Tipping Point.* Some individuals are much better at *selling* ideas than others; some (mavens) are unusual sources of information, for example, knowing who knows what, where important records are kept, and so on; and still others are highly skillful at connecting people, suggesting, for example, that two people the connector knows but who do not know one another need to meet because they have common causes and values.

In a comprehensive article on integrating social network analysis and boundary spanning, Cross, Ernst, and Pasmore (2013) have addressed similar issues to the points we are attempting to clarify in this chapter. For example, they explain the importance of social network analysis as a significant tool for facilitating organization change and define five roles that the network technique helps to identify. These roles are as follows:

- *Connector.* Those who support people in the organization by providing information and assistance. This role is similar to Gladwell's connectors.

- *Expert.* Those who have specific knowledge and experience that may be useful in times of change. This role is also similar to Gladwell's mavens.

- *Broker.* Those who bridge boundaries and are typically trusted by a variety of groups.

- *Energizer.* Network members who enthusiastically support the changes that are needed. These individuals are not unlike Gladwell's salesmen.

- *Resister.* Practically the opposite of energizers, those who tend to block a change effort. As Cross and colleagues put it, these can be only a few people but "5% of employees cause 95% of the misery" (p. 83).

Cross et al. (2013) go on to argue persuasively that many organization change failures are due to an inability and/or perhaps an unwillingness to work across boundaries, such as vertical (hierarchy and status), horizontal (peers, competitors, experts), stakeholder (partners, constituencies), demographic (gender, age, culture), and geographic (location, markets). Their organization change model is therefore an integration of network analysis and boundary spanning; that is, the network analysis helps to identify the key roles for effective boundary spanning.

The point is that attempting to launch and implement successful change in an organization is a complicated endeavor and different players with different skill sets are required. Finally, with respect to selecting and supporting such players for the change process, the context must be taken into account. For example, initiators and salesmen of change may need to come from loose networks and implementers, experts, and connectors from tight networks, although as Gray (2014) has cautioned, connectors may not be able to operate effectively in tight networks because there are less structural holes.

In summary, networks exist as organizations themselves and within larger bureaucracies. Although we usually classify a network as a loosely coupled system, as the Battilana and Casciaro (2012) study demonstrated, networks within these larger systems vary in terms of looseness (structural holes) and tightness (structural closure). As a reminder, the common denominator for networks, as a rule, is characterized as having little if any hierarchy and little if any interdependences among its members.

The technique of choice for studying networks is some form of a social network analysis that serves as both a diagnostic instrument and an intervention. Diagnostically, the assessment provides a map or "picture" of the network with dots or small circles representing individuals in terms of where and how they are connected with one another. Providing this map as feedback to the network members, however, has consequences, thus becoming an intervention into the system. For example, depending on what connective questions are asked and perhaps how permanent or temporary the network is, often people do not want to be identified. In other words, some individuals may be outliers in the network and would not like for that information to be made public. The exact content of the question(s) and how feedback is provided are obviously important.

Loosely Coupled Systems and the Change Process: Additional Potential Interventions

The premise of this chapter is to argue that loosely coupled systems indeed differ from those systems that are tight and, therefore, with respect to change interventions, different approaches should be considered and implemented. Bear in mind, however, that many organization development and change interventions that work well with tightly coupled systems are applicable and appropriate for working with loosely coupled systems. Examples include crafting vision and mission statements, executive coaching, team building, leadership development, negotiation, intergroup conflict resolution, force field analysis, and dealing with resistance, to name a few.

A particularly suitable intervention that can serve either a loosely coupled system or a tightly coupled system effectively is the set of "large system interventions" that include such activities as Fast Cycle Full Participation, Future Search, Open Space Technology, Search Conference, and Workout. For an overview of these interventions and their use, see Bunker and Alban (2002).

The objective of a large system intervention is, if possible, to get the entire organization in the same room (space) at the same time. Achieving this objective for a network can be especially helpful as well as dramatic because coming together could be rare if not a first-time event. Just seeing everyone "all at once" can be a significant intervention itself.

A network that is a stand-alone organization may be more amenable to interventions that have also worked well with large bureaucracies such as the large-group methods noted above, but perhaps less well if not inappropriate for networks that exist within the larger more tightly coupled system. With respect to networks as informal organizations within a larger system, we can think in terms of using these networks as vehicles for implementing change in the more formal system. The *parallel organization* as such a vehicle that emerged in the 1970s comes to mind, also referred to as the collateral organization.

Developed by Zand (1974) and Howard Carlson when he was head of OD at General Motors (GM) in the 1970s (Miller, 1978), elaborated on by Stein and Kanter (1980), and to some extent a precursor to large system interventions that emerged later in the 1980s, the parallel organization was an attempt to recognize and benefit from the informal organization. In Carlson's accounting for how it worked at GM, periodically and typically on a Friday, all members of management and key technical staff from a given plant, foundry, for example, or a division, for example, purchasing, would come together for the day. The primary purpose was to discuss the "undiscussables," thus all formalities were suspended for the day—no one was a boss, anyone could speak his or her mind without fear of retribution, and individuals would work in small groups that represented a cross section of jobs and responsibilities not in a "family" group. If the formal system continued to have too much influence, using, say, the Nominal Group Technique (Delbecq, Van de Ven, & Gustafson, 1975) might help. Fundamental to the technique is that each individual's suggestions and ideas carry the same weight as anyone else's regardless of status and formal power. In any case, the work for the day was to solve problems, some of which may have plagued the organization for years. The intent was that on Monday back in the formal system, people would begin to work differently—more efficiently, openly, and effectively than before.

Consultant as a Broker

Assuming that the change objective is to tighten a loosely coupled system, it may be that the consultant to such a process should not merely be a facilitator. In a consulting project reported by Kaplan (1982), the client was a group of loosely bound mental health services agencies who needed to work together to serve their community as effectively as possible. Kaplan found that the agencies were so loosely bound, he could not determine clearly who the client was, who he was contracting with, what should be facilitated, and so on. Getting focused took an eternity and what we might call a "whole system" simply did not exist. Based on his experience, Kaplan concluded that he needed to form a group that could represent all of the agencies, to "create" the client. In his attempt to help the system come together, at least to some extent, he drew further conclusions that were unusual yet insightful and consistent with Weick's (2001) suggestions for working with loosely coupled systems; that is:

- Feedback should fit looseness; that is, differentiated and limited to subunits, not the "whole system," which in this case had limited existence.

- The consultant needs to have sophisticated political and interpersonal skills and be able to work with relationships. This line of thinking on Kaplan's part is consistent with the views expressed in Chapter 5, "Defining the Client: A Different Perspective," in terms of answering the question "who is the client?" When thinking about an organization's organization chart, the case was made that the client was not any of the individuals whose names and titles were inside the boxes on the chart but in reality the lines that connect the boxes; that is, the relationships.

- "The consultant may need to *convene* people more than *intervene* into the system" (Noumair, Winderman, & Burke, 2010, p. 488).

Not only consistent with Weick's thinking (1976, 2001), Kaplan's conclusion fits comfortably within a systems way of conceptualizing his work. To quote Capra (1996):

All living systems are networks of smaller components and the web of life as a whole is a multilayered structure of living systems within other living systems—networks within networks (pp. 209–210).

The consultant or change leader, particularly when working with a loosely coupled system, will likely need at times to be a broker and connector, to assemble a group, to bring two individuals together to resolve a stalemate, bringing together two groups that had been working on the same problem but didn't know it, and so on.

Tightening a Loose System

What helps to compensate for too much looseness? According to Orton and Weick (1990), there are three points of emphasis:

- *Enhanced leadership.* Recall that a tightly coupled system is characterized especially by hierarchy and interdependence. In the case of a loosely coupled system, imposing hierarchy would probably not be wise. Thus, a form of shared leadership should work better with few if any system members occupying a permanent role of leadership, or if so, that leadership would need to be highly participative and perhaps in the form of servant leadership.
- *Focused attention.* A loose system can be seen as being "all over the place," thus more focus could help. This focus might be in the form of a project that has a beginning, middle, and end. Establishing, say, a permanent program at the larger system level would be more problematic. Planning and conducting a conference for all members to share expertise might be an example. Such a project would clearly help to focus member attention; then the question would become one of deciding whether to have annual conferences, which in turn raises the question of what the mission and purpose of the system are. Not adequately answering this purpose question became the downfall of attempting to change the A.K. Rice Institute, a loosely coupled system (Noumair et al., 2010). Choosing the focus for attention needs to be carefully considered.

- *Shared values.* It is difficult if not impossible to have an organization without at least some common beliefs and values. Even al-Qaida has shared values, beliefs that readers of this chapter are not likely to endorse, but beliefs and values nevertheless that hold them together as a system. Reminding ourselves of why we as a system exist in the first place, our *raison d'etre,* can help tighten an organization, a network, that has become too loose.

Summary Suggestions

Using Weick's (2001) five processes for changing a loosely coupled system (see Table 10.1), let us consider some examples and suggestions for how we might work as change leaders and consultants more effectively:

- *Continuous rather than episodic.* Trying to change a loosely coupled system with an episode ("burning platform")—that is, a jolt to the total system—is like shooting a rifle at a distant target that is scattered rather than finite. Although a shotgun may be somewhat more effective, the analogy begins to break down because a blast is not likely to work very well in the first place. Our interventions therefore need to be focused as much or more on matters of unit efficiency than overall effectiveness. Helping to improve ways of working at small group levels and individual coaching are more likely to be the better choices of interventions.

- *Small rather than large.* Regarding the matter of scale, the fact that the totality is by definition loosely formed and consequently difficult to establish a common focus (often the parts, or at least some of them, are more important than the whole), attempting to launch a large-scale effort is problematic. Remember the Kaplan (1982) study? It is probably better to emphasize and consult with subsystems having the dual aim of (a) helping each unit work more efficiently and effectively, and (b) collaborating with other units (boundary spanning activities) to the degree that such cross-unit activities help each respective unit improve.

- *Improvisational rather than planned.* At a unit level, it may be useful to operate according to Lewin's three steps of unfreeze, change, refreeze, the epitome of planned change, but at the total system level these steps may be overly restrictive for a loose organization. Attempting to unfreeze a total system that is not all that "frozen" in the first place may not be a good use of time and effort. Although a given unit may be stuck in its ways, other units within the system may not be. But as the alternative, what does Weick mean by improvisational? He means essentially how the term is defined—unscripted, spontaneous, invented, extemporaneous, and so on. To help us understand how this form of consulting and change leadership might work, two references may be helpful. First is Schein's (1999) perspective, which provides a set of principles based on process consultation that can serve as a guide for change consultants. His list is fairly extensive, but four of his principles seem to be appropriate for operating improvisationally. Schein's principle #2 is "Always deal with reality." A reality of change leadership is that planned change rarely, if ever, unfolds as planned. To make any change work, we must operate in the moment, or as quickly as possible, by dealing with consequences of an initiation of change that we simply did not anticipate, much less plan (Burke, 2014b). Remember Lewin's dictum referred to in Chapter 9, "Planning and Managing Change": "If you want to understand an organization, try to change it." Organizational members' reactions to an intervention are likely to be more important diagnostically than the intervention itself. Dealing with the reality of the moment is improvisational. Schein's #3 principle is "Access your ignorance"—a scary proposition. Understanding what we do not know can be thought of as a positive. However, a significant problem is when we do not know what it is that we do not know. By admitting ignorance, however, we can spur useful engagement with the client to work together to solve the problem rather than attempting unrealistically to be the expert in all matters of organization change. Principle #7 is "Be prepared for surprises and learn from them." People do not behave all that predictably—even those with whom we are close and have known for years. A way of considering this important principle is when caught by surprise, attempt to control your potential embarrassment and view the situation with curiosity, followed by generating a hypothesis or two as to why the event was novel. And, finally, Schein's principle #8 is "Share the problem." This principle overlaps with the others, of course, and Schein's admonition in all of these principles is to find ways to stay engaged with the client so that the interactive process will lead to innovation and shared responsibility for the overall change process.

A second helpful paper regarding improvisation in consulting endeavors is the one by Van de Ven and Sun (2011). They define four different change models, as follows:

- *Teleology.* A planned organization change approach
- *Life cycle.* Organizational patterns over time
- *Dialectics.* Reasoning and debate about change initiatives and implementations
- *Evolution.* Competition for scarce resources

The argument put forth by these scholars is for an organization change consultant to be versed in all four models but not wed to any given one of them. Being flexible to move from one model to another when warranted is a form of improvisation.

- *Accommodative rather than constrained.* What has been covered by Schein and the article by Van de Ven and Sun are not only relevant for improvisation but for this process of accommodation by Weick as well. In general, the change leader and/or consultant needs to listen to client concerns as well as their suggestions for moving forward even though they may differ from what the change leader and/or consultant think would be best. This potential difference is particularly characteristic of professionals who compose a network or otherwise loosely coupled system such as, say, the humanities faculty of a university who are not change experts as a rule but have strong opinions nevertheless. So, it is not altogether unwise as a change leader to accommodate at times and follow what the client wants, even as one who is knowledgeable in matters of organization change and would not recommend what the client is proposing. Should the client's option not turn out very well, then the change leader can focus on learning, learning about what didn't go so well and what might be a better approach. This accommodating process requires patience and tolerance but the goal then becomes one of learning and the change process for the future can follow.

- *Local rather than cosmopolitan.* Due to the fact that a loosely coupled system is difficult to "get one's arms around," having structural holes with subunits typically having more identification if not influence than the whole, it makes sense to focus more locally than globally; that is, the entire organization. In other words, the change work would be more bottom-up than top-down. The consequences of emphasizing and strengthening subunits means that ultimately the center and total system can be compromised and possibly weakened. Change leaders and consultants must be cognizant of if not vigilant about this potential consequence and, at least at times, raise the question of whether this possible outcome is desirable.

These five processes for changing loosely coupled systems that Weick (2001) has generated and we have contrasted with standard OD practice (Table 10.1) are useful to consider if not follow when working with and perhaps attempting to tighten too much looseness. These are not the only processes, of course. As noted earlier, our loose system may be an internal network or external, a stand-alone organization. As change leaders and consultants, we would work differently if we were attempting to use the internal network, informal organization, as a leverage for change in the formal organization. Even though born from a tightly coupled system, using the parallel organization process, for example, could be beneficial. Following Weick's processes would be more appropriate for stand-alone networks and similar systems such as a university, partnership, consortium, or volunteer agency.

Adapting OD to Loosely Coupled Systems

Weick's (2001) suggestions for working with loosely coupled systems have been helpful—as far as they go. We will now depart from Weick for the time being and return to "normal" OD, as depicted in

Chapters 1, 4, and 9. Let us consider how we might adapt our seven steps of consulting the OD way (entry, contracting, data gathering, and so on) to explore how we might work with loosely coupled systems more effectively. One adaptation to note here at the outset concerns the seven steps of OD practice. With the following seven, we have dropped *planning change* and added *data gathering*. Of course, these two steps are either overt or implicit in both sets of seven steps. With loosely coupled systems, planning the change is much less formal and structured than with tightly coupled systems, and with the former, loose systems, gathering data is a more complex process, often including more constituents and shareholders, thus, data gathering becomes more salient and important.

Entry

With a tightly coupled system (TCS), our initial encounter is typically with an executive or a manager—that is, someone in charge. With a loosely coupled system (LCS), many people are in charge, thus our entry is with anyone in the system who is advocating change, regardless of where in the system and with whom. We therefore seek to establish a relationship if not partnership with that person or persons to explore the possibility of change.

Contracting

Weisbord's (1973) wisdom remains relevant; for example, specifying who is going to do what and by when. Again, in a TCS, the contracting is usually done with a lead person at the top of the organization or at the head of a unit within the larger organization. In this case, we are being attentive to the hierarchy. In an LCS with little hierarchy and interdependence, it might be wise to impose a bit of interdependence by contracting with a group and not an individual. Thus, the two primary issues in contracting are accountability and role clarity of the group members. Without a hierarchy, peer pressure may be the appropriate process to follow, to impose. Then, it becomes a question of contracting with a subunit of the larger system or with a constructed group of individuals who represent key segments of the overall system. In any case, we should think in terms of collectivism, not individualization.

Data Gathering

As with TCS, useful data will be both quantitative—for example, a survey—and qualitative—for example, interviews—as well as archival, such as performance indices and customer satisfaction. With an LCS, in addition to the above, you are likely to need data from stakeholders and related constituents. If there is a board of directors, be sure to interview the members. And if the LCS is a service organization, gather data from the consumers. The point is that with a TCS, interdependence is a basic characteristic and, therefore, everyone does not have to be a data provider—thus being selective and not attempting to touch all data points is in order. With an LCS, all data points are in order. In other words, with an LCS, there is greater differentiation with little integration and typically a proliferation of subunits and groups. With this greater degree of disparate units, there is a greater need to gather data from many more sources in an LCS than would likely be the case for a TCS.

Diagnosis

With greater differentiation of data and data sources in an LCS, diagnosis becomes more complicated. Instead of one story to tell, there are likely to be multiple stories. And we will need ways to summarize and organize the data. As noted earlier, when working with an LCS, the model or framework of choice is a social network analysis. Bearing in mind our personal bias regarding the Burke-Litwin model, albeit founded on the basis of a TCS, this model may still be useful with an LCS. A network analysis shows working and social relationships among people. When concentrating on the arrows, not so much the boxes in the Burke-Litwin model, we are also focusing on relationships but more in terms of organizational functions, for example, mission and strategy, and characteristics, such as culture. This focus comes from the perceptions of people in the system drawn from a survey and/or interviews, but more in terms of their views about such issues as strategic clarity, intent or strategy as it is aligned with structure, how culture affects the organization's reward system, whether or not organizational members see how their jobs and roles contribute to the organization's mission, and so forth—not so much the relationships among individuals.

Feedback

In our work over the years with TCS, we have consistently provided the feedback to the boss first and alone. This has always been an important element of the contract with the client. It is, therefore, a two-step process—first with the boss, then with everyone else. With an LCS, we may not need the first step. In addition to honoring the contract, the purpose of providing feedback is to energize the members of the organization to take action. The initial activity of a large group intervention can be to provide feedback followed by planning action steps accordingly. This kind of process is relevant to both a TCS and an LCS. The feedback process with a TCS, however, is often staggered; that is, conforming to the hierarchy: feedback to the top team, then to the next layer downward, and so forth to the level of first-line supervisors. This takes time, of course, and needs to be orchestrated carefully. With an LCS, it is best, to the degree possible, to have everyone in the same room at the same time. Little interdependence among organizational members coupled with not providing feedback to all simultaneously can cause communication problems, such as misinformation being transmitted, rumor mills, and so forth. In a TCS, communication can be controlled more easily, albeit at times perhaps overcontrolled, whereas in an LCS, without everyone together, the word travels through many channels in turn, creating the possibility of distortion. Large group techniques are, therefore, very useful for an LCS at the feedback stage.

But what if the LCS is essentially virtual and gathering everyone in the same room is not possible? As problematic as this situation might be, you still need to mirror the system as much as possible when providing feedback; that is, virtually. Using software such as Adobe Connect can be an alternative. Skype may help also but could be too limiting. Perhaps some combination of conference call, videoconferencing, and Adobe might be considered. In any case, using whatever technology that can help you to connect and engage the total virtual organization at the same time would be the goal.

Intervention

With respect to intervening into an LCS, the larger the system, the more we should follow Weick's (2001) admonition of keeping the action local rather than at the total system level, or *cosmopolitan* to use his term. But what is local particularly with respect to size? A good rule of thumb is the "magic number of 150," or to be precise regarding Dunbar's research, 147.8. Dunbar (1992) studied what he called *social channel capacity*, or simply put, how many people can we know and keep up with? That is, we do not have to be close friends with this many people; it is more a matter of, for example, knowing who knows what—when I need some information about or help with a particular matter, who would I turn to? In other words, staying at no more than 150 people appears to be the most efficient way to manage a large group. There is considerable evidence for the efficacy of this "magic number." Thus for an LCS of no more than 150 individuals, you can have an efficiently run meeting with everyone at the same time. For an LCS of more than 150, our interventions would need to be held at subunit levels, more local and important to that subunit—not necessarily to the entire system. It might be better to work more with a local school than with an entire district. So, with an LCS, there are multiple choices of entry for an intervention and interventions at these local levels can be any one of many from the OD lexicon of change activities—coaching, team building, conflict resolution between subunits, forming alliances and joint ventures, and leader development. And for more specific examples of potential interventions for spanning boundaries across organizational partnerships, such as reflective intervening, process managing, and brokering, see the contribution by Gray (2008).

Staying with the theme of interventions to tighten an LCS, let us revisit the three suggestions of Orton and Weick (1990) for tightening a loose system: (1) enhanced leadership, (2) focused attention, and (3) shared values.

Enhanced leadership means that selected individuals will be authorized by members of the organization to decide about certain actions that can result in a tightening of the system. This involves power and its use, which has not been addressed directly in this chapter. Let us now at least touch on it.

Richard Beckhard, one of the founders of OD and a mentor for many, was one of the most astute practitioners ever witnessed for quickly and accurately identifying where and who had the power in any given organization. He could practically smell it, not just see it. This ability was, of course, in the context of a tightly coupled system—understanding hierarchy and interdependence. In a loosely coupled system, where power is and who has it is not that easy to identify. Power is dispersed, allusive, situational, and more individualized than a function of position or title. In a loosely coupled system, social power is the key identifier. People who have this form of power are those recognized by Gladwell (2000)—connectors, mavens, and salesmen and by Cross et al. (2013) as connectors, brokers, energizers, and resisters—and those recognized by Battilana and Casciaro (2012) as network members who provide novel ideas that challenge the status quo and those who are talented at getting ideas implemented. Enhancing leadership in a loosely coupled system is a matter of identifying and coaching those who have social power.

With respect to *focused attention,* the intent is to work in small and perhaps accommodative ways, at the local level to identify potential projects that need to be undertaken to improve particularly a given subsystem's efficiency and effectiveness. The project could be devoted to determining how to serve a certain constituency, ones who are served by the network or system, but have not been all that involved or for some reason have been neglected and not well served. For example, in the early days of the OD Network, local groups in major cities across the United States organized to plan and conduct the national meetings. The aim was not only to get the national meetings organized and implemented, but also to facilitate the formation of local, regional chapters, which would hold their own events yet remain loosely connected to the ODN as a whole. And, finally, a consultant might consider having network members attend a workshop on project management.

Shared values underlie an organization's mission, thus a fruitful way to focus on these beliefs is to revisit the mission statement. This was done in the case of attempting to change the A. K. Rice Institute and led to significant change in the system, at least for the short run (Noumair et al., 2010). The mission is the glue that holds the organization together, particularly if the organization is loosely coupled. Revisiting the mission statement from time to time is rarely a waste of time.

Sustainment

As you know, initiating a change effort is one thing and keeping it going is quite another. Over two decades, Jack Welch kept change going at GE by moving from one initiative to another. First, there was workout, then Six Sigma, and later developing a values-oriented culture. That was GE, a large and rather tightly run organization. For an LCS, sustainment of change is probably not one of following a GE model (i.e., the same for everyone). Rather, an effective sustainment process might follow a model of *dispersed differentiation* (i.e., *not* the same for everyone).

But first, let's address sustainment with thinking that is applicable to both a TCS and an LCS. The problem with leading and managing change is the fact that implementation rarely goes according to plan. Thus, fixing unanticipated problems that arise due to interventions into the existing system must take top priority, problems such as new software meant to support the change effort doesn't seem to work or at least work well. (The early days of Obamacare come to mind.) For sustainment problems that emerge from change, interventions must be tackled immediately. Allowing these problems to fester causes a loss of momentum, in essence the death knell of any change effort, with people moaning, "I know this change thing wasn't going to work!" Thus, fixing these unintended consequences of change initiatives must take precedence to sustain the change. See Chapter 2 in Burke (2014b), in particular the section on "The Paradox of Planned Organization Change"; that is, planned change is linear, whereas implementation is nonlinear.

Now with respect to an LCS, intervening with new initiatives can be useful for sustainment but as noted above not for the GE approach. Once a change is launched in an LCS, interventions are likely to be dispersed among local units and different from one another. Local options regarding execution are probably the process to support. Here, the Battilana and Casciaro (2012) study is relevant. The overall change attempted, at least in part, was to increase decision-making authority for nurses, but that took different forms based on the characteristics of the internal network—tight versus structural holes. Fixing unanticipated problems is the same regardless of TCS or LCS. What differs is the content of the problems with much more differentiation for an LCS.

A final thought, perhaps heretical, for sustainment of change in an LCS: A fundamental principle of open system theory is that change in one part of the system has an impact on other parts of the system. How true is this principle for a network? Is it possible that change in a local unit would have no impact on other local units? Yes, we know, the answer is "It depends"; that is, how loose-tight the network is. But it may be that diligently communicating what happens in one locality to all other localities, to foster best practices, for example, may simply not matter that much. It has been said that all politics are local. The more a system is loosely coupled, the more that statement is no doubt valid.

Some scholar-practitioners in the field of organization development and change add an eighth step to this list of seven from entry to sustainment: *evaluation.* This potential eighth step is important—did change actually occur?—but rarely conducted (see Chapter 11, "Does Organization Development Work?"). Many practitioners believe that evaluation takes too much time and effort and doesn't tell you very much. But if incorporated into a change effort from the beginning so that a pre-post comparison can be made, then the time and cost can be worth it. For an LCS, it would need to be conducted locally, of course, and to do so across the entire system may indeed be costly, so it is probably best to keep evaluation as a "local option."

Conclusion

It is not as if we have never heard of a loosely coupled system, perhaps with different language and labels; they have been around since the beginning of human attempts "to get organized." Moses along with help from his brother, Aaron, talked Pharaoh into letting his people go. Moses then more or less led the Israelites, a loose band of people agreeing that wandering in the desert for 40 years was better than slavery, with the dream that reaching the promised land was worth all of the hardships. Moses's band of several thousand was a loose system, a very flat hierarchy with one solitary and rather introverted leader at the top. In fact, years later, Jethro, Moses's son-in-law, thought that Moses was well beyond his limit with respect to leadership and a tightening was needed. So he proposed a hierarchy with Moses having 10 direct reports and with each of them having 10 direct reports, and so forth down the human pyramid. It sounds like a simple solution to Moses's overload. But it was no doubt difficult. As we have attempted to explain, neither loosening a tight system nor tightening a loose system is a cakewalk. Change has never been easy.

What we have also attempted to explain is that we know and have more experience with loosening tight systems and therefore doing so may be less difficult than tightening a loose system. After all, from time to time, Moses would have a rebellion on his hands from his followers. As we now understand, the field of OD is largely based on our accumulative experiences and knowledge from working with tightly coupled systems. Therefore, we have much learning ahead of us regarding the intricacies of changing an LCS. Even so, maybe even now we could make progress with changing an LCS in less than 40 years.

Endnotes

1. This chapter is a slight modification of the article published in the 50th Anniversary special issue of *The Journal of Applied Behavioral Science* (Burke, 2014c).

2. It has been our experience as organization change consultants that a paramount concern on the part of the client is to make sure that we understand their uniqueness as an organization, not how they are similar to others.

11

Does Organization Development Work?

"Does it work?" is one of the first questions managers ask about anything new or different. This chapter therefore responds to the question first by showing that there is substantial evidence that organization development (OD) does indeed work. Caveats will be considered as we respond further to the question. Next, we consider obstacles to conducting an evaluation, the seventh phase of any OD effort, and finally we conclude by arguing the importance of evaluation regardless of the problems involved and the pressures that mitigate such an activity.

Does It Work?

When OD is done according to the principles and practices expounded in this volume, our experience is that OD works. But our experience and others' experiences in "successfully" practicing OD is not enough. So-called hard evidence is needed. And, indeed, there is evidence. French and Bell (1978) selected nine studies that support OD's effectiveness. Four of their nine, for example, were studies by Beckhard and Lake (1971), Kimberly and Nielsen (1975), King (1974), and Marrow, Bowers, and Seashore (1967).

Other studies could be included in the French and Bell list, such as the one by Golembiewski, Hilles, and Kagno (1974).

There are problems, however. From a survey of 63 organizations regarding their knowledge and use of organization development, Heisler (1975) found, among other things, that the major criticism of OD efforts was the difficulty in evaluating their effectiveness. A number of others have made similar observations; see, for example,

Barends, Janssen, ten Have, & ten Have (2014); King, Sherwood, and Manning (1978); Morrison (1978); Porras (1979); and Porras and Patterson (1979).

Researchers, in attempting to evaluate the effectiveness of OD, have relied on a method called meta-analysis. The value of meta-analysis is that it is a statistical technique that summarizes and integrates numerous findings across many studies. As Guzzo, Jette, and Katzell (1985) point out,

> Through meta-analysis, a common yardstick for measuring results of different studies is obtained that furnishes a level of integration of studies not possible through traditional judgmental ways of reviewing a body of literature. In fact, proponents of meta-analysis have criticized traditional literature review methods for their susceptibility to bias and insensitivity to artificial sources of differences in results (p. 276).

In their meta-analysis of 11 types of OD activities, Guzzo et al. showed that these "psychologically based organizational interventions," as they referred to them, raised worker productivity. These interventions included job design, participative management, sociotechnical systems, and team building. This finding was based on their analysis of 98 studies.

In their meta-analysis of 126 research studies, Neuman, Edwards, and Raju (1989) found that OD interventions had a stronger and positive effect on worker attitudes and satisfaction on the job. Their analysis further showed that multiple OD interventions—for example, team building, plus job enrichment, survey feedback, and so on—had a much stronger effect than singular OD interventions.

Considering organization change research since the 1990s and now into the twenty-first century, the focus interestingly has been on the recipients of change as compared with the role and influence of a change leader or agent. In other words, a way of interpreting organization development and change research in the early part of this century is from the perspective of those who have experienced the impact if not the brunt of the change process; that is, attempting to understand the effects on those most affected. This perspective can be considered in two ways: (1) reactions, in general, to organization development and change, and (2) resistance to change.

With respect to (1) reactions to change in general, Oreg, Vakola, and Armenakis (2011) combed through an extensive array of organization development and change studies since 1948, in the neighborhood of 700 publications. Using a primary criterion of methodological rigor, they boiled the numbers down to 79, all being based on quantitative data. Next, they crafted a framework for categorizing the studies resulting in what they referred to as antecedents of recipients' reactions to the organizations' changes:

- Personal characteristics of the change recipients themselves; for example, coping style
- The change process; for example, the extent to which recipients were involved in decision making regarding the change
- The content of the change; for example, a change in organizational structure, a new information technology system, culture change, and so on

Their framework then linked these antecedents to explicit reactions—affective, cognitive, and behavioral—and in turn linked to the consequences of the change such as job satisfaction and organizational performance.

Even with the emphasis for choice of study to be reviewed being methodological rigor, most of these research reports were flawed one way or the other. For example, most studies were based on self-reports from a single source, rarely was a Time 1 measure compared with a Time 2, and most studies were conducted in a single organization or department within a larger organization with no opportunity for comparisons. Even so, Oreg and colleagues were able to draw three primary conclusions from their analyses of the 79 studies; that is, recipients had the most positive reactions to change efforts when there was:

1. A basis of trust especially with top-level executives
2. Involvement of recipients in the decision-making process
3. A positive disposition toward the change by leaders in the organization

Burke's (2014d) conclusion to this work by Oreg et al. (2011) is as follows:

> These consistent findings across studies determined by Oreg and his colleagues are not exactly startling. We have known about the importance of trust, commitment, and benefits of a positive approach to life and work for a long time. It is comforting nevertheless to have (a) established these "truths" with consistency across so many studies and (b) found empirical evidence that supports what is practiced (p. 467).

The second perspective regarding recipients' reactions to organization development and change is the matter of resistance. This perspective is based more on theory and reflections about practice than on research per se.

Although resistance to change is not a universal reaction, some people embrace change, after all, saying such things as "Well, it's about time…." Resistance to change is quite common, nevertheless. Yet in the annals of organization development and change, resistance has usually been considered a given and is something that must be overcome. In fact, the title of the classic study by Coch and French (1948) was "Overcoming resistance to change." *Overcome* has been a part of our lexicon and heritage for a long time. As most of us in the field now know, this mode of thinking has been challenged. Dent and Goldberg (1999) declared that mind-set leads to a we-they process, culminating in a vicious cycle of overcoming met with resistance. This cyclical process eventually led to the downfall of Margaret Thatcher, Prime Minister of the U.K. She classified her constituents as either "for us" or "against us." Those against were not considered as the loyal opposition but rather as disloyal opponents, which, of course, contributed to a strong resistance to change on their part.

But sometimes, perhaps often, what may be perceived as resistance is really nothing more than ambivalence (Piderit, 2000). In such cases, the person "resisting" just needs more information and perhaps a clearer rationale for the proposed change. And, finally, Ford, Ford, and D'Amelio (2008) have joined the more current sentiment regarding resistance to change and argued that it can be seen as a resource rather than a detriment to a change effort that must be overcome. By resource, they mean that resistance requires energy, which is far better than apathy, and that with resistance, organizational members care about something. Thus, it is a matter of maybe seeing resistance as a container for counterproposals and potentially useful ideas and therefore tapping into such different ways of thinking and perspectives might be helpful to the overall change process. The point is that seeing resistance as something to overcome is an oversimplification of reality and that reality encompasses more complexity than we had previously considered. For broader coverage of this more recent way of understanding and dealing with resistance, see the article by Burke (2011a).

In addition to a more nuanced way of considering resistance, there is evidence that organization development and change interventions can and do work. There are problems, nevertheless, in attempting to evaluate organization development and change interventions. We now consider the nature of some of these problems and issues.

Research Issues in Evaluating OD Efforts

The overriding issue in OD evaluation is purpose—whether the research effort is evaluation or knowledge generation, whether it is for the benefit of the client or the social scientist. Because we are discussing evaluation, that should be the obvious concern, not scientific generation of knowledge, but the assessment methodology—how we collect and analyze our information for evaluative purposes—is based on the traditional scientific method. We control and manipulate some independent variables, make some interventions, and see if any difference occurs with respect to some dependent variables. We decide to use team building as an intervention, for example, and we collect information (a dependent variable) to see if it made any difference. We might use a questionnaire to ask team members if they feel more satisfied with and committed to the team, and we might determine if the team's work performance increases after the team-building effort has occurred. Even if our data showed increased satisfaction, commitment, and work performance, it would be difficult to demonstrate that the team-building intervention has *caused* these outcomes unless we had also collected data from a matched control group, a similar team for which no team building had been done, and could compare data for the same period for the two groups. Another critical factor in this evaluation would be the people who collect and analyze the data. Numerous studies have shown that the researcher can affect the outcome (Rosenthal, 1976). This brings up the question of objectivity. To be scientific, or objective, the researcher should be someone other than the team-building consultant or the organization members involved.

Argyris (1968) has argued, however, that the more scientific the evaluation is, the less it is likely to be relevant to and therefore used by the client. Schein (1992) in his study of organizational culture has made similar arguments.

To be more specific, we now examine some primary research issues and problems associated with the evaluation of an organization development effort. The issues and problems are addressed in the form of six questions, which are not necessarily mutually exclusive.

What Is Organizational Effectiveness?

In general, the goal of an OD effort is to improve the organization, to make it more effective, whether the effort is with a large, total system or with a division—a subsystem of a larger organization. It is not a simple matter to define effectiveness (Goodman & Pennings, 1980) or to get people to agree on a definition. Cameron (1980) points out that there are at least four different criteria for organizational effectiveness and that these criteria differ significantly from one organization to another. The differences are particularly apparent when comparing profit-making with nonprofit organizations. The four criteria or models are as follows:

- *The goal model.* Organizational effectiveness is defined in terms of the extent to which the organization accomplishes its goals.

- *The system resource model.* Effectiveness is equated with the ability to acquire needed resources.

- *The process model.* Effectiveness is defined in terms of how smoothly the organization functions, especially the degree of absence of internal strain in the organization.

- *The strategic constituencies model.* Effectiveness is determined by the extent to which the organization satisfies all its strategic constituencies—special interest groups.

As Cameron notes, these models or definitions of effectiveness may be useful or inappropriate, depending on the type of organization and the public or market it tries to serve.

It should thus be apparent that determining organizational effectiveness is not simple.

What Is OD?

As illustrated in this book, OD is many things, and there are seven major phases in an OD effort. For evaluative research purposes, do we consider all these phases or just the intervention phase? Moreover, different OD interventions will also result in different outcomes (Neuman, Edwards, & Raju, 1989; Porras, 1979). The more specific and precise we can be in defining the variety of activities coming under the rubric of OD, the more we will be in a position to evaluate the effectiveness of these activities. A way of increasing this precision is to achieve greater clarity about the remaining four questions.

What Is the Independent Variable?

In an examination of 38 research studies conducted on various aspects of OD, Pate, Nielsen, and Bacon (1977) reported that they had considerable difficulty in categorizing variables from the studies. They could not be sure whether the independent variable was the OD intervention itself or whether OD was only instrumental in the manipulation of some other independent variable. They took the view that OD is instrumental but does not constitute the independent variable as such. "For example, one might expect introduction of participative decision making (OD intervention) to facilitate worker awareness of the rationale for organizational actions (independent variable), which in turn may increase support and commitment to those actions (dependent variables)" (pp. 450–51). Their emphasis of this issue is helpful because we can now be clearer about what activities to evaluate specifically.

How Can We Control Variables?

As organizations are dynamic systems, this is a question of causal attribution—determining whether the consequences of a change can be attributed to organization development. As noted earlier, the more we can control our research conditions (for example, by having a control condition or control group for comparison), the more we will be able to state with confidence what is cause and what is effect. In dynamic, changing organizations, however, this is almost impossible to do. It is difficult, for example, to persuade a manager to subject his or her organization to a series of time-consuming data-collection activities for the purpose of providing a control group. The manager is likely to ask, "What's in it for us?" It is even more difficult to find an appropriate control group. There are rarely two subsystems within an organization, much less two distinct organizations, that do the same things, have the same types of people, and are managed the same way.

With so much going on in the organizational world and with most of this array of activities being impossible to control, we have what Campbell and Stanley (1966) refer to as a problem of internal validity: determining whether what we did by way of change made a measurable difference. In the absence of pure control group conditions, the true experimental design for research purposes, Campbell and Stanley have provided what they call quasi-experimental designs. These designs, though not perfect from a research perspective, provide ways for controlling certain conditions so that validity will be enhanced. Their time-series design is a good example. In this design, several measures are taken at certain intervals *before* the intervention and several measures are taken at essentially the same intervals *after* the intervention.

If it can be shown (1) that there are no significant differences among the first, say, four observations, (2) that there are significant changes from the first four to the fifth observation and beyond (that is, after the intervention), and (3) that there are then no significant differences among, say, four observations after the intervention, then the differences that occurred between preintervention and postintervention must be a result of the change, not merely the passage of time or other variables.

What Changed?

Golembiewski, Billingsley, and Yeager (1976) drew distinctions among three types of change, which they labeled alpha, beta, and gamma. *Alpha* change concerns a difference that occurs along some relatively stable dimension of reality. This change is typically a comparative measure before and after an intervention. If comparative measures of trust among team members showed an increase after a team-building intervention, for example, then we might conclude that our OD intervention had made a difference. Golembiewski et al. assert that most OD evaluation research designs consist of such before-and-after self-reports.

Suppose, however, that a decrease in trust occurred—or no change at all. One study has shown that, although no decrease in trust occurred, neither did a measurable increase occur as a consequence of team-building intervention (Friedlander, 1970). Change may have occurred, however. The difference may be what Golembiewski, Billingsley, and Yeager call a *beta* change, a recalibration of the intervals along some constant dimension of reality. As a result of team-building intervention, team members may view trust very differently. Their basis for judging the nature of trust changed, rather than their perception of a simple increase or decrease in trust along some stable continuum.

A *gamma* change "involves a redefinition or reconceptualization of some domain, a major change in the perspective or frame of reference within which phenomena are perceived and classified, in what is taken to be relevant in some slice of reality" (Golembiewski, Billingsley, and Yeager, 1976, p. 135). This involves change from one state to another. Staying with the example, after the intervention, team members might conclude that trust was not a relevant variable in their team-building experience. They might believe that the gain in their clarity about roles and responsibilities was the relevant factor and that their improvement as a team had nothing to do with trust. In other words, the domain of interest and importance was insufficient clarity regarding team members' roles and responsibilities, not an issue of interpersonal relationships.

Thus, selecting the appropriate dependent variables—determining specifically what might change—is not as simple as it might appear. This is especially important when self-report data are used.

Who Will Conduct the Research and Who Will Use the Results?

The last issue to be addressed is the people involved in the evaluation effort. To avoid the possibility of a Pygmalion effect and to increase the probability of objectivity, it is best that the researcher be someone other than the OD consultant. Both the researcher and the consultant are interveners into the organization, however, and therefore it is imperative that they collaborate. The researcher needs to know not only the consultant's overall strategy—change goals, targets, and so forth—and what interventions might be used, but also the consultant's predictions concerning what should change as a result of the OD effort.

The people who will make decisions as a result of the evaluation research must be involved. These people may or may not be directly involved in the OD process itself, but the decision makers need to be involved by the researcher in much the same way that the organization members who are directly involved in the OD process would be regarding participation in the research goals, methods, and interpretation. This involvement of the decision makers helps ensure that the research results will be valid and will be utilized for further decision making.

In addition to these issues and inherent problems in evaluating OD efforts, there are a number of pressures against conducting this seventh phase of an OD effort. We now examine some of these more important obstacles.

Pressures Opposed to Evaluation

The evaluation process of OD practice can be compared with an annual physical examination: Everyone agrees that it should be done, but no one, except a highly motivated researcher, wants to go to the trouble and expense of making it happen. We examine first some of the reasons for opposing evaluation and then conclude with reasons for going ahead with this phase.

There are at least four sets of people involved in or related to OD evaluation: the manager or decision maker, the organization members who are directly involved in the OD process (the manager or decision maker may or may not be in this process), the OD consultant, and the evaluation researcher. There are pressures on each of these categories of people to ignore evaluation.

The Manager or Decision Maker

Managers want results. If interventions in an OD effort are accompanied by change in certain organizational areas that are important to managers, such as increased profits, decreased absenteeism, or increased morale; that is often all that is necessary for a manager to choose to continue with OD or to move on to other things. Managers want to know *if* it works, not *why* it works. Such managers are usually found in fast-moving, marketing-oriented organizations, where short-term results are rewarded. There are other types of managers, however.

Managers in highly technical, scientific organizations may take the opposite stance. These managers might argue that, unless you can measure the consequences of an organization development effort in a rigorous, scientific manner, an evaluation is not worth doing.

Opposition to evaluation research from managers who are in key decision-making roles may take either extreme: Evaluation research is not necessary because the outcomes are self-evident or because the effects of OD cannot be measured scientifically. Other reasons for opposition from managers could be the cost involved, the amount of extra time it will take, or the undesirability of an outsider coming in to do research on them.

The Organization Members Involved in the OD Effort

Opposition from those directly involved in the OD process may take the same forms as those mentioned with respect to the managers or decision makers. In addition to those possible if not highly potential forms of opposition, organization members may complain about the time it will take for them to answer the questionnaires, for example, when this time could be utilized more productively in getting on with further aspects of the OD effort. They also might argue that the research staff is likely to be more beneficial to the goals of the researcher than to the goals of the organization's change effort.

The OD Consultant

The OD consultant is likely to want an evaluation study but for reasons that differ from those of the manager or decision maker. Managers are interested in OD's impact on outcomes—profits, turnover, costs, productivity—whereas OD consultants may be more interested in process—the impact that OD may have on behavior, attitudes, organizational procedures, changes in authority relationships, and the like. A study by Porras and Wilkens (1980) indicates that many OD consultants may be disappointed with evaluation research on organization development. Porras and Wilkens found that OD in a large organization had a positive impact on outcomes, such as unit performance, but a negative consequence for attitudinal and behavioral variables that described organizational and individual processes. As Porras and Wilkens noted, these latter, unexpected negative findings may reflect a beta change, not an alpha change (Golembiewski, Billingsley, & Yeager, 1976) because their measures of attitudes and behavior were through self-report questionnaires whereas their measures of unit performance came from company records.

The point here is not that OD consultants are uninterested in or opposed to determining OD's impact on outcomes, but that certain factors may be more important to the consultant as a professional.

The Evaluation Researcher

The researcher is interested in both outcome and process measures, but his or her objectives for the use of the research results may differ from those of the other three groups of people concerned with an OD effort. The researcher is often more interested in contributing to the body of knowledge concerning organizations as changing systems or the effectiveness of organization development as a field than in providing information for the organization's decision makers. This difference in objectives or priorities can cause problems with planning and implementing an evaluation research effort, but opposition on the part of a researcher toward conducting an evaluation study is likely to occur for another reason. Most researchers are trained only according to the traditional scientific method of research, which involves distancing oneself from and controlling the subjects of the research (client), not collaborating with them.

Reasons for Conducting the Evaluation Phase

The forces that oppose evaluative research of an organization development effort are formidable and should not be dismissed lightly, but there are also compelling reasons for conducting evaluative research.

Briefly, the primary arguments for an evaluative research study of an OD effort are as follows:

1. An evaluation forces the definition of the change objectives.
2. An evaluation forces the clarification of the change outcomes that are expected.
3. An evaluation forces the clarification of how these change outcomes are to be measured.
4. An evaluation forces specificity with respect to how certain procedures, events, and activities will be implemented.
5. An evaluation helps to signal many of the problems and obstacles to be anticipated in the OD effort.
6. An evaluation facilitates planning for next steps and stages of organizational improvement and development.

As we know from system theory, particularly as applied to organizations, there may be no such thing as a single cause for a single effect. Systematic evaluation will provide many of the causal answers for what occurs and has occurred in organizations. Generally, but perhaps most important, evaluation forces clarity about what *effectiveness* is for an organization.

Finally, it is important to conduct some kind of evaluation rather than none at all. And rather than become embroiled in the issues of whether an outside researcher or the OD practitioner should conduct the evaluation—and in the spirit of OD practice anyway—perhaps the OD practitioner can *facilitate* an evaluative process; that is, help the client do the job himself.

One tool for facilitating an evaluative process is an After Action Review (AAR), borrowed from the U.S. Army. An AAR is an opportunity to review an OD initiative using four questions to guide the process: What was the intent? What actually happened? Why did it happen that way? What was learned? (Garvin, Edmondson, & Gino, 2008). And just as important as an AAR is the Before Action Review (BAR) (Darling, Parry, & Moore, 2005). By conducting a BAR at the outset of an OD effort and asking similar questions to those in an AAR but with an emphasis on the future, the evaluation process is baked into the research from the beginning. As such, AARs and BARs become part of how organizations learn from their experience, an essential outcome of any successful OD initiative. Questions associated with a BAR are: What do we intend to accomplish and how will we know if we have been successful? What do we anticipate will get in the way? What learning have we garnered from similar projects? What will we do to build on our past learning? By engaging these questions up front, at the very least, OD practitioners and clients will not be moving forward with a new initiative without leveraging learning from the past or defining what success looks like in the future.

Conclusion

There is sufficiently strong empirical evidence that OD works. The more recent meta-analysis method of research has contributed significantly to our understanding of whether OD works. Yet, as has been pointed out, there are problems and issues in conducting evaluations of OD efforts. It is important, nevertheless, to conduct some kind of evaluation rather than none at all. The paper by Goodstein and Burke (1991) regarding British Airways is an example of an evaluation that is nonscientific and post hoc but data-based in part. The data are primarily financial, as is the quantitative information reported by Leahey and Kotter (1990) in their case study of British Airways. In these analyses of BA, an assumption is made that OD had an effect in that financial performance significantly improved—but it is assumed, not proven. We can learn from such reports in any case. Moreover, as Argyris, Putnam, and Smith (1985) have indicated, effective OD may actually be inconsistent with rigorous research.

In addition to the contribution of meta-analysis, it may also be that more effective work in the practice of OD has made a positive difference; that is, that OD works. Sashkin and Burke (1987) summarize this point as follows:

We suggest that the clear research demonstration of positive OD impacts owes much to the integration of task structure and behavioral process-based OD approaches and of people-centered with profit-centered OD values. The work on types of change shows an increasingly sophisticated appreciation of the true interdependence of structure and process in OD (p. 405).

12

The Organization Development Consultant

A consultant is one who provides help, counsel, advice, and support, which implies that such a person is wise and would offer sage advice. Although the label *consultant* usually conveys an image of one who provides help, there are obviously many different types of consultants. The purposes of this chapter are to provide a context for the unique role and function of an organization development (OD) consultant, to consider the different roles and functions of an OD consultant including the integration of OD competencies into other organization roles, to explore the kinds of personal characteristics that are needed for OD consultation, to suggest ways for those who want to become OD consultants to do so, to discuss the use of self-as-instrument, and to address the importance of reflective practice as a method of continued professional development.

Context for Roles and Functions

To answer the question of context, two aspects are important. One is where we typically find OD consultants, and the other is how they differ from other consultants.

Where OD Consultants Are Located

Organization development consultants are found either inside an organization, as full-time or part-time employees, or outside organizations, with organizations considered as clients. Internal consultants are usually located within the human resources, people development, or employee relations function. They may be part of an OD department and serve exclusively in an OD capacity, or they may combine OD consultation with other duties, such as learning and development, coaching, research, or career assessment and development. Thus, internal OD consultants are usually in a staff function, and line managers throughout the organization are their clients.

External OD consultants may be employed by a consulting firm, may be self-employed, or may have academic appointments and consult only part of the time. In the past, external OD consultants usually came from colleges and universities. Now they are more likely to come from large consulting firms, as discussed in Chapter 2, "Organization Development Then and Now," or work on their own as full-time independent consultants.

A change in the field since the last revision of this book is that there is now a much greater incidence of line managers across functions integrating OD competencies into their work. We view the expansion of OD skills into a wide array of organization functions as a consequence of change being a constant in contemporary organizational life. Rather than solely partnering with OD consultants, line managers are enhancing their own leadership skills by becoming proficient in organization change and development in order to lead change and manage more effectively. Thus, while we elaborate on the role of OD consultants, the material covered in this chapter is also relevant for line managers. Additionally, we address line managers directly in the section on developing OD competencies.

Comparisons of the OD Consultant with Other Types of Consultants

Edgar Schein (1987; 1988; 1999) contrasts the process consultant role, a primary but not exclusive role and function of an OD consultant, with the purchase model and the doctor-patient model. According to Schein, the purchase model is the most prevalent form of consultation, essentially consisting of the client's purchase of expert services, such as information about the marketplace and competitors, latest technology, surveys and polls, and so forth. A client's employment of a consultant to conduct a market research study is an example of purchasing both expert service and information. The doctor-patient model consists of the client telling the consultant the symptoms of what is wrong with the organization ("Our turnover is too high," "We're losing market share with respect to product X," "Our management information system is a mess") and then expecting the consultant to prescribe a remedy for the problem.

Schein contrasts these two models with the process consultant, one who helps the client organization diagnose its own strengths and weaknesses more effectively, learn how to see organizational problems more clearly, and with the consultant generate a remedy. Schein states:

> It is a key assumption of change that the client must share in the process of diagnosing what may be wrong (or learn to see the problem for himself), and must be actively involved in the process of generating a remedy because only the client ultimately knows what is possible and what will work in his culture and situation (1987, p. 30).

Thus, the primary though not exclusive function of OD consultants is to help clients learn how to help themselves more effectively. Although consultants occasionally provide expert information and may sometimes prescribe a remedy, their more typical mode of operating is *facilitation.*

Although a typical mode, facilitation is not the only function or role of OD consultants. The next section summarizes the array of consultant roles from which OD consultants may choose; more likely, they may use a combination of these roles within one client engagement.

Roles and Functions

As an introduction to the roles and functions of the OD practitioner, let us start with Beckhard's broad categories, as noted in Witherspoon and White (1996). Beckhard viewed the OD practitioner as playing at least four roles:

- *Expert.* Solving a problem or providing solutions and recommendations; this is similar to the purchase and doctor-patient models defined by Schein (1988).

- *Consultant.* Helping the client to address an issue while keeping the responsibility for the concern with the client; this is the same as the process consultant role as defined by Schein (1988).

- *Trainer or educator.* Providing information through teaching the client; for example, giving a brief lecture on content or identifying a teachable moment.

- *Counselor.* Advising the client and facilitating learning in the client. Today Beckhard would probably rename the Counselor a Coach, given the prevalence and popularity of coaching in OD. Coaching as an aspect of the OD consultant role is addressed in Chapter 13, "Coaching and Organization Development."

Beckhard's four categories are useful as they expand on Schein's process consultation model, which is the *sine qua non* of OD practice. One challenge of process consultation, however, is that it is often *perceived* as not bringing expertise to bear on the problem and there is concern that clients will not see the added value of a consultant who uses process consultation. Although eventually the expertise required for process consultation is apparent, it is often not an easy sell to those in the early stages of learning it. Thus, Beckhard's more expansive definition of the consultant role allows one to serve as an expert, teacher, and advisor, and provides a model for how to engage a client in other ways besides solely through process consultation. Depending on client needs, a consultant would use a combination of these roles within one client engagement, and sometimes within one client meeting.

Lippitt and Lippitt (1975) provide us with a more nuanced view of the role of consultant. Using a continuum from directive to nondirective, Lippitt and Lippitt devised a descriptive model of eight different roles for a consultant. By *directive,* Lippitt and Lippitt mean that the consultant's behavior assumes a leadership posture and that he or she initiates activities, whereas at the opposite extreme—nondirective—the consultant merely provides data for the client to use or not. All along the continuum, the consultant is active; what varies is how directive or nondirective this activity becomes. The eight roles from directive to nondirective are *advocate, technical specialist, trainer* or *educator, collaborator* (in problem solving), *alternative identifier, fact finder, process specialist,* and *reflector.* Lippitt and Lippitt also note that these roles are not mutually exclusive. The consultant may, for example, serve as a trainer and educator and as an advocate at the same time.

Marginality

As noted earlier in Chapter 5, "Defining the Client: A Different Perspective," Margulies (1978) has described the consultant's role differently and more generically. He argues that the OD consultant role is a marginal one. *Marginal* implies being on the periphery, and, accordingly, another term that Margulies uses is *boundary.*

First, Margulies contrasts two models of consulting with which we are already familiar: the *technical consulting* model and the *process consulting* model. His technical consulting model is like Schein's purchase and doctor-patient models and like Lippitt and Lippitt's technical specialist role, and his process model is the same as Schein's process consultation model. Margulies makes an analogy of technical-process with rational-intuitive and with the idea of the two-sided person represented by the two hemispheres of the brain. The OD consultant's role, he argues, is to function between these two halves, in the margin, being neither too technically oriented nor too process-oriented. Both sets of consultant expertise are appropriate, but for the OD consultant neither should be emphasized to the exclusion of the other. The consultant operates within the boundary of these two models of consultation, totally endorsing neither yet accepting both.

Margulies includes two other boundaries: the activities boundary and the membership boundary. For both, the OD consultant should operate at the boundary, in a marginal capacity. With respect to change activities, particularly implementation, the consultant must help but not be directly involved. Suppose, for example, an off-site team-building session for a manager and his subordinates was forthcoming. The consultant would help the manager with the design and process of the meeting but would not lead the meeting.

With respect to membership, the OD consultant is never quite in nor quite out. Although the consultant must be involved, he or she cannot be a member of the client organization. Being a member means that there is vested interest, a relative lack of objectivity. Being totally removed, however, means that the consultant cannot sense, cannot be empathetic, and cannot use his or her own feelings as data for understanding the client organization more thoroughly. Being marginal with respect to membership means that the consultant becomes involved enough to understand client members' feelings and perceptions yet distant enough to be able to see these feelings and perceptions for what they are—someone else's—rather than as an extension of oneself. An example of being marginal with respect to membership is when a client once described me (Noumair) in my role as consultant as "Switzerland," moving between and among subsystems in the organization in order to understand each unit's position but interacting with each one as a neutral party. Marginality, in this case, allowed me to be empathetic with each unit while also remaining apolitical with respect to any unit's agenda.

Being marginal is critical for both an external consultant and an internal consultant. The major concern regarding the internal OD consultant's role is that he or she can never be a consultant to his or her own group. If the group is an OD department, a member of this department, no matter how skilled, cannot be an effective consultant to it. It is also difficult for an internal OD practitioner to be a consultant to any group that is within the same vertical path or chain of the managerial hierarchy as he or she may be. Because the OD function is often a part of the corporate human resource function, it would be difficult for the internal OD consultant to play a marginal role in consulting with any of the groups within this corporate function because the consultant would be a primary organization member of that function. Consulting with marketing, research and development, technology, or manufacturing within one's organization, for example, would be far more feasible and appropriate because the OD consultant could more easily maintain a marginal role.

It is understandable that an OD consultant's role can be a lonely one. The role can also create anxiety about one's accuracy of perception (no one to check it with but the client) and about one's choice of intervention (whether it is the right thing for the moment). Joining in fully, being a member, helps alleviate this loneliness and anxiety. Staying removed, distant, and aloof can also relieve the anxiety because feelings are not involved. Doing either, however, lessens one's effectiveness as a consultant significantly. An obvious way to alleviate the problems of loneliness and anxiety is to co-consult. Working as an external and internal consultant team is probably the best way.

Shadow Consultation

If a co-consultant arrangement is not possible, an alternative is for a consultant to invite a colleague to partner as a *shadow consultant* for a client engagement. A shadow consultant as defined by Schröder (1974) is a "consultant who, at the request of a colleague (or a team of colleagues) and by means of a series of discussions, helps assess, and if necessary, change that colleague's diagnosis, tactics, or role in a specific assignment" (p. 580). Alban (1974), in her commentary on Schröder's article on shadow consultation, corroborates that consulting is a lonely experience, and that support from a colleague as a shadow consultant can mitigate loneliness and improve one's work.

The purpose of partnering with a shadow consultant is to help a consultant improve her or his work on a particular project, however, without administrative responsibility or authority for the work of the consultant. The absence of responsibility or authority is the greatest single difference between a shadow consultant and a supervisor.

In order for shadow consultation to work well, certain conditions must be in place. First, to consider working together in this way, there must be reciprocal trust between consultant and shadow consultant. Next, the consultant and shadow consultant must establish clear boundaries around each person's authority and role and above all, both must have clarity regarding the task of their joint work. Finally, they must each take responsibility for maintaining a learning orientation.

As important as establishing a set of working agreements, the consultant and shadow consultant need to be aware of the risks that are inherent in such partnerships. For the consultant, the risks include avoiding asking for help for fear of appearing vulnerable, in effect, not holding a learning orientation. This could manifest in withholding information. The consultant could also become too passive or too easily influenced by the shadow consultant and give up too quickly her or his own point of view; or the opposite, the consultant could become too wrapped up in his or her own ideas and not fully consider the ideas of the shadow consultant.

For the shadow consultant, the risks are complementary to those of the consultant. The shadow consultant could also not maintain a learning orientation and become impatient with, or not offer constructive feedback to, the consultant. As a counterpart to the consultant who relinquishes his or her point of view, the shadow consultant could mismanage the power associated with the role and get carried away with his or her own ideas and not fully take in the ideas of the consultant.

Having defined shadow consultation and identified the necessary conditions for effective partnerships as well as the risks involved, we end the discussion of shadow consultation with Kilburg's (2002) commentary on the importance of shadow consultation as his point of view is in keeping with our perspective on learning and collaboration as essential to the organizational consultation enterprise.

> It is not easy for any of us to admit that we may not know everything or that we get into trouble in our consultations. Being willing to do so, I believe, is one of the hallmarks of true professionalism. For it is only when we become aware of what we do not know that I think we can stretch ourselves into full maturity. It is mostly our defensiveness and more primitive psychological conflicts that keep us from reaching out for assistance in our continuing efforts to grow.

> When done well, shadow consultation creates a safe, interpersonal containment in which a consultant and a colleague can reflect carefully on any and all dimensions that may be creating impacts on a project. It can lead to dramatic improvements in the ability to be self-aware and therefore self-managing and self-confident in consulting assignments. It also creates a safety net through which a mature practitioner is unlikely to fall when inevitable problems occur in our very difficult work. For new or less experienced practitioners, it is a wonderful way to stretch the learning curve and to do so quickly with live material that has immediate impact on performance (p. 92).

Consultant Abilities

We believe that 12 primary abilities are key to an OD consultant's effectiveness. Most of these abilities can be learned, but because of individual differences in personality or basic temperament, some of them would be easier for some people to learn than for others. The effective consultant should have the following abilities:

- *The ability to tolerate ambiguity.* Every organization is different, and what worked before may not work now. Regardless of the genesis of an OD effort, it is best to enter a client engagement, either as an internal or external consultant, with few preconceived notions other than with the general characteristics that we know about social systems. One must then be able to tolerate ambiguity while also moving the work forward; that is, acting without complete certainty.

- *The ability to influence.* Having some talent for persuasion and enjoying power enable the OD practitioner to be successful; without it, he or she is likely to succeed in only minor ways in OD. Working with client systems on organization development and change is not for the faint of heart; intellectual and emotional engagement is a prerequisite for survival.

- *The ability to "read" a group or "read" the room.* Reading a group or room involves observing nonverbal behavior that does not conform to what people are saying; there is some disconnect between the audio and the video. OD consultants are always collecting data and inconsistent data are critical to developing a robust understanding of a client system.

- *The ability to confront difficult issues.* Much of OD work consists of exposing issues that organization members are reluctant to face. Sometimes, the most important function of an OD consultant is to serve as a "container" for undiscussable issues and to "hold" organization members in a safe place as they engage in difficult conversations.

- *The ability to support and nurture others.* This ability is particularly important in times of conflict and stress, as noted above. It is also critical just before and during a manager's first experience with team building.

- *The ability to listen well and empathize.* This is always important, an essential competency, and especially during interviews, in conflict situations, and when client stress is high.

- *The ability to recognize one's own feelings and intuitions quickly.* It is important to be able to distinguish one's own perceptions from those of the client and also be able to use these feelings and intuitions as interventions when appropriate and timely. We will consider this point in more detail in the section dedicated to developing expertise in self-as-instrument.

- *The ability to self-manage.* Working effectively as a consultant often means setting up your client to "look good" and get the credit; therefore, management of one's own ego is essential. Management of one's impatience is also required as change usually takes longer than planned and observable metrics of success are difficult to come by.

- *The ability to conceptualize.* It is necessary to think and express in understandable terms certain relationships, such as the cause-and-effect and if-then linkages that exist within the systemic context of the client organization. Models and frameworks can be supportive of this ability.

- *The ability to discover and mobilize human energy, both within oneself and within the client organization.* There is energy in resistance, for example, and the consultant's interventions are likely to be most effective when they tap existing energy within the organization and provide direction for the productive use of the energy.

- *The ability to teach or find that teachable moment and the capacity to create learning opportunities.* This ability should not be reserved for classroom activities, but should be utilized as part of the consultant role, within the mainstream of the overall change effort. Associated with this is the ability to learn in public. Consultants serve as role models for clients and if a consultant cannot allow him or herself to be vulnerable and learn in the moment, how can clients be expected to do so?

- *The ability to maintain a sense of humor, both on the client's behalf and to help sustain perspective.* Humor can be useful for reducing tension. It is also useful for the consultant to be able to laugh at himself or herself; not taking oneself too seriously is critical for maintaining perspective about an OD effort, especially because nothing ever goes exactly according to plan, even though OD is supposed to be a *planned* change effort.

In addition to these abilities, it is important, of course, for OD consultants to have self-confidence and to be interpersonally competent (Argyris, 1962); that is, to express feelings, own up, and experiment or take risks. Finally, we think it is helpful for consultants to have a sense of mission about their work as OD practitioners. They should believe that what they are doing is worthwhile and potentially helpful to others. This belief helps to sustain energy, to lessen feelings of loneliness and anxiety, and to provide a reason for continuing to work with organizations that appear recalcitrant and impossible to change.

OD Values

Following the line of thought and belief that OD constitutes culture change, it is obviously important that we understand the nature of organizational values as thoroughly as possible. We also need to understand the value system of the field of OD itself and the carriers of this professional culture—OD practitioners and consultants. Thus, in this section, we examine the values represented by the field of organization development.

We can gain some understanding of the values represented by OD by referring to the field's roots, especially sensitivity training (see Chapter 3, "Where Did Organization Development Come From?"). This method of education and change has a humanistic value orientation, the belief that it is worthwhile for people to have the opportunity throughout their lives to learn and develop personally toward a full realization and actualization of individual potential. Some people believe that this preference not only is worthwhile but also should be a right or entitlement.

Another OD value that came even more directly from sensitivity training is that people's feelings are just as important a source of data for diagnosis and have as much implication for change as do facts or so-called hard data and people's thoughts and opinions, and that these feelings should be considered as legitimate for expression in the organization as any thought, fact, or opinion.

Yet another OD value stemming from sensitivity training is that conflict, whether interpersonal or intergroup, should be brought to the surface and dealt with directly, rather than ignored, avoided, or manipulated. When sensitivity training was at the height of its popularity in the United States, Schein and Bennis (1965) stated what they considered to be its two main value systems: a spirit of inquiry and democracy.

The spirit of inquiry comes from the values of science. Two parts of it are relevant: the hypothetical spirit—being tentative checking on the validity of assumptions and allowing for error—and experimentalism—putting ideas or assumptions to the test. In sensitivity training, "all experienced behavior is subject to questioning and examination, limited only by the threshold of tolerance to truth and new ideas" (Schein & Bennis, 1965, p. 32). A corollary value mentioned by Schein and Bennis is being authentic in interpersonal relations.

The second main value system, the democratic value, has two elements: collaboration and conflict resolution through rational means. The learning process in sensitivity training is collaborative between participant and trainer, not a traditional authoritarian student-teacher relationship. By conflict resolution through rational means, Schein and Bennis did not mean that irrational behavior or emotion was off limits, but "that there is a problem-solving orientation to conflict rather than the more traditional approaches based on bargains, power plays, suppression, or compromise" (p. 34).

Most important—what Schein and Bennis called the "overarching and fundamental value" (p. 35)—is the matter of choice. Freedom from coercion and from the arbitrary exercise of authority is the most preferred end state of existence.

Schein and Bennis wrote about and espoused those values in the 1960s, when individualism, rebellion toward authority, and questioning the rights of certain traditional institutions were in vogue. What about OD today?

Similar to his work with Bennis in the 1960s, Schein (2014) addresses the values of OD today in his examination of the role of coercive persuasion in education and learning. The importance of Schein's analysis is that experiential learning of interpersonal, group, and interorganizational relationships, what he refers to as the "human side of enterprise, that is management and leadership" (p. 2) continue to be important components of OD. In his discussion, Schein emphasizes the importance of animating clients and students through valid and agreed-upon goals by involving them in the diagnostic and intervention process, always ensuring the matter of choice, just as he stated with Bennis almost 50 years earlier. However, while attending to the human side of organizational life remains an OD value, Schein asks, "Can a networked multicultural world design experiential learning settings that animate learners or will we invent yet another mode of learning without the intense face to face contact that animation seems to depend on?" (p. 23). We understand this question from Schein as a way of preserving OD values that began with sensitivity training at the same time as recognizing the opportunities for OD today.

Burke and colleagues (Church & Burke, 1993; Church, Burke, & Van Eynde, 1994) addressed the question of "what about OD today?" at the time of the second edition of this book and again, recently (Shull, Church, & Burke, 2013). Both times, they surveyed OD practitioners about their perceptions of the field, values, motivators, and intervention activities; the recent study compares the findings to the earlier one.

The current findings (Shull, Church, & Burke, 2013) were both similar to and different from findings in the 1993 study regarding perceptions of the field. Following are the five primary findings:

1. Practitioners once again reported a perceived weakening of traditional values in OD today, and the trend was significantly more pronounced than in the past, particularly regarding new entrants into the field.

2. Practitioners continue to agree that OD work should focus on business effectiveness and efficiency, and the perception that OD is too interpersonal, touchy-feely, or missionary in orientation has declined from years past.

3. Practitioners have aligned in greater numbers against the misuse of power and authority in organizational life and have become much more committed to their organizations.

4. Practitioners see coaching as an integral part of OD today.

5. Despite other trends, practitioners are very optimistic about the future of OD and only a fifth see the field in a state of crisis (pp. 13–20).

These findings as discussed by Shull et al. (2013) are relevant to our discussion of values, preparation for the role of OD consultant, and the future of OD. The perceived weakening of traditional values of OD, and that those with more experience viewed new colleagues in the field as lacking in academic preparation and without sufficient knowledge of how the current practice of OD is informed by early research and theory development, is addressed in the next section on preparation for the role of OD consultant. Regarding continued agreement that the focus of OD should be on business effectiveness and efficiency suggests some degree of clarity about the purpose of OD and is not surprising given the increased demand on HR and OD professionals to engage as business partners and demonstrate their capacity to add value as strategic thought partners. The finding that the commitment to addressing the misuse of power and authority in organizations is even stronger than it was 20 years ago may be related to the greater incidence (or reporting) of the abuse of power between 1993 and 2013 and the shift in organizational structures and accompanying models of authority. The finding that coaching was perceived as integral to OD is addressed in Chapter 13 and our view about the perception of optimism in the field is addressed in Chapter 14, "Organization Development and the Future."

Overall, we agree with Shull et al. (2013) about the importance of understanding the core values of the field as espoused by the founders of OD. As stated at the beginning, given that OD work is about culture change and culture change is about behavior, attitudes, and values, how can one engage in culture change—that is, OD work—without a firm grounding in the roots, and therefore values, of the field? As culture carriers, OD practitioners have a responsibility and obligation to represent the field accurately. In the next section, we provide our recommendations for requisite training and experience in OD.

Becoming an OD Consultant and Integrating OD Competencies into Other Organizational Roles

Like any other field that consists of applying skills and implementing a particular kind of practice, experience is the best teacher for OD practice—or rather, experience accompanied by related feedback is the most impactful. One can have numerous experiences, but unless one receives feedback about which experiences are more related to effective practice, then learning rarely occurs. Thus, one should try to obtain experience in and feedback on consultative activities.

As discussed in the section on values, in addition to experience, it is also necessary to learn the fundamentals of the field and to gain an understanding and appreciation for the history of OD. There is no substitute for academic learning and nonacademic training for becoming an OD consultant as well as for integrating OD competencies into other organizational roles.

Academic Learning

We suggest the following 12 areas to provide a good background for OD practice. These courses are fairly common, sometimes offered as a comprehensive OD curriculum within a university, and also available as stand-alone courses. Obtaining education in these domains would be most useful:

- *Organizational psychology or organizational behavior.* The former is typically offered in a department of psychology, the latter in a school of business or management. Either course provides the necessary background for understanding human behavior in an organizational context.

- *Organization theory.* This course should follow the basic course on organizational behavior or organizational psychology. Usually this kind of course helps one learn about organizational design, effectiveness (performance criteria), and the organization as a system.

- *Group dynamics.* This kind of course is a must. Organizations are composed of subsystems, usually in the form of work groups or teams. Understanding the theory, research, and conceptual aspects of group behavior as well as the applicability of this knowledge helps one understand the utility of groups and teams in organizations, and adds to one's understanding of system dynamics.

  Most group dynamics courses include an experiential component as it is virtually impossible to learn about group dynamics without actually experiencing group dynamics in the "here and now" followed by opportunities for reflection, meaning-making, and application work.

- *Organization development.* The course may not be called OD; instead it may be titled "organization change," "action research and consultation," "managing change," and so forth. Such courses usually include opportunities to learn specific skills associated with consultation as well as experience in data collection for diagnosis, feedback, and planned change.

- *Process consultation.* A course with this title is not likely to be available, but any course that provides an understanding of what process is and experience in working with it as a consultant would be useful. Sometimes this topic is covered in a group dynamics course and/or in an OD course. To clarify:

  > The process consultant seeks to give the client insight into what is going on around him, within him, and between him and other people. Based on such insight, the consultant then helps the client to figure out what he should do about the situation. But the core of this model is that the client must be helped to remain "pro-active," in the sense of retaining both the diagnostic and remedial initiative (Schein, 1988, p. 11).

  Identifying a course that would provide what Schein describes is what is most important.

- *Research methods.* Field research methods are preferable because they are the most applicable for learning about applied research, data collection and analysis in organizations, evaluation methods, and evidence-based practice.

- *Adult learning.* This type of course is useful for understanding how organization members may learn from their experiences on the job as well as for knowing more about the appropriate rationale for designing teaching and learning opportunities. A related course on *Training and Development* provides useful information about design of programs and about how to conduct certain learning activities associated with talent development.

- *Social equality and diversity in organizations.* As the world population changes, so does the demographic composition of organizations. As a result, work practices come under scrutiny and often require change and innovation; differences among and between individuals and groups must be addressed. Understanding how to leverage diversity and create inclusive work environments is an area of expertise that clients expect from OD practitioners.

- *Negotiation and conflict resolution.* Organization development and change often involves trying to gain alignment between and among individuals, teams, and organizations with conflicting interests. Additionally, culture change is usually concomitant with greater ambiguity and anxiety as well as fallout from unanticipated consequences; these conditions are often accompanied by an increase in conflict. Being well versed in the theories and techniques associated with negotiation and conflict resolution are requisite for the OD practitioner.

- *Coaching.* This kind of course can provide critical skills for specific help to individual organization members and often to a team or subunit within a client system. Coaching courses usually have a blended design focused on theory and practice.

- *Human resource management.* This course provides the necessary grounding in the organizational function that is most related to OD. A closely associated course is *Career Development* as OD consultants are frequently involved in designing career development programs and are involved in human resources planning and talent development.

- *Functions of organizations.* This course might be subtitled "crash course in business." Such a course is designed for students who have no background in business or in how organizations actually function. Thus, there are classes on accounting, finance, budgeting, operations, marketing, strategy, and the manager's role. It is a course about learning a new language as we believe strongly that to be effective as an organizational psychologist, in general, and as an organization consultant, in particular, one needs to know at least some of the basics about how organizations operate and function as well as the language of management.

We purposely limited ourselves to 12 areas, conforming to a typical master's degree program requiring 36 to 45 credits.

Nonacademic Training

Several professional development programs are offered by training organizations or by the continuing or executive education divisions of universities. These provide useful training in both the knowledge and skills appropriate to OD practice, but the weight is usually on the side of skill development. The following are five avenues or programs for developing oneself toward becoming an OD practitioner:

- *Laboratory training programs*
  - A program devoted to improving one's interpersonal competence—a T-group, Gestalt group, or something very similar.
  - Instead of emphasizing interpersonal development, a program that focuses on intrapersonal understanding. Because the primary instrument in OD work is the consultant practitioner, it is important that one know this instrument as well as possible.
  - A Tavistock group relations conference focused on learning group dynamics by examining behavior at the group level, and considering unconscious forces that influence individuals, groups, and systems. A group relations perspective enables OD consultant practitioners to diagnose organizational problems systemically, expanding options for interventions and solutions.

- *Organization development training programs*
  - OD programs usually provide an introduction to the field and practice in consulting. This type of program is ideal because it offers a safe environment for testing untried skills.
  - Advanced OD programs for professional development are designed for experienced OD practitioners and provide an opportunity for more advanced development and networking with experienced professionals.

- *Supervised experience*

  Sometimes such an experience is provided as part of a consultation skills training program; otherwise, one needs to consult with an actual client and arrange some form of supervision from an experienced OD consultant. Having a mentor is a related avenue for professional and personal development.

- *Internal consultant with large organization*

  An excellent way to get started in OD is to work for an organization that has an internal OD service for its managers. We emphasize *large* organizations because the opportunities would be greater and more varied. One may not be able to join an internal OD group immediately; given that, the entry job should be at least closely associated with OD work, such as learning and development, career development, talent development, or as a human resource generalist or human resource business partner. One can then develop a network that will facilitate entry to other OD opportunities such as supervised experience.

- *Professional associations*

  Belonging to and attending the meetings of certain associations devoted to OD can of course help one learn about and keep up with the field. Such organizations are the OD Network, the Association for Talent Development (formerly American Society for Training & Development), the Society for Human Resource Management, the Academy of Management Division of Organization Development and Change, the American Psychological Association Division of Consulting Psychology (Division 13) and the Society of Industrial and Organizational Psychology (Division 14), and regional groups of these associations in the United States and globally.

In the Executive Masters Program in Change Leadership at Teachers College, Columbia University, the curriculum reflects nine clusters of competencies culled from professional organizations that serve as arbiters of the basic requirements for professions related to change leadership. The nine clusters are the following:

- Knowledge of organizational frameworks and models, and systems thinking;
- Knowledge of the consulting cycle (entry and contracting, data collection, diagnosis, feedback, planning change, intervention, and evaluation);
- Knowledge of strategy and organization design;
- Leadership and management (knowledge, skills, and abilities);
- Applied research and evaluation;
- Ability to use self-as-instrument (to be reflective and self-examining);
- Awareness of group dynamics, power and authority dynamics, and diversity and intercultural dynamics;
- Individual and group facilitation and coaching skills; and
- Collaboration and conflict negotiation skills.

Engaging in academic and nonacademic training programs detailed here provides opportunities to develop these nine clusters of competencies.

Being an OD consultant means being a practitioner. We practice OD much as lawyers and physicians practice law and medicine, but there are no bar or boards to pass and there is no licensing procedure. Short of such a procedure, we believe that some combination of academic training and professional development is the next best approach to becoming an OD consultant.

Line managers who want to integrate OD knowledge and skills into their repertoire can pursue academic and nonacademic learning opportunities similar to individuals who want OD to be central to their professional identities. It would be important, however, for line managers to be aware that some of what is taught in academic and nonacademic OD programs requires translation before leveraging the knowledge and skills in service of more effective management and change leadership. Exploring the theory and research that under-girds evidence-based OD practice is akin to learning what informs evidence-based management. Based on our experience with executives across functions, sectors, and geographies via consulting, coaching, executive education programs, and our degree programs in Social-Organizational Psychology at Teachers College, Columbia University, integrating evidence-based management and evidence-based OD practice is an effective combination.

Self-as-Instrument

Taken together, the skills and abilities necessary to work as an OD consultant that have been discussed fall into four buckets: content knowledge, facilitation skill, personal characteristics, and expertise in self-as-instrument. We have allotted a special section to developing expertise in self-as-instrument for several reasons. First, content knowledge can be acquired through academic, and to a lesser extent through nonacademic, training. Similarly, facilitation skills can be learned by participation in laboratory and organization development training programs. Personal characteristics, as noted, are related to personality or basic temperament and can be enhanced through achieving a high level of self-awareness, specifically, and more generally, through developing emotional intelligence.

The Emotional Intelligence framework as developed by Goleman, Boyatzis, and McKee (2002) consists of a 2×2, with *Self* and *Social* on the vertical axis and *Awareness* and *Management* on the horizontal axis. Within each quadrant is a set of competencies: Self-Awareness includes Emotional Self-Awareness, Accurate Self-Assessment, and Self-Confidence; Self-Management includes Self-Management, Transparency, Adaptability, Achievement, Initiative, and Optimism; Social Awareness includes Empathy, Organizational Awareness, and Service; Relationship Management includes Inspiration, Influence, Developing Others, Change Catalyst, Conflict Management, and Teamwork and Collaboration. Many of these competencies are included in the section on Consultant Abilities and while we have made the case for their importance in working in the organization development and change arena, emotional intelligence is necessary for using oneself as an instrument in OD work. More specifically, developing expertise in self-as-instrument requires the capacity to not only be self-aware and self-manage, have social awareness, and manage relationships, but to also know *how* to use one's emotional intelligence and lived experience in the "here and now" in service of understanding, and working with, a client system.

Burke (1982, 1994) as well as Levinson (1972a) and others (Berg & Smith, 1985; Berg & Smith, 1988; Cheung-Judge, 2001; McCormick & White, 2000; Smith, 1995) have spoken of the self as the most important instrument an OD consultant has and as such, like any instrument, keeping it well tuned requires ongoing discipline, rigor, and practice. As noted in Chapter 6, "Understanding Organizations: The Process of Diagnosis," Levinson includes consultant observations and feelings as one set of information that adds to the diagnosis, and an example of using self-as-instrument data for diagnosis and intervention is an aspect of the case study in Chapter 8, "Understanding Organizations: Covert Processes."

Including consultant observations and feelings in the diagnosis, however, is a complex skill, as the consultant needs to act as a thermometer of sorts, able to discern what is about the self and what is about the client. It is for this reason that self-knowledge is essential. As stated in the Talmud, "You do not see things as they are but as you are." For example, if a consultant always feels anxious when entering a client system, anxiety may not be a differentiator about a particular client system. If, however, anxiety emerges as the consultant becomes more engaged with the client and it is not indicative of a common emotional tenor of the consultant, then it is more likely to be a data point about something inside the client system. Still though, we would not expect a consultant to do anything more than take note of the anxiety until he or she has other data with which to triangulate the anxiety (McCormick & White, 2000).

I (Noumair) have found using self-as-instrument most powerful when my experience in the client system aligns with data collected through other methods and I am able to include my experience in the dialogue when the client is struggling to engage in joint diagnosis with me. It is as if the client cannot deny my experience because it brings to life the very issues that the organization is attempting to address in the change effort. At such times, it is the consultant's marginality as discussed earlier (Margulies, 1978) that is critical to the veracity of the self-as-instrument data, and to the client perceiving it as legitimate. Its legitimacy is a key factor in making the diagnosis real for the client, thereby facilitating greater ownership of the issues to be addressed. If the consultant is perceived as too much a member of the client system, the data will not be seen as sufficiently differentiated from other organization members to be useful. If the consultant is seen as too distant from the client system, the self-as-instrument data may not be rich or nuanced enough to make a difference.

OD is a practice of art and craft as well as the application of behavioral science. It requires rigorous professional knowledge grounded in data-based research and practice. Developing expertise in using self-as-instrument is at the intersection of art, craft, and behavioral science and when expertly employed, it is one tool of data-based research and practice. The next section on reflective practice describes how to tune one's self-as-instrument as well as introduces other tools essential to the art and craft of OD practice.

Reflective Practice

Introduced by Schön in *The Reflective Practitioner* (1983), "[R]eflective practice is the capacity to reflect on action so as to engage in a process of continuous learning" (p. 62). It provides opportunities to critically review what has been successful in the past and what can be improved in the future. Gillette (1995), introducing reflection in general, and Schön's work in particular, defines reflection:

> The ability to reflect consists of being able to step out of an experience and generate, through a different perspective on that experience. It is not a flight from self but a dialogue with self. I often imagine it as the generation of an internal dialogue, between a temporarily created new "me" and the "me" who is filled with the experiences. It is sort of an internal debriefing process (p. 21).

This internal dialogue is what Schön is known for from his study of unusually competent performers. Schön introduced two concepts that are central to reflective practice: Reflection-in-Action and

Reflection-on-Action. Reflection-in-Action is the ability of a practitioner to "think on her or his feet." Within any given moment, when faced with a professional issue, a practitioner usually connects with his or her feelings, emotions, and prior experiences to attend to a situation in the moment. Connecting feelings and emotions with prior experiences is what allows a practitioner to use past learning in service of working differently in the present. In effect, reflective practitioners (and OD consultants) work as improvisation artists (Schein, 2013b; Schön, 1987).

Some examples of Reflection-in-Action include Self-as-Instrument as already discussed, Surfacing Undiscussables, and Getting on the Balcony (Heifetz & Linsky, 2002). Surfacing undiscussables refers to becoming aware in the moment of an "elephant in the room" that, if discussed, would be helpful to the task at hand, and then creating conditions for the important yet difficult conversation to occur. Often serving as a safe container for such conversations is one of the most important functions an OD consultant can serve.

Getting on the balcony, a concept introduced by Heifetz and Linsky (2002), involves getting off the dance floor and going to the balcony in order to temporarily pause the action and gain perspective. By doing so, one is then able to rejoin the dance floor with a greater sense of clarity having observed patterns of behavior and dynamics. It is an iterative process and if one can move swiftly between the dance floor and the balcony, metaphorically speaking, it is a tool for Reflection-in-Action. If going to the balcony takes one out of the action for a considerable period of time, it is a tool for Reflection-on-Action.

Reflection-on-Action occurs after an experience when a practitioner analyzes her or his reaction to a situation and explores the reasons for, and consequences of, her or his actions. This usually occurs through a documented reflection of the situation. Central to Schön's work is the idea that professional growth begins when the practitioner starts to view things with a critical lens and develops the capacity to doubt his or her behavior. Developing this capacity occurs as a result of cumulating experience as discernment can only occur as a result of examining oneself across differentiated situations.

Related to Reflection-on-Action, Argyris and Schön (1978) developed the concept of single and double loop learning. Single loop learning is when there is an action and a consequence of the action followed by another action. Cycles of single loop learning repeat themselves identically without interruption, even when the consequence of the action is not what was intended. Double loop learning is when there is an action, a consequence of the action, followed by reflection before the next action is taken. By establishing a cycle of action-reflection, reflection-action, a pause is created long enough to reflect and learn, hopefully producing better results the next time an action is taken.

Examples of Reflection-on-Action to create double loop learning are the Left-Hand Column Exercise, developed by Argyris and Schön (1974); After Action Reviews (AARs) and Before Action Reviews (BARs) (Darling, Parry, & Moore, 2005) as discussed in Chapter 11, "Does Organization Development Work?"; regularly keeping a journal in which one responds to questions that facilitate the identification of feelings and associated thoughts in order to "connect the dots"; and seeking feedback on a piece of work witnessed by a mentor, colleague, or coach. For an application of double loop learning to coaching, see Witherspoon (2014). All of these create a structure for reflecting on action and provide opportunities to learn from experience. As best stated by John Dewey (1938), "We do not learn from experience, we learn from reflecting on experience."

Conclusion

In this chapter, we have considered the values of the field and the role, characteristics, and abilities of the OD consultant. In the broadest sense, the role of the OD practitioner contains four functions, that of expert, educator or trainer, counselor or coach, and consultant. The consultant may behave in a directive manner, perhaps even as an advocate, or, at the opposite extreme, may behave very nondirectively, serving perhaps as a reflector, primarily raising questions. For the most part, however, the OD consultant serves in a facilitative capacity, helping clients learn how to learn, and learn how to change, in order to solve their own problems more effectively.

We also considered the role of the OD consultant from another perspective. Remaining marginal, at the boundary or interface between individuals, especially managers and direct reports, and between groups and subsystems, is critical to effective consultation, at least from the vantage point of organization development practice. In this marginal role, the consultant functions in an organic way, attempting to intervene in a timely manner and according to what the client needs at the time. Consulting organically means that the practitioner must use himself or herself as an instrument—sensing client need by paying attention not only to what may be observed but also to his or her own feelings and intuitions. This form of consultation is not easy and is highly dependent on the skills of the consultant and subject to bias according to the consultant's personal values and attitudes. Obviously, the effective OD consultant will be sensitive to these issues, be aware of what values are espoused by the field he or she represents, and work hard to be consistent in word and deed. Toward this ideal, we discussed the importance of shadow consultation as well as ongoing reflective practice in order to ensure that individuals keep their self-as-instrument well tuned throughout their professional practice.

In addition to considering the role of OD consultant as a professional identity, we also acknowledged that line managers are incorporating OD knowledge and skill into their repertoire as change is now a constant in contemporary organizational life. We included information on academic and nonacademic training that can facilitate entry into the field as well as how to develop OD competencies as an expansion of other organizational roles. The next chapter, "Coaching and Organization Development," addresses similar issues regarding coaching; that is, a role with its own professional identity as well as a skill set that is integrated into other roles across functions in organizations.

13

Coaching and Organization Development

An executive coaching engagement begins following a leadership development program in which the coach worked with the client on her multi-rater feedback. The client was recently promoted and coaching was offered as one means of support for her leadership transition. During the contracting process, the coach learns that not only is the client undergoing a leadership transition, the organization is challenged by the ambivalent succession of a beloved leader who is also the manager and longstanding sponsor and mentor of her client. While the coaching engagement is viewed by the organization as an individual level intervention, the coach recognizes that in order to facilitate a successful leadership transition of her client, she must also work on succession of the revered leader with the organization, with her client, and with the revered leader, himself, as the two are inextricably linked. Is this a coaching engagement or an organizational consultation or both?

As will be discussed in this chapter, we locate coaching as a component of OD and view this vignette of an actual case as indicative of the challenges that OD consultants and coaches must address. These are relatively new challenges because when the second edition of this book was published, 1994, coaching was just beginning to have a presence in organization development (OD).

Grant (2011) reported that although the first peer-reviewed article in coaching was published in 1937, publications of coaching-related research did not significantly increase until 1995, with outcome studies surging beginning in 2000. *Consulting Psychology: Theory and Practice* produced five special issues of executive coaching between 1996 and 2008 (Diedrich, 2008). Recounting the history of executive coaching, Maltbia, Marsick, and Ghosh (2014) note that the first professional association for coaching began in 1994. Nearly twenty years later, one of five major findings reported in a 2013 survey of OD practitioners was that coaching is seen as "valuable and relevant to the practice of OD" (Shull, Church, & Burke, 2013, p. 20).

Although it has emerged very rapidly, coaching remains young in its development and insufficiently bounded (Feldman & Lankau, 2005; Kauffman & Coutou, 2009; Pavur, 2013; Peterson, 2011). Numerous questions exist concerning the differences among coaching, therapy, consulting, mentoring, and training (Alderfer, 2014; Evers, Brouwers, & Tomic, 2006; Kauffman & Coutou, 2009; Schein, 2000). There are also concerns that anyone can identify as a coach, be paid for services, and perform poorly without sanction. Further, how to classify coaching—as an intervention within organizational consultation, as a role, or as its own profession—is also under consideration in the literature (Sperry, 2008). More recently, deHaan et al. (2013) stated, "It is apparent that the coaching field is in a state of flux and only just beginning to be regulated as a profession" (p. 41).

Several efforts are under way to address these concerns; notably, the Graduate School Alliance for Executive Coaching (GSAEC) is working to advance executive and organizational coaching as an academic discipline (Maltbia et al., 2014). A study to identify coaching competencies by two divisions within the American Psychological Association—the Society of Consulting Psychology (SCP) and the Society for Industrial and Organizational Psychology (SIOP)—is in progress. The expectation is that the results will be used to develop a competency model to serve as a guide for psychologists regarding the basic knowledge and skills required for effective coaching. Benefits will accrue to consumers of coaching and their organizations, and to psychologists and graduate training programs in psychology.

With the nascent state of coaching, in this chapter we consider coaching as it is currently practiced. We examine coaching as a set of competencies within the role of OD consultant, as a function within the role of internal consultant, as a role with its own professional identity, external coach, and as a system-level intervention. We focus on coaching roles in which the coach has no formal authority over a client. Across roles and contexts, we discuss types of coaching and coaching process, including our point of view on coaching. Concluding thoughts focus on abilities, skills, and knowledge domains that are requisite for coaching as well as suggested learning opportunities.

Definitions

The word "coach" dates back to the 1500s when it referred to a carriage that moved valuable people from where they were to where they wanted to be. Although this concept remains true today, coaching as an enterprise is fast moving and a case in which practice is well ahead of theory and research (Bennett, 2006; Evers et al., 2006; Feldman & Lankau, 2005). Coaching has come to have multiple meanings, spanning a number of disciplines and domains (Sperry, 2008, 2013). As a point of departure, we define coaching as a process of learning and development that leads to new perspectives, attitudes, behaviors, and skills. We view coaching as a tool to support individual, team, and organization learning, and as a lever for change. Our focus is on coaching that is conducted within the domain of organizational life.

One origin of coaching is sports, where every athlete has a coach. In sports, coaching is an integral component of work, the game, and performance, whereas that is not true in organizations. Linking it to sports, however, allows coaching to be viewed as normative and absent any taboo. This association, we believe, is one driver of the explosion of executive and organizational coaching. Coaching is an acceptable way of helping individuals, teams, and organizations improve performance.

The idea of a taboo emerges from the seeming similarity of coaching with therapy. Kauffman and Coutou (2009) conducted a study in which they examined perceptions of similarities and differences among coaching, consulting, and therapy. In their report, coaching is differentiated from therapy as it focuses on individual performance in an organizational context rather than on diagnosis and treatment of dysfunctionality. This perception that therapy is about fixing something that is personally broken in an individual is the stigma that threatens coaching. Depending on the organizational culture and the meaning of coaching in that organization, engaging in coaching may be viewed as treatment for the dysfunctional behavior of an individual. The opposite is also true; in some organizations, coaching may be viewed as a reward for high performance and symbolic of an organization's investment in an individual.

As a licensed psychologist who was initially trained as a therapist and later as a consultant and coach, I (Noumair) can attest to the differences between therapy and coaching from first-hand experience. With my first forays into executive coaching, I was able to facilitate greater self-awareness in my clients; they appreciated my empathetic responses to their organizational challenges. My colleagues would send all their "difficult" coaching cases to me, which was an implicit way of stating that what they thought the client really needed was therapy. While increasing self-awareness was part of the task of coaching and I was competent to work with "difficult" cases, it often felt as if I was doing psychotherapy at work and because it was labeled "executive coaching" it was acceptable to the executives and viewed as appropriate by their organizations. However, my work as an executive coach improved when I invited clients to align enhanced self-awareness, behavioral change, and strategic organizational objectives. This shift meant that the focus of coaching was on the individual in his or her organizational role inside an organizational system, and as a result, the boundary conditions for the work were clear and in service of both the individual and the organization. The adjustments I made to my practice of coaching are best described in Dotlich and Cairo's (1999) book, *Action Coaching*. "Action coaching is a process that fosters self-awareness and that results in the motivation to change, as well as the guidance needed if change is to take place in ways that meet organizational needs" (p. 18).

Further, Dotlich and Cairo describe differences between what they refer to as *traditional coaching* versus *action coaching*. The culmination of these shifts from traditional coaching to action coaching is that coaching focuses on an individual in an organizational role within a specific context and highlights the importance of establishing a coaching contract that has alignment between an individual's goals and the organization's goals as central to the work. These differences in role dictate a different kind of practice and reflect my experience of moving from therapist to executive coach.

In the Kauffman and Coutou (2009) report, coaching is differentiated from consulting as having more of a focus on individual performance within an organizational context rather than a direct focus on organizational performance. A consultant's responsibility is to the organization as a whole even when the consultation may be with a subset of the organization. A coach's responsibility is to the individual while holding a systems view of the context as well as the client's perception of the context. And although it is true that as a rule coaching is an individual-level intervention, it must not be overlooked that coaching is always conducted within context. The context can be cultural, hierarchical, interdependent, values-based, and a myriad of other aspects of one's environment. A fundamental of coaching, therefore, is to help the client articulate how the context influences his or her actions, and how one might in turn influence these con-textual factors. In this regard, it is essential that the coach and client consider the context in which coaching takes place, including who initiated coaching, terms of the contract including scope and timeframe, metrics, limits of confidentiality, and who is responsible for paying for coaching services. Boundary conditions differentiate coaching and consulting from therapy. Coaches and consultants usually work with clients at the client's organization, whereas therapy occurs in the therapist's office. Organizations usually contract and pay for coaching and consulting, whereas therapy is paid for by the individual or through medical insurance. Because coaching is usually located in a client's organization and paid for by a client's organization, the organization is an ever-present factor influencing the purpose of coaching and the coaching relationship.

Although confidentiality is an aspect of all three helping relationships (therapy, consulting, and coaching), therapists are bound by a different code of ethics than coaches and consultants. In practice, this means that in therapy, confidentiality is only broken without prior consent if the client is at risk for harming her/himself or others. In coaching, confidentiality is more limited as the contract usually involves multiple parties—the client, the manager, and an HR professional—and must be negotiated.

It is also important to differentiate coaching from mentoring. Alderfer (2014), discussing the classic work of Levinson, Darrow, Klein, Levinson, and McKee (1978) and Levinson and Levinson (1996), makes a case for the original meaning of mentoring:

The relationship consists of senior people helping junior colleagues develop the younger person's sense of personal authority based on *the junior person's Dream of themselves in a mature adult role.* It is decidedly not imposing (or subtly promoting) an organization's or a mentor's version of what that person should become. It is helping the younger person listen to their inner voice and learn to act in accord with it. It is a disservice to both protégé and mentor if the older person consciously or inadvertently acts otherwise. When this occurs, neither protégé nor mentor will reap the benefits of the relationship, which fundamentally are intrinsic for both parties (p. 7).

From Alderfer's discussion of Levinson's work on mentoring, the differences between coaching and mentoring are clear. Coaching is fundamentally about improving performance, and in the context of organizational life, the client will not be the sole arbiter of providing evidence for improved performance. The manager and HR professional usually determine the metrics for improved performance based on organizational goals rather than on the client's *Dream* (Levinson et al., 1978; Levinson & Levinson, 1996). Another difference between mentoring and coaching is the source of authority. In mentoring relationships as discussed by Alderfer (2014), authority emanates from the protégé. In coaching relationships, authority is shared by the coach, the client, and the organizational sponsor of the work.

Authority relations also help to distinguish training and coaching. Training offers another avenue for leadership development and performance improvement. The organization and the trainer drive the agenda more than the individual seeking development (Evers et al., 2006). Trainers provide learning opportunities that are designed for groups rather than individuals and as such must have broader appeal to larger audiences usually providing actionable information, instruction, and advice (deHaan et al., 2013). Coaching, in contrast, is a customized solution tailored uniquely for an individual client and co-created by the coach, the client, and the organizational sponsor of the work.

Types of Coaching

Having differentiated coaching from therapy, consulting, mentoring, and training, it is important to discuss types of coaching. Peterson (2011) in the *Handbook of Industrial-Organizational Psychology* presents a taxonomy of four types of coaches: *feedback, insight and accountability, content,* and *development-process* coaches. We discuss each type within Peterson's frame (2011) and elaborate on its relevance to OD work.

Feedback coaches (Peterson, 2011) focus on facilitating understanding of results from assessments, such as multi-rater feedback, personality, emotional intelligence, learning styles, learning agility, interpersonal relations, communication preferences, conflict style, and cultural awareness, with the aim of creating a development plan that can be implemented and monitored until goals are accomplished. "Assessment is an essential element of coaching. It is important because people in the workplace tend to avoid frankness when they deal with one another, especially when they interact with people to whom they report—bosses and those who formally evaluate and pay them" (Peltier, 2010, p. 1). Relatedly, Hogan (2006) argues that assessment should be of a leader's reputation rather than identity, as individuals are notoriously poor self-raters.

Assessment-anchored coaching engagements are usually brief, one or two sessions either as independent assignments or may occur as part of a leadership development program. Although additional research is needed on all aspects of coaching, there is some agreement that multi-rater feedback with coaching or feedback facilitation is more effective in increasing self-awareness and perceived behavioral change than reviewing multi-rater feedback alone (Luthans & Peterson, 2003; Nowack & Mashihi, 2012; Siefert, Yukl, & McDonald, 2003; Smither, London, Flautt, Vargas, and Kucine, 2003). The best use of multi-rater feedback is as a catalyst for important conversations, and working with a feedback coach can provide the often much-needed support for important conversations.

An example of multi-rater feedback as a catalyst for important conversations occurred with a client that I (Noumair) coached in a leadership development program. During a coaching session focused on reviewing his multi-rater feedback, the client expressed rage at his direct reports for not sharing their feedback with him directly but instead anonymously responding to a survey online. Observing his body language and hearing his language—pounding his fist, raising his voice, and expressing anger at their "cowardly behavior"—I suggested that if this is how he might have behaved had they shared their feedback directly with him, I understood why they did not. His anger then expanded to include me. After completing the coaching engagement within the program, with some trepidation I followed up with him one month later. At that time I learned that although the program, and especially the multi-rater feedback and coaching, had been emotionally painful for him, it did lead to important conversations. He returned to work and initiated a conversation with his team about the feedback given to him. A radical departure from his usual way of leading and managing, he invited dialogue and created space for shared action planning. Moreover, he shared his feedback with his wife and daughter, and they said that he behaved similarly at home as he did at work. That was the important conversation that led to a change in his behavior and also fueled his motivation to make changes in both domains, changes he was sure would be sustainable.

Another function that feedback coaches serve within OD is to support organization culture change by coaching in company-specific leadership development programs. Programs of this kind typically include a multi-rater feedback instrument custom designed to make explicit leadership practices that reflect the behaviors, attitudes, and values of the organization's desired state. In turn, the leadership practices help to create a shared definition of effective leadership and a common language for performance feedback across the company. By working with executives in leadership development programs, coaches support executives in learning how to implement desired leadership practices, provide consistent feedback on agreed upon leadership behaviors, and initiate meaningful conversations in service of organizational culture change.

Insight-accountability coaches (Peterson, 2011) focus on helping a client identify goals related to a future desired state and a plan for achieving those goals. Important to this type of coaching is creating an accountability plan that is feasible and owned by the client. For example, imagine a participant who, at the conclusion of a leadership development program, is energized to implement her learning and change her behavior. Feeling more self-possessed with action plan in hand, she returns to the same environment she worked in prior to the program. Unless her plan includes responding to the context in new ways, the insight she gained in the program may quickly fade. Insight-accountability coaches are helpful in this regard as short-term goals with accompanying action plans and regular meetings can support the learning gained in a leadership development program and enable the client to strategize new responses to her old context.

Content coaches (Peterson, 2011) are subject matter experts who coach individuals in a content area such as strategy or on a specific skill set such as executive presentation skills. An example from executive education involves ex-theatre professionals teaching leadership presence and storytelling to participants. At the end of a daylong workshop, participants stand and deliver their leadership story, with leadership presence, in effect, providing initial evidence that learning has occurred. An important consideration, however, is the extent to which knowledge obtained or skills mastered through content coaching are transferred to the workplace, and sustained over time.

Development-process coaches (Peterson, 2011), in contrast to content coaches, are focused on facilitating learning related to individual and organizational behavior and usually have a sequential coaching process that they follow, similar to OD consultants adhering to phases of consulting. As noted by Peterson, "Coaches in this category often have backgrounds in psychology or other behavioral sciences, extensive consulting experience, and significant life experience dealing with people and their development" (p. 530). These characteristics are noted because development-process coaching has a broader mandate than a specific content area or skill set, which is usually best served by coaches with more experience.

Similar to Peterson's typology, Witherspoon and White (1996) conceptualized executive coaching by differentiating four agendas: coaching for skills to develop competence in relation to a specific job (content), coaching for performance to enhance and increase an executive's functioning in her or his current role (insight-accountability), coaching for development in which learning is focused on a future role (development-process), and coaching for an executive's agenda—for example, achieving better work-life balance or increasing emotional intelligence.

More recently, Witherspoon (2014) introduced double loop coaching (DLC), which applies the Argyris & Schön (1978) concept of double loop learning to coaching. As discussed in Chapter 12, "The Organization Development Consultant," double loop learning is foundational to reflective practice (Schön, 1983) and serves the same function in coaching; it is a framework for learning from experience. Witherspoon differentiates DLC from single loop coaching that focuses solely on coaching for performance to achieve results. He states, "In contrast, double-loop coaching requires leaders to reflect critically on their thinking, assess their reactions and their frame of reference (which may inadvertently contribute to problems), and then consider change" (p. 262). Given its roots in reflective practice, it seems likely that double loop coaching will be integrated into OD practice as well as a stand-alone framework for coaching and leader development.

Coaching Process

Having reviewed different types of coaching, we now discuss the coaching process. Many coaching models emphasize steps or phases similar to action research: entry and contracting; data collection and feedback; action planning; implementation and follow-through; evaluation, including debriefing and termination of the contract or recycling through the phases.

O'Neill's (2007) four-step process is useful, because in addition to emphasizing a primary task for each phase, a set of core principles guide executive coaching. The principles are coaching with *backbone and heart. Backbone* is about saying what your position is, whether it is popular or not, and *heart* is about staying in relationship and reaching out even when the relationship is in conflict. Given that difficulties in interpersonal relationships are often the catalyst for coaching, experiencing *backbone and heart* in the coaching relationship has the potential to transform relationships for the client outside of the coaching relationship.

These principles are evident in the four phases of coaching: *contracting, planning, live action coaching,* and *debriefing.* The primary task in *contracting* is to find a way to be a partner and establish a working alliance. It is the most important phase as it defines what the coach and client are going to do and how they are going to do it. It is also the most delicate as questions abound for both coach and client regarding what it will be like to work together.

Planning involves interacting with the client as a partner while keeping the client as owner of the issue. At its core, coaching is a helping relationship and helping involves facilitating and supporting a client owning his or her concerns. If the coach facilitates ownership by the client at the outset, ownership will likely continue with the client collaborating as an owner of the coaching process as well as ownership of the solution.

Live action coaching involves making use of the here and now and requires that the coach have expertise in using self-as-instrument (Chapter 12). O'Neill refers to the task of live action coaching as: "Strike while the iron is hot. Live action coaching is more like improvised jazz than a choreographed dance. You intervene in unexpected yet useful ways to help your client achieve his goal in the session" (p. 175). Live action coaching, then, is similar to consulting to a loosely coupled system (Chapter 10, "Understanding and Changing Loosely Coupled Systems") in which improvisation is also required.

Live action coaching often occurs when shadowing a client, for example, attending a meeting in a client's workplace and while observing him or her in action, the coach shares an observation with the expressed purpose of increasing awareness in the moment, shifting the dynamics at play, and facilitating behavior change. Live action coaching also occurs in the work between coach and client absent observers. More than any other phase, live action coaching requires trust as coach and client are working in the here and now in which the next moment in time is unknown (Kagan, 1984).

Debriefing focuses on reviewing what occurred during the coaching engagement and specifically what was learned, about the client individually and about the environment in which the client is working. This phase is akin to reflective practice, specifically reflection-on-action (Chapter 12). As such, identifying what was learned and how the learning will be carried forward is what makes coaching sustainable.

Coaching Roles and Contexts

Having defined coaching, differentiated it from other helping relationships, and identified types of coaching and coaching processes, we now discuss coaching roles and contexts. We consider three roles: coach as one function within the broader role of OD consultant, coach as one function within the broader role of internal consultant, and external coach. Regarding context, we discuss coaching as an individual level intervention inside an organizational system and as a system level intervention in which the focus is on creating a coaching culture.

OD Consultant as Coach

As one component of an OD consultant's role, coaching occurs within the boundaries of an OD consultation as an intervention employed to support accomplishment of the overall objectives. Thus, consultants and practitioners must have the skills needed to coach individuals, work pairs, and teams. While coaching may not be part of the formal, explicit contract with an OD client, it is expected that coaching will be required as the change process unfolds. Given the complexity of organization change, the nature of resistance, the likelihood of unintended consequences and subsequent adaptations, coaching as a component of an OD engagement is often necessary. Furthermore, the aims of coaching are consistent with those of OD. Whitmore (2009) defines coaching as, "…unlocking people's potential to maximize their own performance. It is helping them to learn rather than teaching them" (p. 10). This view of coaching, focused on helping an individual to learn, is similar to OD as a process of helping organizations learn, and more specifically, learn how to change.

Schein, originator of process consultation (1987; 1988; 1999; Chapters 3 and 12, "Where Did Organization Development Come From?" and "The Organization Development Consultant," respectively), defines coaching as: "a set of behaviors on the part of the coach (consultant) that helps the client to develop a new way of seeing, feeling about, and behaving in situations that are defined by the client as problematic" (2000, p. 19). He continues by stating that he sees coaching as a "subset of consultation and believes the coach should have the ability to move easily between the roles of process consultant, content expert, and diagnostician/prescriber" (2000, p. 17).

We agree with Schein and offer an example that illustrates the use of coaching within a consulting project. As part of an OD engagement, I (Noumair) coached the leader of an organization as it became apparent that she needed to further develop her emotional intelligence. Rather than only trusting her head, she needed to also intuit the feelings of her team and to lead in ways that would foster greater engagement. Rather than taking an authoritarian stance, she needed to invite participation. Changes in her behavior occurred as a result of coaching her in the context of the OD work; it became clear to her that if she wanted to lead a culture change, she would have to behave differently. The behavior that was required was not her natural inclination; it required greater emotional intelligence (Goleman, Boyatzis, & McKee, 2002); that is, more self-awareness and social awareness and a greater capacity for self-management and relationship management. Coaching was an iterative process that occurred simultaneous to the OD work and because it was concurrent, the leader was able to see the impact of her new behavior on her colleagues as well as the organizational culture change that was in progress. As described by Schein, I was able to shift roles throughout the engagement, sometimes acting as coach, other times as process consultant, and, less frequently, as diagnostician/prescriber. Although coaching was emergent and required contracting midstream, it was no less integral to accomplishing the objectives of the OD engagement.

Coaching is also a component of OD when creating a new culture is the goal and leadership development is the primary strategy; for example, with a merger of two organizations. In such cases, organizations may develop a leadership development program designed for their senior most executives as a means of bringing together key powerbrokers of the organization with the intent of increasing buy-in with the new direction. The CEO and senior team usually lead the program, creating opportunities for the delivery of key messages regarding the organization's future and opportunities for dialogue among senior executives. In addition, assessment-anchored coaching may be used to support individual leadership development of participants.

Coaches are engaged to work with participants to understand their assessment results and to facilitate the alignment of individual development goals with organization development goals.

Both internal and external coaches support OD initiatives by coaching in such leadership development programs.

Internal Coach

Coaching is an individual-level intervention conducted by internal practitioners within organizations, usually situated in Human Resources, Organization Development, and Learning and Development functions. The most common aims of internal coaching are to support leadership development and improve or enhance individual and organizational performance. As noted by Frisch (2001), although some professionals in the functions noted above would say that coaching has always been part of their role, internal coaching as a recognized function inside organizations has gained more recognition in tandem with the rapid growth of executive coaching. Frisch provides the following definition:

> Internal coaching is a one-on-one developmental intervention supported by the organization and provided by a colleague of those coached who is trusted to shape and deliver a program yielding individual professional growth. From the standpoint of setting standards, however, there are several implications of this definition that should be made explicit. Internal coaches should be outside the usual chain of command of those they coach, to differentiate it from the job coaching that all effective managers do. Also, whereas external coaches usually use a standardized assessment at the beginning of coaching applicable to a wide range of situations, internal coaches can often be more flexible. They will know extensive background information about the situation and have access to the results of organizational processes, such as performance appraisals and multi-rater feedback surveys. They can therefore shape an assessment that targets the key development issues without overmeasuring. Finally, derived from both the importance of a trusted relationship and the presence of a

development plan, multiple coaching meetings are assumed. A single chat may be interesting and useful but should not be defined as a coaching relationship (p. 242).

Frisch's definition of internal coaching reveals that the advantages of internal coaching are also the disadvantages. Having familiarity with the context in which a client works can be a benefit as one has knowledge of the organization, its position in the external environment, mission and strategy, leadership, and culture as well as information and perceptions of the client and the client's reputation; it can facilitate the work because much is already known. However, for this knowledge to truly be an advantage, the coach and client must explore the client's perceptions of the organization and the situation and not assume that because they both work in the same organization, they actually work in the *same* organization. Although it might seem like an obvious best practice, internal coaches must overcome the perception that because they are internal they have a biased point of view about the organization and about the internal client.

One difference between internal and external coaches is that external coaches are immediately perceived as credible because they are external and therefore not viewed as "contaminated" by being a member of the same organization.

Another difference between internal and external coaches is that internal coaches have relationships that may interfere with the task of coaching. As aptly stated by Hunt and Weintraub (2006), "The internal coach does...face a political landscape slightly different from that of the external coach. Presumably with more at stake, it may be difficult for the internal coach to 'speak truth to power'" (p. 20).

We have found that partnerships between externals and internals, similar to partnerships between internal and external consultants, may be best for the client and for the organization as the combination of insider knowledge with an outsider perspective leverages the positionality of each role in relation to the client and the organization. Such partnerships, however, are expensive and therefore more likely to be implemented solely for senior executives and organization leaders.

External Coach

Similar to internal coaching, organizations hire external coaches to work with executives to support their leadership development and improve or enhance performance. However, some organizations employ external coaches as a last-ditch effort before exiting an employee or as a way to outsource difficult conversations regarding development feedback that ought to be part of a manager's role. External coaches are also engaged in service of complex and complicated political issues because they are external, and therefore not part of the organizational hierarchy and political landscape. It is precisely because they are not part of the ongoing organization that external coaches have more freedom to discuss the "undiscussable"; their outsider status serves the individual and the organization. As executives advance and their power and authority increase, their colleagues are less likely to tell them the truth (Peltier, 2010); in these cases, the value of an inner circle to offer a third opinion (Joni, 2004) or an external coach increases as well.

An example of how external coaches may be used in service of a manager's or organization's agenda is a case in which I (Noumair) was in the process of being hired by an organization to coach someone whom I had coached in a leadership development program sponsored by the company. I was informed that before I was hired, my potential client's manager wanted to have a "chemistry" conversation with me, which I assumed meant that the manager wanted to vet me. After speaking to the manager for some time, he began to close the conversation and I noted my surprise that I thought he had wanted to vet me and we did not seem to engage in that process. He said that vetting was not the intention. Instead, he wanted to give me his view of the issues with my potential client before I was actually hired as a coach because once in the role of his direct report's coach, I would have a different relationship with him as my client's manager. He was explicit that he wanted to have his say before we were in a formal, contractual relationship in which he knew that the working agreements would dictate a different discourse between us. He said that after the coaching engagement ended he would talk with me, offline, and I could tell him if he was "right." The conversation provided me with a plethora of data about my client's manager, the relationship between my client and his manager, and the culture of the organization. I learned that communication is largely indirect, difficult feedback is given by a coach rather than a manager, and that being "right" is very important, and perhaps more so, than resolving conflict. Understanding these dynamics enabled me to enter the coaching engagement with a more informed sense of the manager's expectations, his views of my client, and what work was necessary if we were to align my client's goals, his manager's goals, and the goals of the organization. As the coaching ensued, I was able to work with my client as well as with him and his manager as a work pair because I understood from the outset what the explicit, and implicit, expectations were of coaching and what role I, as an external coach, served for the organization.

While initial conversations with a client's manager are not always as revealing as the one in the example, external coaching engagements do involve contracting with multiple parties (usually a client, client's manager, and HR professional), identifying agreed-upon change objectives, and negotiating boundary conditions for work. Each of these tasks provides an external coach with an opportunity to learn about the client, the client's manager, and the HR professional, individually and collectively, and also about the culture of the organization.

In the above instance, the stated reason I was hired as an external coach was to support my client's leadership development and increase his performance. However, it was also the case that the difficult feedback regarding his performance was outsourced to me rather than addressed by his manager. Given the culture of polite conversation, indirect feedback, and the importance of being right rather than resolving conflict, an external coach was viewed as the appropriate intervention. As I came to understand these issues, I explored them with my client and his manager and at that point, I no longer felt as if I was in collusion with my client's manager. I felt I could use my external position as leverage for accomplishing individual and organizational objectives.

Coaching Culture

Coaching is also a system intervention in which an organization develops a coaching culture. Organizations create coaching cultures as part of overall culture change initiatives, which is the primary purpose of OD. Rather than utilizing coaching as a stand-alone intervention, coaching is intentionally integrated into the fabric of the organization; that is, into "how we do things around here" (Deal & Kennedy, 1982). In such cases, coaching can help ensure that actual organizational behavior is assessed against espoused behavior (Argyris & Schön, 1974).

Several definitions of coaching culture exist in the literature. Clutterbuck and Meggison (2005) define a coaching culture as, "Coaching is the predominant style of managing and working together, and where a commitment to grow the organization is embedded in a parallel commitment to grow the people in the organization" (p. 19). Meggison and Clutterbuck (2006) offer six dimensions of a coaching culture, which can be assessed over time with the intent of answering the question: "To what extent is your organization as a whole (or the part of it you are interested in) moving to integrate coaching into its deep processes of performance and renewal?" (p. 233). The six dimensions are: "1. Coaching linked to business drivers. 2. Being a coachee is encouraged and supported. 3. Provide coach training. 4. Reward and recognize coaching. 5. Systemic perspective. 6. The move to coaching is managed" (p. 233).

For Hunt and Weintraub (2006), "A coaching organization makes effective and regular use of coaching as a means of promoting both individual development and organization learning in the service of the organization's larger goals" (p. 15). In such a coaching culture (Hunt & Weintraub, 2006), everyone in the organization believes that learning is critical to individual and organizational success. Decision making is developed closest to those who implement the decisions and individuals are given freedom to take risks and set their own goals. Having a mentor or a coach is viewed positively, and people are encouraged to seek mentoring or coaching support at various stages in their career and for various reasons. Leaders of the organization use a nondirective leadership style; that is, they use a similar coaching style with direct reports as they use with peers. Developing others and creating a learning environment are major responsibilities of managers. In this environment, peers coach one another to share knowledge, to pass on expertise to help one another, and also to raise their own standards and general standards of professionalism.

Both descriptions of coaching cultures are consistent with OD and are offered here as a means of conceptualizing coaching as a system-level intervention as OD practitioners must be able to intervene across multiple levels within the same organization. An example is an OD engagement that began by my (Noumair) working with the senior team and ended by my working with the whole organization to create a coaching culture. In that organization, the idea for creating a coaching culture emerged from trying to increase the level of engagement of employees with lower rank and less tenure. Rather than an organizational culture depicted by a lack of psychological safety in which there was fear and anxiety about speaking in public, the ideal culture for this organization would be more relaxed and encouraging of spontaneous contributions; employees would freely share their ideas. Colleagues would support one another's work by offering information, expertise, and learning from past experience. A learning orientation, as opposed to a performance orientation, would be the modus operandi. Throughout the organization, learning would occur in peer relationships as often as in hierarchical relationships, the quality of strategic thinking and dialogue would be enhanced, and ultimately, individual, team, and organizational performance would improve.

In order to work toward the ideal state as depicted above, the organization engaged in a combination of strategies and practices discussed by Meggison and Clutterbuck (2006) and Hunt and Weintraub (2006). Additionally, this was an organization already using the Burke-Litwin model (1992) to guide the overall culture change and the decision to create a coaching culture easily mapped onto the model. First, the senior team decided that creating a coaching culture would support the overall culture change that was already in process; that is, alignment of the transformational boxes of the Burke-Litwin model. Having made the decision, the first step was to invest in training the entire staff in coaching. Once all members of the organization were learning new skills together, they spontaneously began to practice coaching with each other. By learning together, the climate began to shift toward more openness and participation; staff appeared to have more energy. These levers for change comprise the spine of the Burke-Litwin model, the center boxes aligned vertically: leadership, management practices, work unit climate, motivation, and individual and organizational performance.

As this organization continued on its journey toward creating a coaching culture, it used learning together as one means to accomplish their culture change objectives. Similar to Hunt and Weintraub (2006), they intentionally linked individual development and organizational learning to the organization's performance, and similar to Meggison and Clutterbuck (2006), they implemented four of the six dimensions of a coaching culture; that is, encouraging and supporting coaching, providing coach training, embracing a systemic perspective, and managing coaching. It is significant that the two dimensions that were lagging behind the others were linking coaching to business drivers and recognizing and rewarding coaching. Although not simple, and certainly not linear in positive growth, the steps they did take enabled them to recover more easily when they did revert to old behaviors that slowed their progress toward their "ideal" state.

Point of View

First and foremost, we adhere to the Lewin formula (1951), Bf P/E: Behavior is a function of the interaction between a person and his or her perceived environment. Although the coaching conversation may be a dialogue between two individuals, other people as well as contextual factors are also present in the minds of the coach and client. For this reason, we contract for collecting data through the use of assessments and we view assessment results as data about the "person" component of the Lewin formula (Burke & Noumair, 2002). Self-ratings on a multi-rater feedback assessment are one source of data of an individual's perception of her/himself in the environment. Multi-rater feedback contributes to an environmental perspective by providing data on how those in his or her surroundings perceive an individual; for example, manager, peers, direct reports, and customers/clients.

Analyzing the environment means applying a systems perspective in which the focus of coaching is a person in an organizational role inside an organizational system. A systems perspective includes the conceptual framework introduced in Chapter 8, "Understanding Organizations: Covert Processes," which combines the use of group relations (psychodynamic theory, a group-as-a-whole level of analysis, and social-structural concepts) with OD frameworks and concepts. Including "Beneath the Surface of the Burke-Litwin Model" allows access to covert processes, as important in coaching as in OD work. The focus on perceptions of the environment and covert processes requires that a coach, similar to an OD consultant, maintain a well-tuned self-as-instrument. This conceptual framework creates space for considering the links between emotional processes, group development, and organizational behavior.

Holding a systems perspective allows a client to consider the impact of environmental forces, both overt and covert, and as a result removes some pressure from an individual shouldering all of the responsibility for a situation, problem, or challenge. First, taking the context into account usually changes the kinds of questions that are asked; questions shift from why a situation occurred to how it occurred. Second, when feedback is focused more on role rather than on person, it provokes less defensiveness. It allows unconscious and covert processes to surface and become more conscious and overt. Third, as a result, once systemic factors are understood and responsibility is shared, individuals are usually more able to own their contribution to the situation, problem, or challenge. Finally, by considering patterns of behavior across contexts, clients learn what part of any given situation, problem, or challenge is about the person and what part is about the context. In this way, clients, too, come to hold a Lewinian perspective, which contributes to making their learning more sustainable.

The following example helps to illuminate our approach to coaching. A woman underrated herself on 50 percent of items on a multi-rater feedback survey and rather than employ an intrapersonal explanation such as low self-esteem or being excessively self-critical (common explanations for underrating), she stated that her ratings reflected the fact that she was hired to lead change in the organization and the organization was change-resistant. Thus, she evaluated herself against her charge and found herself wanting. She perceived her ratings as an accurate evaluation of her performance. Interestingly, her raters, in the same environment, did not view her performance as about her as an individual. Instead, they viewed her performance as about the context, stating that regardless of who was hired as a change agent, they (the organization) would have undermined the change efforts. Realizing that she and her colleagues perceived the same situation differently enabled her to consider further her behavior in context. Viewing what occurred through the lens of person-role-system, she realized that she overemphasized her person and underemphasized her role and the system. As a result, she was able to reengage and experiment with new ways of leading change. Although certainly not easy nor fast, eventually she was able to accomplish some of the initial goals related to the desired change.

Moreover, she reflected on her longstanding pattern of behavior in which she realized that she usually takes more responsibility than is hers for a given situation, problem, or challenge. This insight enabled her to understand how she underrated herself on the multi-rater feedback assessment and essentially was blind to the systemic forces that also contributed to her performance. Rather than continue to act as if she, alone, were responsible for the stalled change initiative, she understood the context more deeply and her change leadership was reinvigorated. This example points to the importance of considering the interaction between the person and his or her *perceived* environment as well as holding a systems perspective.

Conclusion

Throughout this chapter, we have discussed coaching within the domain of OD, as one role that comprises the identity of an OD consultant, as well as a role with its own professional identity, that of internal coach and external coach. To be effective, both groups of professionals require knowledge, skills, and abilities of OD and of coaching. However, the roles have different emphases and, therefore, some variation in requisite preparation.

The set of abilities for OD consultants, and the courses listed under academic training in Chapter 12, represent what we believe are foundational for OD consulting and serve as background for coaching. Developing expertise in self-as-instrument and reflective practice, both essential to the repertoire of effective coaches, are also covered in Chapter 12.

In addition, the following abilities, knowledge, and skills are required for coaches and recommended for OD consultants invested in developing further the role of coach:

- *Knowledge of coaching process,* how to create a coaching partnership, collect data, make sense of it and feed it back, engage in coaching conversations, and build commitment for action planning.
- *Skills in person-centered approach to coaching,* including congruence, unconditional positive regard, and empathetic understanding. These skills are considered core competencies that are foundational across theories, approaches, and models, and are essential for establishing a working alliance and for the management of resistance to coaching.
- *Theory related to a coaching-specific theoretical orientation,* to serve as a guiding framework for coaching beyond core competencies.
- *Awareness of coaching models in general, as well as a specific model of coaching to guide theory in use;* for example, a model that is available in the academic or business literature, one that is an extension of a theoretical orientation, or one that is eclectic. At its core, a model should include a theoretical perspective on how individuals change, and also, how individuals resist change.
- *Individual interviewing skills* are needed to collect data from clients and key stakeholders.
- *Knowledge of assessments, including psychometrics and interpretation, and specific instruments,* such as multi-rater feedback, personality, emotional intelligence, learning styles, learning agility, interpersonal relations, communication preferences, conflict style, and cultural awareness.
- *Familiarity with organizational models* to assess context and provide a systemic perspective for individual coaching.
- *Skills for working with diverse clients* including awareness of one's own social identity and understanding the impact of social identity on the interaction between the client and his or her environment and on the interaction between the client and coach.

- *Ability to surface "undiscussables" and "speak truth to power,"* the bounded role of coach permits conversations to occur outside formal organizational authority structures and supports moving work forward.

- *Understanding the importance of the interdependence among individual, group, and organizational levels for coaching individuals,* including the conceptual framework that combines group relations and organization development discussed in Chapter 8.

Multiple avenues exist for gaining knowledge in these content areas, developing abilities and skills, and pursuing coach training. One of the challenges in selecting a path for coach training, however, is the current state of the field: There is no agreed-upon definition of coaching, no entry-level criteria, multiple professional organizations offering credentialing, and much needed research to claim evidence-based coaching. Thus, we offer three recommendations we view as necessary but not sufficient for developing coaching competencies:

- Participate in a training model known as Interpersonal Process Recall (IPR) (Kagan, 1984). IPR provides opportunities to engage in videotaped coaching conversations followed by debriefing with the coach, client, and "inquirer." The role of inquirer is to facilitate the recall of the coaching conversation by asking exploratory, open-ended, nonjudgmental questions of the coach and client. While watching the videotape, the coach and client recall their experience by exploring thoughts and feelings that were unsaid during the coaching conversation; that is, what was covert but nonetheless influencing the interaction between them. In addition to learning in the roles of coach and client, practicing the role of inquirer, and facilitating "learning by discovery" of the coach and client, the inquirer furthers his or her development as a coach.

Schein corroborates the importance of internalizing the role of inquirer as an essential component of coach training in his book, *Humble Inquiry* (2013a): "Humble inquiry is the skill and art of drawing someone out, of asking questions to which you do not already know the answer, of building a relationship based on curiosity and interest in the other person" (p. 21). By learning how to take the role of inquirer in IPR, one learns how to put "humble inquiry" into practice. The skills of the inquirer, and of humble inquiry, build trust and promote open communication and collaboration, which are essential for developing effective coaching relationships. For more on IPR, see Kagan (1984).

- Develop a coaching model that includes the purpose of coaching, the coaching process, theory/theories that undergird the model, key elements of the coaching relationship, skills needed, coach's style based on knowledge of self-as-instrument, how the coach will work with people whose styles are different, and ethical guidelines that guide the coaching model. Model development is akin to identifying one's point of view on coaching and even if a coach decides to use a model already in existence, it is imperative that the coach be aware of why he or she selected the model and how it is reflective of the coach's point of view. For more on developing a coaching model, see Lennard (2010).

- Coaching engagements in organizations often involve leadership development, and thus, it is helpful for coaches to have led an enterprise of any kind, regardless of size or type, as it provides the coach with a lived experience of what it takes to motivate others to work on one's behalf and to align others in service of a shared task.

In keeping with our conviction that coaching requires knowledge of organizational development as well as of individual coaching, those wishing to pursue training in coaching ideally should seek out programs that locate coaching within the domain of OD. In so doing, the coach will be organizationally knowledgeable and individually knowledgeable, which in our view is requisite for effective coaching.

14

Organization Development and the Future

With the publication of this third edition of our book devoted to an explanation and examination of a field that is now some 56 years of age, organization development (OD) is well beyond adolescence. Considering all of the criticism thrown at OD regarding its relevance, squishiness, growing departure from its scholarly and value-based roots, and lack of innovation in recent times (Burke, 2011a), it is a wonder that the field remains in existence. For example, in the book coedited by Bradford and Burke (2005), a critique of OD, a chapter by Jerry Harvey is entitled "The Future of OD, or Why Don't They Take the Tubes Out of Grandma?" Grandma seems to have survived. And there are now grandchildren active in the field. But problems remain, a serious one being the departure of OD as practiced today from its scholarly roots (Bartunek, 2014).

The dual purpose of this final chapter, therefore, is first to provide a quick summary of the final chapter in the second edition and then to move on to thoughts regarding the future and where OD needs to go developmentally to ensure relevance and organization change expertise.

Summary of the Final Chapter in the Second Edition

In the second edition, the final chapter was entitled "New Dimensions of Organization Development." Noteworthy was the observation that the term *culture* was a widely accepted concept at the time compared with the 1970s and early '80s. In other words, executives and managers in the early 1990s, and especially today, readily talk about their organization's culture and often use the term before the OD practitioner does. It is not clear if many executives and managers believe that organizational culture can be changed, but they are usually willing to discuss the matter.

A second observation at the time was that health-care organizations were beginning to explore OD possibilities as never before. That trend has lasted and today many health-care systems work with OD practitioners. Also, the delivery of OD in 1994 was expanding beyond the human resource function as the exclusive source of expertise. Information technology people began to explore OD as a possible tool in their toolkits. That trend has also continued.

The bulk of the relatively short final chapter in the second edition focused on the question of whether OD should be no more than a facilitative, contingent process or normative; for example, advocating a cultural change that would help to humanize the organization and advise that certain values, if lived, would improve organizational effectiveness such as operating in teams with considerable employee participation and engagement rather than managing individuals in a command-and-control manner. For empirical support regarding this advocacy statement, see the study by McClelland and Burnham (1976).

To see what some of the primary ingredients of an organization's culture advocated by an OD consultant with a normative perspective might look like, see the list of nine provided by Burke (1994) in that last chapter (p.197), for example, "Members feel a sense of ownership of the organization's mission and objectives" and "Conflict is dealt with openly and systematically, rather than ignored, avoided, or handled in a typical win-lose fashion." Beckhard's (1969) list of ten were perhaps less value-laden than Burke's, but similar nevertheless; for example, two of his were "Decisions are made by and near the sources of information, regardless of where these sources are located on the organizational chart," and "There is high conflict (clash of ideas) about tasks and projects and relatively little energy spent in clashing over *interpersonal* difficulties, because they generally have been worked through" (pp. 10–11).

These lists from Burke and Beckhard were drawn from their experiences as OD consultants and from personal beliefs and viewpoints. Not covered in the second edition, but highly related to goals for an organization's culture that could also be considered normative and in any case described as *adaptive,* is the work of Kotter and Heskett (1992). They were probably the first researchers to show a clear relationship between organizational culture and performance. They began with consideration of more than 200 companies and in the end selected 10 that had made a successful culture change. Among the 10 were British Airways, General Electric, Imperial Chemicals Industry, ConAgra, and Scandinavian Airlines Systems. These final 10 were companies that had the best record of performance and the capacity to make changes when needed. What these organizations had in common was what Kotter and Heskett called an *adaptive* culture. The following list describes the 11 characteristics of an adaptive culture according to the work of Kotter and Heskett (1992) and for our purposes serves as a possible norm and a set of goals for culture change:

1. Willingness to make changes in culturally ingrained behaviors
2. Emphasis on identifying problems before they occur and rapidly implementing workable solutions
3. Focus on innovation
4. Shared feelings of confidence about managing problems and opportunities
5. Emphasis on trust
6. Willingness to take risks
7. Spirit of enthusiasm
8. Candor
9. Internal flexibility in response to external demands
10. Consistency in word and action
11. Long-term focus

Now, what about today, 15 years into the twenty-first century?

Current and Future Trends in Organization Development

Organizations that last with growth and maturity tend over time to differentiate their operations more than they integrate them (Lawrence & Lorsch, 1967). New and different ways of thinking about how to sustain whatever success the organization has realized emerge, such as starting a new line of business or just as often if not more so, acquiring an organization that will serve the same objective of new and different.

But OD is a field, not an organization. Yet similarities regarding the emergence of different ideas and values exist. For example, Pasmore (2014) has characterized this differentiation as *three ODs*. Answering the question of "what is OD" would depend on which of the three different OD practitioners you asked. The three ODs, or factions as Pasmore refers to them, are humanistic/altruistic, whole systems, and bottom line/efficiency. To give a flavor of these factions we consider three of his nine comparisons:

	Humanistic/ Altruistic	Whole Systems	Bottom Line/ Efficiency
Primary Objective	Self-actualization, more humanistic workplaces, improved teamwork, self-awareness, achieving human potential, collaboration, discovering common ground	Improved system functioning, sustainable outcomes, high commitment and high performance, scientific proof	Immediate bottom line results
Representative Interventions	T-groups, team building, coaching, survey-feedback, employee engagement, training, environmental sustainability, diversity, positive psychology, search conferences	Sociotechnical systems, high-performance work systems, talent development/ succession planning, innovation, change leadership, customer focus, rewards, vision, culture, design thinking	Reengineering, total quality, rightsizing, organization design, strategy, M&A, goal setting, performance management, change management for ERP installments, selection/ assessment

	Humanistic/ Altruistic	Whole Systems	Bottom Line/ Efficiency
Slogan	Do the right thing	Do what is possible and proven	Do things right

Source: Pasmore (2014)

Incidentally, we, the authors of this book about OD, see ourselves as *factionally dualistic*—a combination of humanistic/altruistic and whole system.

Now let us consider differentiation from the perspective of emerging trends for the future. The first trend covered is dialogic OD, which represents a clear differentiation in the field of OD. The remaining three trends that we summarize are less differentiators and more concerned with new emphases at least for inclusion within the field of OD. They are leadership development, positive psychology, and agility.

Dialogic Organization Development

The primary advocates of this trend or movement in the field are Gervase Bushe and Robert Marshak. They have been prolific with their writings and publication, but we will refer primarily to their most recent work, an overview of what they refer to as the *dialogic mindset* (Bushe & Marshak, 2014). They contrast this kind of mindset to what they label as diagnostic OD. In any case, the fundamental difference is that the latter approach to OD emphasizes gathering data as objectively as possible on the part of the OD practitioners with the primary objective of changing *behavior,* whereas the dialogic approach emphasizes communication—what people say, how they say it, what they espouse, and what they believe. The primary objective with a dialogic approach is to capture the "generative image" of what organizational members talk about, what picture of the organization they generate via discussion, which constitutes a mind-set. The target of change is the mind-set, not so much their behavior. The primary database for this dialogic approach is, therefore, the conversation, the stories organizational members relate about how the organization functions and why it seems to operate the way it does.

What is not new here are the many examples of this approach—dialogic. Although this approach to understanding and changing organizations may be conducted at any level—one-on-one coaching for example—most dialogic activities consist of large group interventions. What is new, then, is Bushe and Marshak's (and others) attempts to conceptualize and provide theoretical ideas for making sense of a plethora of organizational activities that are largely based on large group interventions. Bushe and Marshak list 27 such interventions and then concentrate on 6 to illustrate their points. To give a sense of these activities, what follows are brief descriptions of their 6 primary examples:

1. *Open space technology (Owen, 2008).* From one to as much as three days, a group convenes around an issue of common concern. Participants propose topics for discussion and a schedule with small assignments is created. Participants are free to move from one small group to another—"as the spirit moves." The meeting conclusion is in the total group where what has been learned and decided is discussed.

2. *Emergent engagement (Homan, 2010).* Essentially an extension of Owen's open space technology. Both take cues from complexity theory, for example, Prigogine and Stengers (1984), with Homan's convenor/facilitator being a bit more directive; it guides her facilitation according to a three-step process—disruption, differentiation, and coherence. The intent with disruption is to disturb the status quo followed by reorganization of thought, which in turn can lead to action. It is a matter of finding new levels of coherence.

3. *Complex responsive processes of relating (Griffen, 2002; Shaw, 2002; Stacey, 2011).* According to Stacey and his associates, Griffen and Shaw, there is no objective reality; all reality is created and re-created within the relationships and discussions among people, like Homan's point, again based on complexity theory, disruption must occur for change to be realized. As Stacey (2001) puts it, "...without such disruption to current patterns of collaboration and power relations there could be no emergent novelty in communicative interaction and hence no novelty in any form of human action. The reason for saying this

is that disruptions generate diversity. One of the central insights of the complexity sciences is how the spontaneous emergence of novelty depends upon diversity" (p. 149).

The three preceding examples link to complexity theory, whereas the following three, according to Bushe and Marshak (2014), are what they label as *interpretive perspectives*.

4. *Coordinated management of meaning (Pearce & Cronen, 1980).* Pearce and Cronen are more interested in developing people than producing theory. Meaning comes from the interactions of people. Four fundamental questions guide their interventions: (1) What are we making together? (2) How are we making it? (3) What are we becoming? (4) How do we make better social worlds? These questions guide the conversations among people and talk is a form of action, not a substitute for it. Their process as consultants/practitioners is one of "mapping" the episodes that occur as people engage one another. These maps can lead to further interventions and actions.

5. *Organization discourse (Grant & Oswick, 1996; Grant & Marshak, 2011).* The interpretive perspectives for this approach to dialogic OD are metaphor and story lines. The consultant listens carefully to what clients say, especially the stories they tell and the metaphors they use. The consultants develop ideas, hunches about the meaning of the client's language and stories, and then provide feedback to the client based on these hunches as well as suggestions for modifying current assumptions and thinking.

6. *Appreciative inquiry (Cooperrider & Srivastva, 1987; Barrett & Cooperrider, 1990; Cooperrider, Whitney, & Stavros, 2008).* Appreciative inquiry (AI) is a significant example of the positive psychology movement, both having emerged at about the same time in the mid-1980s. AI is also another example of discourse and narrative as processes for organizational change. Moreover, these dialogues, which emphasize strengths, usually occur in a large group setting (Cooperrider, 2012). AI sessions often last up to four days and follow four phases: Discovery, dream, design, and destiny/deployment, a set of processes that are similar to the Open Space Technology approach (Owen, 2008). AI emphasizes the emergent nature of change rather

than the standard OD approach; for example, the seven steps of consultation—entry, contracting, data gathering, and so on. (Cooperrider, Whitney, & Stavros, 2008).

In summary regarding dialogic OD, Bushe and Marshak's (2014) contribution comes from their extensive accumulation of interventions based largely on dialogue and generative imagery. In other words, their propositions concerning dialogic OD are based on a set of organization change theory and methodologies usually associated with large group activities. The common denominator for these methods and interventions is discourse, that is, paying attention to the characteristics and nature of dialogue, what people say and how they say it, for example, with a metaphor. Dialogic OD represents a differentiation within the larger field of organization development and change. A fair question to ask is why such differentiation?

One reason is Bushe and Marshak's attempt to explain the proliferation of certain methods that promote organization change but do not follow the "regular" steps of OD, unfreeze, change, refreeze. Finding similarities and consistencies across these methods, which may occur via one-on-one coaching but more often in group settings, have encouraged these scholar-practitioners to make further sense of it all. Thus, dialogic OD.

Another reason, as Bushe and Marshak (2014) note, is the problem with organization change overall; that is, the high degree of failure. Successful organization change is less than 50 percent and may be as low as 30 percent. They suggest that normal OD does not exactly have a great track record; therefore, variations and other approaches are in order. They conclude their article with three propositions that if followed should make a difference with respect to organization change regardless of what specific method is used. Their propositions are as follows:

1. A disruption in the ongoing social construction of reality is stimulated or engaged in a way that leads to a more complex reorganization.

2. A change to one or more core narratives takes place.

3. A generative image is introduced or surfaces that provides new and compelling alternatives for thinking and acting.

At the risk of oversimplification, what Bushe and Marshak are advocating is that organization change occurs as a consequence of organizational members' increased understanding of how they have construed their work life as manifested in the language they use and the stories they tell, and that this construction, a social one, may not be the one they want or that will lead to greater effectiveness as a team or organization as a whole. Reaching a different mind-set will then constitute the change.

Leadership Development

Family feuds are known to occur in family-owned businesses, but the one making the news during the summer of 2014 was most unusual. Market Basket, a grocery chain of 71 stores in three New England states, Massachusetts, Maine, and New Hampshire, was owned by the Demoulas family, not brothers, however, but two cousins: Arthur S. Demoulas, chair of the seven-member board of directors and majority owner of the business, and Arthur T. Demoulas, the CEO. The dispute between the two cousins was wide-ranging but focused particularly on how profits were to be distributed. The chair, Arthur S., wanted the owners and stockholders to gain most from the profits, but the CEO, Arthur T., wanted the majority to be shared among the employees. In any case, the feuding cousins could not come to a resolution and consequently the chair, with backing from the board, fired his cousin, the CEO. The employees, demonstrating fierce loyalty to Arthur T. calling him "our leader," went on strike, vacating the stores and protesting in front of the stores with placards calling for a reinstatement of their leader. Customers joined the protest. Fearing financial collapse, eventually a deal was made for Arthur T. to purchase the remaining stock in the company (up to that point, he had 49.5 percent ownership) and be reinstated as CEO. The dedicated employees of Market Basket had pushed the company to the brink, but in the end, they won the day and got their much-beloved leader returned to the helm. Thomas Kochan, a professor at the Sloan School of Management at MIT, was quoted as saying that "employees are the most valuable asset in this business." In other words, they saved the business. Professor Kochan went on to declare that "Market Basket has done more to educate us on how to manage a business than any business case study that's been written to date" (Seelye & de la Merced, 2014, p. A17). In a time of crisis, the followers became leaders.

To say that "Artie T," as he is called, has loyal employees and customers is an understatement. His employees risked losing their jobs and their customers joined them in the revolt. Artie T may be a "natural" leader and needs little if any development. But he is a rare breed. Most of us who seek or are cast into leadership positions could benefit from some form of development. Previous evidence has shown that the failure rate for people in positions of leadership ranges from 50 to 67 percent with an overall average of at least one out of every two not meeting goals for the positions that they hold (Hogan, Curphy, & Hogan, 1994). It is likely that this failure rate is much the same today, which may account for, at least in part, the recent increase in leadership development activities. A survey of OD practitioners comparing their values and interventions in 1994 with those some 20 years later showed that leadership development was the top priority for OD practice by 2014 (Shull, Church, & Burke, 2013). Clearly the need is there. Moreover, Burke (2011a) has argued that leadership development is one of four areas of "unfinished business" for OD scholars and practitioners (the other three being culture change, loosely coupled systems, and resistance). This increase regarding leadership development is therefore good news. Yet there remain at least two areas of concern.

Many, if not most, leadership development activities currently consist of programs that include multi-rater feedback and other assessments as well as sessions that help to provide an acculturation for leaders and potential leaders into the organizations. These efforts are fine as far as they go. Receiving feedback often helps with increasing one's self-awareness and such processes can lead to enhanced performance; see, for example, Atwater and Yammarino (1992), Church (1997), and Chapter 14 in Burke (2014b). Few organizations conform to the 70-20-10 model (Burke, 2011a; McCall, 2010), however: 70 percent of leadership development being focused on arranging for potential leaders to have different and challenging job experiences, 20 percent being activities that help the potential leader to learn from those experiences via reflection, coaching, and mentoring, and 10 percent devoted to skill development such as public speaking. The next frontier, then, is getting leadership development right. Experiences alone will not do it. *Learning* from the experiences is the necessary ingredient, the 20 percent part of the model.

The second concern is about the field of OD itself. Leadership development should be supported, for sure, but the emphasis is at the individual level of an organization. OD is about system change, particularly culture, at the organizational level. In other words, leadership development may be a distraction from OD. But it doesn't have to be, provided leadership development efforts are in support of overall organization change; that is, to ensure that the learning for leaders consists of behaviors and practices that will move the organization in the desired change direction.

Positive Psychology

The so-called positive psychology movement emerged in the mid-1980s. Appreciative inquiry was an early part of this emergence. Some 15 years later, a special issue of the *American Psychologist* edited by Seligman and Csikszentmihalyi (2000) signaled that such a movement had indeed arrived and was having an impact. Topics associated with such positives as optimism, courage, spirituality, hope, creativity, and wisdom were discussed. Psychological research had largely been focused on negatives, the *problem* to be investigated. This predominance may still be true today, but the positive emphasis by researchers has gained ground. One of the reasons why emphasizing negative forces remains significant is because negative findings by researchers in psychology have a more powerful impact on study results than is the case for positive findings. These more powerful findings get published more easily; see the article by Baumeister, Bratslavsky, Finkenauer, and Vohs (2001).

Positive psychology is concerned with life-giving domains of interest and study rather than life-depleting ones. Life-giving behaviors are more naturally embraced than those focused on the negative.

Kim Cameron has taken the lead regarding the application of positive psychology to organization development and change. And he has done his homework. His article on the paradox of positive organizational change (Cameron, 2008) covers more than 160 references. A positive approach regarding organization change means that the emphasis is on strengths, capabilities, and possibilities rather than on problems, threats, and weaknesses. The paradox that Cameron addresses is that a positive approach leads to effectiveness and change, but a negative emphasis has more impact. A couple of examples may illustrate the paradoxical point:

- People judge positive phenomena more accurately than negative phenomena; for example, managers are more accurate in rating subordinates' competencies and proficiencies when they perform correctly than when they perform incorrectly. Yet people pay more attention to negative feedback than positive feedback.

- A positive event is remembered more accurately and longer, but a negative event has more effect on immediate memory and salience in the short run.

So Cameron (2008) concludes that both positive and negative reactions are evolutionarily adaptive but function in different ways; that is, negative reactions are typically more intense. Most life events are positive, at least for most of us, and therefore negative events are more unique. Cameron puts it this way:

> Just as movement in a still room attracts attention, so negative (novel) events capture more attention than positive (normal) patterns. Furthermore, negative events often indicate maladaptation and a need to change, (and) one single negative thing can cause a system to fail, but one single positive thing cannot guarantee success (2008, p.15).

We have three final points regarding this trend of positive psychology. First, it seems clear that both positive and negative effects are, or at least can be, significant aspects of organizational change. The negative aspect may be a strong need to change due to, say, a competitor's superior strategy and tactics in the marketplace, and the positive aspect might be a new and inspiring vision for the future. Second, it also seems clear that to accentuate the positive over the negative requires extra effort and commitment. Thus, change leaders must be willing to "stay the course" when it comes to, say, concentrating on strengths of the organization, rewarding people who champion change, and when negative outcomes occur with change implementation, which are typical, change leaders must move quickly to fix the implementation problem, for example, a computer software glitch, so that ultimately the negative does not overpower the positive, thus not allowing the effects of positive change tactics to be realized.

And, finally, the third point concerns research evidence regarding positive organizational change. In a study of highly effective teachers in K-12 public schools, Quinn, Heynoski, Thomas, and Spreitzer (2014) found that the use of positive approaches in helping students to learn was the predominant mode of interaction between teacher and student. These researchers also drew parallels between facilitating learning and leadership. In these cases of highly effective teachers, the positive outweighed the negative. Thus, these researchers concluded that this imbalance of positive over negative was no doubt the differentiator for the highly effective teachers, and the same should be true for leaders in a variety of settings. At a much broader level, Cameron and McNaughton (2014) provide an overview of research conducted in recent years on the effects of positive organizational change. A considerable number of studies show strong empirical evidence that when positive factors—compassionate support for employees, forgiving mistakes and avoiding blame, expressing gratitude and showing kindness—are given greater emphasis than negative factors—blaming employees for mistakes, downsizing, disciplinary actions and related measures of punishment—individual and organizational productivity as well as high job satisfaction and loyalty to the organization are significantly higher. For guidelines on how to facilitate positive organizational change, see Cameron's (2013) book.

Much is yet to be learned and studied regarding this trend of positive organizational change, but there is now sufficient evidence to encourage the pursuit thereof.

Agility: Organizational and Individual

Our fourth and final trend to be considered for now and in the future is the notion of agility briefly considered in Chapter 2, "Organization Development Then and Now," as one of the major trends for the future, and now explained in more depth.

As we know, a fundamental ingredient of the American culture is our love of "the latest"—be it a fad, clear trend if not movement, the magic pill for weight loss, or the silver bullet that will fix a problem. One such phenomenon at the present time is *agility*. The concept is touted at both the organizational and individual levels. At the individual level, the primary focus is on learning; that is, learning agility, being able and willing to grasp new ideas, tackle challenging projects, and make oneself vulnerable in the interest of learning something new in a behavioral manner that is quick and flexible. Many assume that agile learners are high performers. Evidence to support this assumption is yet to emerge, but the excitement about this concept and its implications remains. We have more to say about learning agility momentarily. For now, let us turn briefly to the organization.

At the organizational level, similar language is used. The titles of three recent books set the tone: *The Agility Factor* by Worley, Williams, and Lawler (2014), *Cultural Agility* by Caligiuri (2012), and *Quick and Nimble* by Bryant (2014). The Worley et al. book looked at high-performing companies as measured by profitability and, in particular, return on assets across 17 industries. They found that the 11 top performers from a total of 243 large firms could be characterized as agile in terms of how management conducted their businesses. Agility was defined in terms of rapidly changing the firm's strategy when needed by staying in constant touch with the external environment and its changing dynamics (think the Burke-Litwin model in Chapter 7, "The Burke-Litwin Model of Organizational Performance and Change") followed by testing new ideas, learning from these tests, and then implementing change accordingly. Interestingly, this book seems to confirm the earlier position taken by Lawler and Worley (2006) that organizations "built to change" are the ones that will last.

Caligiuri's book, as the title signals, emphasizes the importance of having a flexible culture. She argues that this agile culture must be led by the human resource function. And Bryant's *Quick and Nimble* book has a subtitle that helps to explain his thesis—*Lessons from Leading CEOs on How to Create a Culture of Innovation*—which is based on numerous interviews that he has conducted over the years for his *New York Times* column based on "insights from the corner office." His main conclusion from these interviews is that for CEOs to be successful in creating an innovative culture, they must themselves be agile, or in his words, quick and nimble.

Returning to the individual level, the term is not individual agility exactly but, instead, it is *learning* agility. It is likely that the notion of learning agility, irrespective of precise language, has been considered if not discussed for a long time. After all, what is often lauded as new isn't. What's the phrase, "What's old is new again"? The idea of learning agility could have been considered as long as 3,000 years ago. Assuming that Malcolm Gladwell got his biblical story about *David and Goliath* (Gladwell, 2013) reasonably correct, we could easily conclude that David was high on learning agility. He had learned much at an early age to have accomplished what he did. Whether the concept has been known this long or not, it is nevertheless rather difficult to define, much less measure, learning agility in the twenty-first century. But we will make an attempt. And whether learning agility is a fad or not, we think that it is important and, thus, we will take a stab at a definition followed by a brief discussion.

Learning agility: What is it? There are two components: One is skill and the other is motivation. The skill of being agile is highly important, especially when confronted with a novel and different situation. The learning aspect concerns whether what one has learned from experience, how one thinks and behaves, is applicable to the new and different situation and if not, what does one then do? This question leads to the second component, motivation, that is, one's willingness to take risks in attempting to deal with a novel situation when not knowing exactly what to do. Coupled with risk-taking is seeking feedback about how one is doing regardless of how threatening this action might be to one's self esteem. Relevant terms to further our understanding include (a) flexibility, being adaptable, not rigid, when trying something for the first time and getting feedback as soon as possible, (b) speed, trying new approaches quickly and learning about the consequences in the moment retaining some of the thoughts and behaviors and discarding others that do not appear to add anything to one's learning, and (c) avoiding defensiveness, justifying one's actions regardless of their efficacy regarding the uniqueness of the situation. In summary, learning agility is a combination of motivation; that is, being willing to face new and perhaps ambiguous situations by taking actions that help one to stay engaged, and the skill to discern quickly the consequences of these actions and then determine what to do next in order to continue the process of learning.

These are early days of studying agility, but the scholarly work is under way. The definitive paper so far is the one published by DeRue, Ashford, and Myers (2012). These organizational psychologists note that discussion, practice, and enthusiasm about learning agility are ahead of theory and research and that the concept is poorly defined and inadequately measured. They provide a complex yet useful model for understanding learning agility, which encompasses individual differences, for example, openness to experience, contextual factors, such as a culture, and climate for learning. Then, they address learning agility per se in terms of both cognitive processes, for example, pattern recognition, and behavioral processes, for example, experimentation and reflection. DeRue and his colleagues have helped us to understand more broadly and deeply the concept of learning agility—the good news—but also point out at the same time the lack of an adequate measure—the bad news. But work is under way regarding measurement, which is better news; see, for example, the commentary article reacting to the DeRue et al. piece regarding the issue of rigor versus relevance by Mitchinson, Gerard, Roloff, and Burke (2012).

To conclude this section on the final trend, let us briefly address what may help to explain the popularity of the term *agility.* We will therefore consider two possible explanations. First, it may represent a, if not *the,* primary coping mechanism for dealing with the complexity and speed of change in these and future times. Change is now considered to be constant with stability being a quality of the past, and trying to keep up is evermore challenging if not at times agonizing. Rigidity in thought and behavior is clearly not the way to cope. Also recall that agility is not new. As noted earlier, Kotter and Heskett (1992) investigated this idea at the organizational culture level and labeled it adaptive. What feels new perhaps is simply the more rapid nature of change, which contributes to feelings of intensity and discomfort, and at times, experiencing a feeling of being overwhelmed. Learning flexible and adaptive behaviors can help.

A second possible explanation returns us to a discussion we considered in the section on dialogic OD; that is, the way we conduct

OD may be unnecessarily inflexible. Maybe we cannot always have a diagnosis that precedes an intervention, and, besides, a diagnosis *is* an intervention. The question has arisen, at least in part, as a consequence of the poor track record regarding successful organization change; that is, the failure rate is somewhere in the neighborhood of 70 percent. Obviously, this record is unacceptable. A key concept in most definitions of OD is the word *planned.* And steps or phases are followed: unfreeze, change, refreeze; contracting, data gathering, and so on; and present state-transition state-future state. With the rapidity of change in the external environment, we simply do not have the luxury of planning the change effort as thoroughly as we might like. By the time we plan step 2 or 3, step 4 is already in our laps. Proceeding with dialogue at the outset as advocated by Bushe and Marshak (2014) has appeal, as does operating an organization with a high degree of agility where planning and action meld together as Worley and colleagues argue (Worley, Williams, & Lawler, 2014). We can also consider ideas from consulting work with loosely coupled systems where, for example, improvisation is appropriate; see Chapter 10, "Understanding and Changing Loosely Coupled Systems." So, the point is that some OD work needs to be done on OD with a goal in mind of increasing adaptability, or if you prefer, agility. There is nothing inherently wrong with planned change. It is a matter of adaptation to current and future circumstances.

On the other hand, the field of OD seems to have been under constant criticism; for example, see the chapters in the book coedited by Bradford and Burke (2005), and adaptation may have occurred more than we know. Surely OD practitioners are not resistant to change! Moreover, while we as OD practitioners may not like and readily embrace feedback that goes against the grain, we are, after all, in the change business. This means that from time to time we give bad news to our clients and hope that they do not kill the messenger. In any case, what is good for our clients should be good for us. In addition to being in the change business, we are also in the learning business—check the subtitle of this book. Also consider the possibility that constant examination and criticism of OD may have contributed to the field's survival rather than having caused a deadly blow. Perhaps another 56 years is on the horizon.

Conclusion

We began this concluding chapter with a brief summary of the final chapter of the second edition noting that organizational culture was an accepted term and concept beyond OD. Our clients often use the term before we OD practitioners speak about it. Also noted was OD being accepted in health-care organizations more than had been true in the past. Most of that chapter in 1994, however, was devoted to coverage of values underlying the field of OD. Moving to the present, we covered Pasmore's (2014) *three ODs* of humanistic/altruistic, whole systems, and bottom line/efficiency, which reflect different values. The problem of defining OD, according to Pasmore, is the existence of these three different factions in the field.

Regarding the future of OD, we covered four trends: (1) dialogic OD, a composite, in part, of large group interventions and what they have in common regarding OD practice; (2) leadership development where we pointed to the importance of learning from different work experiences; (3) positive psychology, a trend if not movement of emphasizing life-giving interventions in the world of organization change and development; and (4) agility and its importance at both the individual and organizational levels.

These four trends are not the only ones. We could have returned to Chapter 2, for example, and elaborated on one or more of the trends discussed earlier, such as the inequities of the "haves" versus the "have nots," particularly regarding compensation of CEOs and high-level executives compared with the remainder of employees in the organization. Our overall intent, nevertheless, with Chapter 2 and this final one has been to draw our attention to the many complexities of the world we now live in and the role that OD may have with respect to coping and dealing with these complexities while at the same time helping organizations to change. To do this well, it may be that OD needs to do some changing as well. In most societies, practicing what one preaches is rarely, if ever, a bad thing.

References

Ackoff, R. L. (1981). *Creating the corporate future.* New York, NY: Wiley.

Adizes, I. (1979). Organizational passages: Diagnosing and treating lifecycle problems of organizations. *Organizational Dynamics, 8*(1), 2–25.

Alban, B. (1974). Further questions about and by a shadow consultant. *Journal of Applied Behavioral Science, 10,* 595–597.

Alderfer, C. P. (2014). Clarifying the meaning of mentor-protégé relationships. *Consulting Psychology: Practice and Research, 66*(1), 6–19.

Allport, G. W. (1945). *The nature of prejudice.* Cambridge, MA: Addison-Wesley.

Argyris, C. (1971). *Management and organizational development.* New York, NY: McGraw-Hill.

Argyris, C. (1970). *Intervention theory and method.* Reading, MA: Addison-Wesley.

Argyris, C. (1968). Some unintended consequences of rigorous research. *Psychological Bulletin, 70,* 185–197.

Argyris, C. (1965). Explorations in interpersonal competence, II. *Journal of Applied Behavioral Science, 1,* 255–269.

Argyris, C. (1962). *Interpersonal competence and organizational effectiveness.* Homewood, IL: Dorsey Press.

Argyris, C., Putnam, R., & Smith, D. M. (1985). *Action science.* San Francisco, CA: Jossey-Bass.

Argyris, C., & Schön, D. A. (1978). *Organizational learning: A theory of action perspective.* Reading, MA: Addison-Wesley.

Argyris, C., & Schön, D. A. (1974). *Theory in practice: Increasing professional effectiveness.* San Francisco, CA: Jossey-Bass.

Armenakis, A. A., Bernerth, J. B., Pitts, J. P., & Walker, H. J. (2007). Organizational change recipients' beliefs scale: Development of an assessment instrument. *Journal of Applied Behavioral Science, 43,* 481–505.

Armenakis, A. A., Harris, S. G., & Mossholder, K. W. (1993). Creating readiness for organizational change. *Human Relations, 46,* 681–703.

"At Emery Air Freight: Positive Reinforcement Boosts Performance." (1973). *Organizational Dynamics, 1*(3), 41–67.

Atwater, L., & Yammarino, F. (1992). Does self-other agreement on leadership perceptions moderate the validity of leadership predictions? *Personal Psychology, 45,* 141–164.

Barends, E., Janssen, B., ten Have, W., & ten Have, S. (2014). Effects of change interventions: What kind of evidence do we really have? *Journal of Applied Behavioral Science, 50,* 5–27.

Baron, J. N., & Hannan, M. T. (2002). Organizational blueprints for success in high-tech start-ups: Lessons from the Stanford Project on Emerging Companies. *California Management Review, 44*(3), 8–36.

Barrett, F. J., & Cooperrider, D. L. (1990). Generative metaphor intervention: A new approach for working with systems divided by conflict and caught in defensive perception. *Journal of Applied Behavioral Science, 26,* 219–239.

Bartunek, J. M. (2014). Academic practitioner relationships: What NTL started and what management scholarship keeps developing. *Journal of Applied Behavioral Science, 50,* 401–422.

Bass, B. M. (1985). *Leadership and performance beyond expectations.* New York, NY: The Free Press.

Battilana, J., & Casciaro, T. (2012). Change agents, networks, and institutions: A contingency theory of organizational change. *Academy of Management Journal, 55,* 381–398.

Bauman, R. P., Jackson, P., & Lawrence, J. T. (1997). *From promise to performance: A journey of transformation at Smithkline Beecham.* Boston, MA: Harvard Business School Press.

Baumeister, R. F., Bratslavsky, E., Finkenauer, C., & Vohs, K. D. (2001). Bad is stronger than good. *Review of General Psychology, 5,* 323–370.

Beckhard, R. (1977). *Organizational transitions: Managing complex change.* Reading, MA: Addison-Wesley.

Beckhard, R. (1972). Team-building efforts. *Journal of Contemporary Business, 1*, 23–32.

Beckhard, R. (1969). *Organization development: Strategies and models.* Reading, MA: Addison-Wesley.

Beckhard, R. (1967). The confrontation meeting. *Harvard Business Review, 45*(2), 149–155.

Beckhard, R., & Harris, R. T. (1987). *Organizational transitions: Managing complex change* (2nd ed.). Reading, MA: Addison-Wesley.

Beckhard, R., & Lake, D. G. (1971). Short- and long-range effects of a team development effort. In H. A. Hornstein, B. B. Bunker, W. W. Burke, M. Gindes, & R. J. Lewicki (Eds.), *Social interventions: A behavioral science approach* (pp. 421–439). New York, NY: Free Press.

Beckhard, R., & Pritchard, W. (1992). *Changing the essence: The art of creating and leading fundamental change in organizations.* San Francisco, CA: Jossey-Bass.

Bennett, J. L. (2006). An agenda for coaching-related research: A challenge for researchers. *Consulting Psychology Journal: Practice and Research, 58*(1), 240–249.

Bennis, W. G., & Nanus, B. (1985). *Leaders: The strategies for taking charge.* New York, NY: Harper & Row.

Berg, D. N., & Smith, K. K. (Eds.). (1988). *The self in social inquiry: Researching methods.* Newbury Park, CA: Sage.

Berg, D. N., & Smith, K. K. (Eds.). (1985). *Exploring clinical methods for social research.* Thousand Oaks, CA: Sage.

Bernstein, W. M., & Burke, W. W. (1989). Modeling organizational meaning systems. In R. W. Woodman & W. A. Pasmore (Eds.), *Research in organizational change and development* (pp. 117–159). Greenwich, CT: JAI Press.

Bion, W. R. (1961). *Experiences in groups.* New York, NY: Basic Books.

Blake, R. R., & Mouton, J. S. (1982). A comparative analysis of situationalism and 9,9 management by principle. *Organizational Dynamics, 10*(4), 20–30.

Blake, R. R., & Mouton, J. S. (1981). *Toward resolution of the situationalism vs. "One Best Style..." controversy in leadership theory, research, and practice.* Austin, TX: Scientific Methods.

Blake, R. R., & Mouton, J. S. (1978). *The new managerial grid.* Houston, TX: Gulf.

Blake, R. R., & Mouton, J. S. (1968). *Corporate excellence through grid organization development.* Houston, TX: Gulf.

Blake, R. R., & Mouton, J. S. (1964). *The managerial grid.* Houston, TX: Gulf.

Blake, R. R., Mouton, J. S., Barnes, L. B., & Greiner, L. E. (1964). Breakthrough in organizational development. *Harvard Business Review, 42* (November), 133–155.

Boss, R. W. (1989). *Organization development in health care.* Reading, MA: Addison-Wesley.

Bowers, D. G. (1973). OD techniques and their results in 23 organizations: The Michigan ICL study. *Journal of Applied Behavioral Science, 9,* 21–43.

Bracken, D. W., Timmreck, C. W., & Church, A. H. (Eds.). (2001). *Handbook of multisource feedback.* San Francisco, CA: Jossey-Bass.

Bradford, D. L., & Burke, W. W. (Eds.). (2005). *Reinventing organization development.* San Francisco, CA: Pfeiffer/Wiley.

Brockner, J. (1992). Managing the effects of layoffs on survivors. *California Management Review, 34*(2), 9–28.

Brockner, J. (1988). *Self-esteem at work: Research, theory and practice.* Lexington, MA: Lexington Books.

Brockner, J., Greenberg, L., Brockner, A., Bortz, J., Davy, J., & Carter, C. (1986). Layoffs, equity theory and work performance: Further evidence of the impact of survivor guilt. *Academy of Management Journal, 29,* 373–384.

Brown, L. D. (1972). Research action: Organizational feedback, understanding, and change. *Journal of Applied Behavioral Science, 8,* 697–711.

Bryant, A. (2014). *Quick and nimble: Lessons from leading CEOs on how to create a culture of innovation.* New York, NY: Times Books.

Bunker, B. B., & Alban, B. T. (2002). Understanding and using large system interventions. In J. Waclawski & A. H. Church (Eds.), *Organization development: Data-driven methods for change* (pp. 222–241). New York, NY: Wiley.

Burck, G. (1965). Union Carbide's patient schemers. *Fortune* (December), 147–149.

Burke, W. W. (2014a). Conflict in organizations. In P. T. Coleman, M. Deutsch, & E. C. Marcus (Eds.), *The handbook of conflict resolution: Theory and practice* (3rd ed.) (website). San Francisco, CA: Jossey-Bass.

Burke, W. W. (2014b). *Organization change: Theory and practice* (4th ed.). Thousand Oaks, CA: Sage.

Burke, W. W. (2014c). Changing loosely coupled systems. *Journal of Applied Behavioral Science, 50*, 423–444.

Burke, W. W. (2014d). Organizational change. In B. Schneider & K. M. Barbara (Eds.). *The Oxford handbook of organizational climate and culture* (pp. 457–483). Oxford, UK: Oxford University Press.

Burke, W. W. (2011a). A perspective on the field of organization development and change: The Zeigarnik effect. *The Journal of Applied Behavioral Science, 47*, 143–167.

Burke, W. W. (2011b). *Organization change: Theory and practice* (3rd ed.). Thousand Oaks, CA: Sage.

Burke, W. W. (1994). *Organization development: A process of learning and changing* (2nd ed.). Reading, MA: Addison-Wesley.

Burke, W. W. (1993). The changing world of organization change. *Consulting Psychology Journal, 45*(1), 9–17.

Burke, W. W. (1991). Practicing organization development. In *Working with organizations and their people: A guide to human resources practice* (pp. 95–130). D. W. Bray & Associates, New York, NY: Guilford.

Burke, W. W. (1988). Team building. In W. B. Ready & K. Jamison (Eds.), *Team building: Blueprints for productivity and satisfaction* (pp. 3–14). Alexandria, VA: NTL Institute.

Burke, W. W. (1986). Leadership as empowering others. In S. Srivastva & Associates. *Executive power: How executives influence people and organizations* (pp. 51–77). San Francisco, CA: Jossey-Bass.

Burke, W. W. (1982). *Organization development: Principles and practices.* Boston, MA: Little, Brown.

Burke, W. W. (1980). Systems theory, gestalt therapy, and organization development. In T. G. Cummings (Ed.), *Systems training for organization development* (pp. 209–222). London, England: John Wiley and Sons.

Burke, W. W. (1976). Organization development in transition. *Journal of Applied Behavioral Science, 12*, 22–43.

Burke, W. W. (1974). Managing conflict between groups. In J. D. Adams (Ed.), *New technologies in organizational development: 2* (pp. 255–268). San Diego, CA: University Associates.

Burke, W. W., & Biggart, N. W. (1997). Interorganizational relations. In D. Druckman, J. E. Singer, & H. van Cott (Eds.), *Enhancing organizational performance* (pp. 120–149). Washington, DC: National Academy Press.

Burke, W. W., Clark, L. P., & Koopman, C. (1984). Improve your OD project's chances for success. *Training and Development Journal, 38*(8), 62–68.

Burke, W. W., & Hornstein, H. A. (Eds.). (1972). *The social technology of organization development.* La Jolla, CA: University Associates.

Burke, W. W., & Jackson, P. (1991). Making the Smith Kline Beecham merger work. *Human Resource Management, 30*, 69–87.

Burke, W. W., & Litwin, G. H. (1992). A causal model of organizational performance and change. *Journal of Management, 18*, 532–545.

Burke, W. W., & Litwin, G. H. (1989). A causal model of organizational change and performance. In J. W. Pfeiffer (Ed.), *1989 Annual: Developing human resources* (pp. 277–288). San Diego, CA: University Associates.

Burke, W. W., & Myers, R. A. (1982). *Assessment of executive competence.* Technical Report. Washington, DC: National Aeronautics and Space Administration.

Burke, W. W., & Noumair, D. A. (2002). The role of personality assessment in organization development. In J. Waclawski & A. H. Church (Eds.), *Organization development: A data drive approach to organizational change* (pp. 55–77). San Francisco, CA: Jossey-Bass.

Burke, W. W., & Schmidt, W. H. (1971). Primary target for change: The manager or the organization? In H. A. Hornstein, B. B. Bunker, W. W. Burke, M. Gindes, and R. J. Lewicki (Eds.), *Social intervention: A behavioral science approach* (pp. 373–385). New York, NY: The Free Press.

Burnes, B. (2004). Kurt Lewin and the planned approach to change: A reappraisal. *Journal of Management Studies, 41*, 977–1002.

Burns, J. M. (1978). *Leadership.* New York, NY: Harper & Row.

Burns, J. M., & Stalker, G. (1961). *The management of innovation.* London, England: Tavistock.

Burt, R. (2005). *Brokerage and closure: An introduction to social conflict.* Oxford, England: Oxford University Press.

Bush, R. G., & McCord, S. A. (2010). Technologies to support interactive and connective OD in a virtual world. In W. J. Rothwell, J. M. Stavros, R. L. Sullivan, & A. Sullivan (Eds.), *Practicing organization development: A guide for leading change* (3rd ed.) (pp. 502–515). San Francisco, CA: Pfeiffer.

Bushe, G. R., & Marshak, R. J. (2014). The dialogic mindset in organization development. In A. B. Shani & D. A. Noumair (Eds.), *Research in organizational change and development*, Vol. 22 (pp. 55–98). United Kingdom: Emerald Group Publishing.

Bushe, G. R., & Shani, A. B. (1991). *Parallel learning structures: Increasing innovation in bureaucracies.* Reading, MA: Addison-Wesley.

Caligiuri, P. (2012). *Cultural agility: Building a pipeline of successful global professionals.* San Francisco, CA: Jossey-Bass.

Callimachi, R. (2013, December 30). $0.60 for cake: Al-Qaida records every expense. *Associated Press.* Retrieved from http://bigstory.ap.org/article/060-cake-al-qaida-records-every-expense.

Cameron, K. (2008). Paradox in positive organizational change. *Journal of Applied Behavioral Science, 44*, 7–24.

Cameron, K. (1980). Critical questions in assessing organizational effectiveness. *Organizational Dynamics, 9*(2), 66–80.

Cameron, K., & McNaughton, J. (2014). Positive organizational change. *Journal of Applied Behavioral Science, 50*, 445–462.

Cameron, K. S. (2013). *Practicing positive leadership: Tools and techniques that create extraordinary results.* San Francisco, CA: Berrett Koehler.

Campbell, T. D., & Stanley, J. C. (1966). *Experimental and quasi-experimental designs for research.* Chicago, IL: Rand McNally.

Capra, F. (1996). *The web of life.* New York, NY: Anchor Books.

Capra, F. (1983). *The turning point: Science, society, and the rising culture.* New York, NY: Bantam Books.

Capra, F. (1977). The Tao of physics: Reflections on the 'cosmic dance'. *Saturday Review, 5*(6), 21–23, 28.

Capra, F. (1976). *The Tao of physics: An exploration of the parallels between modern physics and eastern mysticism* (2nd ed.). Boulder, CO: Shambhala Publications.

Carlzon, J. (1987). *Moments of truth: New strategies for today's customer-driven economy.* Cambridge, MA: Ballinger.

Chandler, A. (1962). *Strategy and structure.* Cambridge, MA: MIT Press.

Chatman, J. A., Polzer, J. T., Barsade, S. G., & Neale, M. A. (1998). Being different yet feeling similar: The influence of demographic composition and organizational culture on work processes and outcomes. *Administrative Science Quarterly, 43*, 749–780.

Chatman, J. A., & Spataro, S. E. (2005). Using self categorization theory to understand relational demography–based variations in people's responsiveness to organizational culture. *Academy of Management Journal, 48*, 321–331.

Cheung-Judge, M. Y. (2001). The self as an instrument: A cornerstone of the future of OD. *OD Practitioner, 33*(3), 11–16.

Christensen, C. M. (1997). *The innovator's dilemma.* Boston, MA: Harvard Business School Press.

Christensen, C. M., & Raynor, M. E. (2003). *The innovator's solution: creating and sustaining successful growth.* Boston, MA: Harvard Business School Press.

Church, A. H. (2014). What do we know about developing leadership potential? The role of OD in strategic talent management. *OD Practitioner, 46*(3), 52–61.

Church, A. H. (2013). Engagement is in the eye of the beholder. *OD Practitioner, 45*(2), 42–48.

Church, A. H. (1997). Managerial self-awareness in high-performing individuals in organizations. *Journal of Applied Psychology, 82*, 281–292.

Church, A. H., & Burke, W. W. (1993). What are the basic values of OD? *Academy of Management ODC Division Newsletter. Winter: 1*, 7–11.

Church, A. H., Burke, W. W., & Van Eynde, D. F. (1994). Values, motives, and interventions of organization development practitioners. *Group and Organization Management, 19*, 5–50.

Church, A. H., & Dutta, S. (2013). The promise of big data for OD: Old wine in new bottles or the next generation of data-driven methods for change? *OD Practitioner, 45*(4), 23–31.

Clutterbuck, D., & Meggison, D. (2005). *Making coaching work: Creating a coaching culture.* UK: Chartered Institute of Personnel and Development.

Coch, L., & French, J. R. P. (1948). Overcoming resistance to change. *Human Relations 1*, 512–532.

Collier, J. (1945). United States Indian Administration as a laboratory of ethnic relations. *Social Research, 12* (May), 275–276.

Cooperrider, D. L. (2012). The concentration effect of strengths: How the whole system "AI" summit brings out the best in human enterprise. *Organizational Dynamics, 41*(2), 106-117.

Cooperrider, D. L., & Srivastva, S. (1987). Appreciative inquiry in organizational life. In W. A. Pasmore & R. W. Woodman (Eds.), *Research in organizational change and development* (Vol. 1). Greenwich, CT: JAI Press.

Cooperrider, D. L., & Whitney, D., & Stavros, J. M. (2008). *Appreciative inquiry handbook* (2nd ed.). Brunswick, OH: Crown Custom Publishing.

Cross, R., Ernst, C., & Pasmore, B. (2013). A bridge too far? How boundary spanning networks drive organizational change and effectiveness. *Organizational Dynamics, 42* (2), 81–91.

Cummings, T. G., & Worley, C. G. (2014). *Organization development and change.* Stamford, CT: Cengage Learning.

Cytrynbaum, S., & Noumair, D. A. (2004). *Group dynamics, organizational irrationality, and social complexity: Group relations reader 3.* Jupiter, FL: A. K. Rice Institute for the Study of Social Systems.

Darling, M., Parry, C., & Moore, J. (2005). Learning in the thick of it. *Harvard Business Review*, June-July, 2005.

Davis, S. A. (1967). An organic problem-solving method of organizational change. *Journal of Applied Behavioral Science, 3*, 3–21.

Dawson, P. (1994). *Organizational change: A processual approach.* London, England: Paul Chapman Publishing.

deHaan, E., Duckworth, A., Birch, D., & Jones, C. (2013). Executive coaching outcome research: The contribution of common factors such as relationship, personality match, and self-efficacy. *Consulting Psychology Journal: Practice and Research*, 65, 40-57.

Deal, T. E., & Kennedy, A. A. (1982). *Corporate cultures: The rites and rituals of corporate life.* Reading, MA: Addison-Wesley.

Delbecq, A. L., Van de Ven, A. H., & Gustafson, D. H. (1975). *Group techniques for program planning: A guide to nominal group and Delphi processes*. Glenview, IL: Scott Foresman.

Dent, E. B., & Goldberg, S. G. (1999). Challenging "resistance to change." *Journal of Applied Behavioral Science, 35,* 25-41.

DeRue, D. S., Ashford, S. J., & Myers, C. G. (2012). Learning agility: In search of conceptual clarity and theoretical grounding. *Industrial and Organizational Psychology: Perspectives on Science and Practice, 5,* 258–279.

Dewey, J. (1938). *Experience & education*. New York, NY: Simon & Schuster.

Diedrich, R. C. (2008). Still more about coaching? *Consulting Psychology: Practice and Research, 60,* 4–6.

Dotlich, D. L., & Cairo, P. C. (1999). *Action coaching: How to leverage individual performance for company success*. San Francisco, CA: Jossey-Bass.

Dowling, W. F. (1975). System 4 builds performance and profits. *Organizational Dynamics, 3*(3), 23–38.

Dunbar, R. I. M. (1992). Neocortex size as a constraint on group size in primates. *Journal of Human Evolution, 20,* 469–493.

Duvall, S., & Wicklund, R. A. (1972). *A theory of objective self awareness*. New York, NY: Academic Press.

Evers, J. G., Brouwers, A., & Tomic, W. (2006). A quasi-experimental study on management coaching effectiveness. *Consulting Psychology Journal: Practice and Research, 58,* 174–182.

Fagenson, E. A., & Burke, W. W. (1990). Organization development practitioners' activities and interventions in organizations during the 1980s. *Journal of Applied Behavioral Science, 26,* 285–297.

Feldman, D. C., & Lankau, M. J. (2005). Executive coaching: A review and agenda for future research. *Journal of Management Development, 31,* 829–848.

Follett, M. P. (1996). The essentials of leadership. In P. Graham (Ed.), *Mary Parker Follett - prophet of management: A celebration of writings from the 1920s* (pp. 163–181). Boston, MA: Harvard Business School Press.

Foltz, J. A., Harvey, J. B., & McLaughlin, J. (1974). Organization development: A line management function. In J. D. Adams (Ed.), *Theory and method in organization development: An evolutionary process* (pp. 373–385). Arlington, VA: NTL Institute.

Ford, J. D., Ford, L. W., & D'Amelio, A. (2008). Resistance to change: The rest of the story. *Academy of Management Review, 33,* 362-377.

Fox, M. M. (1990). The role of individual perceptions of organizational culture in predicting perceptions of work unit climate and organizational performance. Unpublished doctoral dissertation, Columbia University, New York.

Freeman, L. (2006). *The development of social network analysis.* Vancouver, British Columbia, Canada: Empirical Press.

French, J. R. P., Jr., & Raven, B. H. (1959). The bases of social power. In D. Cartwright (Ed.), *Studies in social power* (pp. 150–167). Ann Arbor, MI: Institute for Social Research.

French, W. L. (1969). Organization development: Objectives, assumptions, and strategies. *California Management Review, 12* (Winter), 23–34.

French, W. L., & Bell, C. H., Jr. (1978). *Organization development* (2nd ed.). Englewood Cliffs, NJ: Prentice-Hall.

Friedlander, F. (1976). OD reaches adolescence: An exploration of its underlying values. *Journal of Applied Behavioral Science, 12,* 7–21.

Friedlander, F. (1970). The primacy of trust as a facilitator of further group accomplishment. *Journal of Applied Behavioral Science, 6,* 387–400.

Friedlander, F., & Brown, L. D. (1974). Organization development. *Annual Review of Psychology, 25,* 313–341.

Frisch, M. H. (2001). The emerging role of internal coach. *Consulting Psychology: Practice and Research, 53*(4), 240–250.

Frohman, M. A., Sashkin, M., & Kavanagh, M. J. (1976). Action research as applied to organization development. *Organization and Administrative Sciences, 7,* 129–142.

Frost, P. J., Moore, L. F., Louis, M. R., Lundberg, C. C., & Martin, J. (Eds.). (1991). *Reframing organizational culture.* Newbury Park, CA: Sage.

Gabarro, J. J., & Kotter, J. P. (1980). Managing your boss. *Harvard Business Review* (January-February), 92–100.

Galbraith, J. R. (1982). Designing the innovating organization. *Organizational Dynamics, 10*(1), 5–25.

Galbraith, J. R. (1977). *Organization design.* Reading, MA: Addison-Wesley.

Garvin, D. A., Edmondson, A., & Gino, F. (2008). Is yours a learning organization? *Harvard Business Review, 86* (3), 109-120.

Gillette, J. (1995). Toward a practice of learning. In J. Gillette & M. McCollom (Eds.), *Groups in Context: A New Perspective on Group Dynamics* (pp. 15–33). University Press of America.

Gladwell, M. (2013). *David and Goliath: Underdogs, misfits, and the art of battling giants.* New York, NY: Little, Brown.

Gladwell, M. (2000). *The tipping point: How little things can make a big difference.* Boston, MA: Little, Brown.

Gleick, J. (1987). *Chaos: making a new science.* New York, NY: Viking.

Goleman, D., Boyatzis, R., & McKee, A. (2002). *Primal intelligence: Learning to lead with emotional intelligence.* Boston, MA: Harvard Business School Press.

Golembiewski, R. T., Billingsley, K., & Yeager, S. (1976). Measuring change and persistence in human affairs: Types of change generated by OD designs. *Journal of Applied Behavioral Science, 12,* 133–157.

Golembiewski, R. T., Hilles, R., & Kagno, M. S. (1974). A longitudinal study of flex-time effects: Some consequences of an OD structural intervention. *Journal of Applied Behavioral Science, 10,* 503–532.

Goodman, P. S., & Pennings, J. M. (1980). Critical issues in assessing organizational effectiveness. In E. E. Lawler, D. A. Nadler, and C. Cammann (Eds.), *Organizational assessment: Perspectives on the measurement of organizational behavior and the quality of work life* (pp.185–215). New York, NY: Wiley-Interscience.

Goodstein, L. D., & Burke, W. W. (1991). Creating successful organizational change. *Organizational Dynamics, 19*(4), 5–17.

Gould, L. J. (2004). Fraternal disciplines: Group relations training and systems psychodynamic consultation. In L. J. Gould, L. F. Stapley, & M. Stein (Eds.), *Experiential learning in organizations: Applications of the Tavistock group relations approach* (pp. 39–62). London, England: Karnac.

Grant, A. M. (2011). *Workplace, executive and life coaching: An annotated bibliography from the behavioural science and business literature.* Coaching Psychology Unit, University of Sydney.

Grant, D., & Marshak, R. J. (2011). Toward a discourse-centered understanding of organizational change. *Journal of Applied Behavioral Science, 47*, 204–235.

Grant, D., & Oswick, C. (1996). *Metaphor and organization*. London, England: Sage.

Gray, B. (2014). *Discussant* for symposium on fifty years of powerful words: A retrospective and prospective look at the impact of *The Journal of Applied Behavioral Science*. Annual Meeting, *Academy of Management*, Philadelphia, August 4.

Gray, B. (2008). Intervening to improve inter-organizational partnerships. In S. Cropper, M. Ebers, & P. S. Ring (Eds.), *The Oxford handbook of inter-organizational relations* (pp. 664–690). Oxford, England: Oxford University Press.

Green, Z. G., & Molenkamp, R. J. (2005). *The BART system of group and organizational analysis: Boundary, authority, role, and task*. Unpublished manuscript.

Greiner, L. E. (1972). Evolution and revolution as organizations grow. *Harvard Business Review, 50*(4), 37–46.

Griffen, D. (2002). *The emergence of leadership*. London, England: Routledge.

Guidelines for education and training at the doctoral and postdoctoral levels in consulting psychology/organizational consulting psychology (2007). *American Psychologist, 62*(9), 980–992.

Gustafson, J. P., & Cooper, L. (1992). After basic assumptions: On holding a specialized versus a generalized theory of participant observation in small groups. In M. Pines (Ed.), *Bion and group psychotherapy* (pp. 157–175). London and Philadelphia: Jessica Kingsley Publishers.

Guzzo, R. A., Jette, R. D., & Katzell, R. A. (1985). The effects of psychologically based intervention programs on worker productivity: A meta-analysis. *Personnel Psychology, 38*, 275–291.

Hackman, J. R., (Ed.). (1989). *Groups that work (and those that don't): Creating conditions for effective teamwork*. San Francisco, CA: Jossey-Bass.

Hackman, J. R., & Oldham, G. R. (1980). *Work redesign*. Reading, MA: Addison-Wesley.

Hackman, J. R., & Oldham, G. R. (1975). Development of the job diagnostic survey. *Journal of Applied Psychology, 60*, 159–170.

Hall, J. (1976). To achieve or not: The manager's choice. *California Management Review, 18*(4), 5–18.

Halton, W. (1994). Some unconscious aspects of organizational life: Contributions from psychoanalysis. In A. Obholzer & V. Zagier Roberts (Eds.), *The Unconscious at Work*. London, England: Routledge.

Hanna, D. P. (1988). *Designing organizations for high performance.* Reading, MA: Addison-Wesley.

Harvey, J. B. (1988). *The Abilene Paradox and other meditations on management.* Lexington, MA: Lexington Books.

Harvey, J. B. (1974). The Abilene Paradox: The management of agreement. *Organizational Dynamics, 3*(2), 63–80.

Hatch, M. J. (1997). *Organization theory: Modern, symbolic and postmodern perspectives.* Oxford, England: Oxford University Press.

Heifetz, R. (1994). *Leadership without easy answers.* Cambridge, MA: Belknap Press.

Heifetz, R., & Linsky, M. (2002). *Leadership on the line: Staying alive through the dangers of leading.* Boston: Harvard Business Review Press.

Heisler, W. J. (1975). Patterns of OD in practice. *Business Horizons* (February), 77–84.

Hersey, P., & Blanchard, K. H. (1993). *Management of organizational behavior: Utilizing human resources (6th ed.).* Englewood Cliffs, NJ: Prentice Hall.

Herzberg, F. (1966). *Work and the nature of man.* Cleveland, OH: World.

Herzberg, F., Mausner, B., & Snyderman, B. (1959). *The motivation to work.* New York, NY: Wiley.

Hirschhorn, L. (1988). *The workplace within: Psychodynamics of organizational life.* Cambridge, MA: The MIT Press.

Hogan, R. (2006). *Personality and the fate of the organization.* Hillsdale, NJ: Lawrence Erlbaum Associates.

Hogan, R. J., Curphy, G. J., & Hogan, J. (1994). What we know about leadership: Effectiveness and personality. *American Psychologist, 49*(6), 493–504.

Holt, D. T., Armenakis, A. A., Feild, H. S., & Harris, S. G. (2007). Readiness for organizational change: The systematic development of a scale. *Journal of Applied Behavioral Science, 43*, 232–255.

Homan, P. (2010). *Engaging emergence. Turning upheaval into opportunity.* San Francisco, CA: Berrett-Koehler.

Homans, G. C. (1950). *The human group.* New York, NY: Harcourt Brace.

Hornstein, H. A., Bunker, B. B., Burke, W. W., Gindes, M., & Lewicki, R. J. (1971). *Social intervention: A behavioral science approach.* New York, NY: Free Press.

Hornstein, H. A., & Tichy, N. M. (1973). *Organization diagnosis and improvement strategies.* New York, NY: Behavioral Science Associates.

Hunt, J. M., & Weintraub, J. R. (2007). *The coaching organization: A strategy for developing leaders.* Thousand Oaks, CA: Sage.

Hunt, J. M., & Weintraub, J. R. (2006). *The coaching manager: Developing top talent in business* (2nd ed.). Thousand Oaks, CA: Sage.

Huselid, M. (1995). The impact of human resource management practices on turnover, productivity, and corporate financial performance. *Academy of Management Journal, 38,* 635–672.

Jamieson, D., & O'Mara, J. (1991). *Managing workforce 2000: Gaining the diversity advantage.* San Francisco, CA: Jossey-Bass.

Janis, I. L. (1972). *Victims of groupthink: A psychological study of foreign policy decisions and fiascoes.* Boston, MA: Houghton Mifflin.

Jantsch, E. (1980). *The self-organizing universe: Scientific and human implications of the emerging paradigm of evolution.* Elmsford, NY: Pergamon Press.

Jones, J. E. (1980). Quality control of OD practitioners and practice. In W. W. Burke & L. D. Goodstein (Eds.), *Trends and issues in OD: Current theory and practice* (pp. 333–345). San Diego, CA: University Associates.

Joni, S.A. (2004). *The third opinion.* New York, NY: Penguin Group.

Kagan, N. I. (1984). Interpersonal process recall: Basic methods and recent research. In D. Larson (Ed.), *Teaching psychological skills: Models for giving psychology away* (pp. 229–244). Monterey, CA: Brooks Cole.

Kaiser, R. B., Hogan, R., & Craig, S. B. (2008). Leadership and the fate of organizations. *American Psychologist, 63*(2), 96–110.

Kanter, R. M. (1989). *When giants learn to dance: Mastering the challenges of strategy, management, and careers in the 1990s.* New York, NY: Simon and Schuster.

Kanter, R. M. (1984). *The change masters: Innovating for productivity in the American corporation*. New York, NY: Warner Books.

Kanter, R. M. (1982). Dilemmas of managing participation. *Organizational Dynamics, 11*(1), 5–27.

Kanter, R. M., Stein, B. A., & Jick, T. D. (1992). *The challenge of organizational change*. New York, NY: Free Press.

Kaplan, R. E. (1982). Intervention in a loosely organized system: An encounter with non-being. *Journal of Applied Behavioral Science, 18*, 415–432.

Kaplan, S. (2005). Technology and organization development. In W. J. Rothwell & R. L. Sullivan (Eds.), *Practicing organization development: A guide for consultants* (2nd ed.) (pp. 550–582). San Francisco, CA: Pfeiffer.

Katz, D., & Kahn, R. L. (1978). *The social psychology of organizations* (2nd ed.). New York, NY: Wiley.

Kauffman, C., & Coutou, D. (2009). HBR research report: The realities of executive coaching. *Harvard Business Review*, available at coachingreport.hbr.org.

Kayes, A. B., Kayes, D. C., & Kolb, D. A. (2005). Experiential learning in teams. *Simulation & Gaming*, 36(X), 1–25.

Kessler, E. H. (Ed). (2013). *Encyclopedia of management theory*, Volume two (pp. 542–547). Thousand Oaks, CA: Sage.

Kets De Vries, M. F. R., Krotov, K., & Florent-Treacy, E. (2007). *Coach and couch: The psychology of making better leaders.* New York, NY: Palgrave Macmillan.

Kilburg, R. R. (2002). Shadow consultation: A reflective approach for preventing disasters. *Consulting Psychology Journal: Practice and Research, 54*, pp. 75–92.

Kilduff, M., & Tsai, W. (2003). *Social networks and organizations*. London, England: Sage.

Kimberly, J. R., & Nielsen, W. R. (1975). Organization development and change in organizational performance. *Administrative Science Quarterly, 20*, 191–206.

King, A. (1974). Expectation effects in organizational change. *Administrative Science Quarterly, 19*, 221–230.

King, D.C., Sherwood, J. J., & Manning, M. R. (1978). OD's research base: How to expand and utilize it. In W. W. Burke (Ed.), *The cutting edge: Current theory and practice in organization development* (pp. 133–148). La Jolla, CA: University Associates.

Kissler, G. D. (1991). *The change riders: Managing the power of change.* Reading, MA: Addison-Wesley.

Kizilos, M., Cummings, T., & Strickstein, A. (1994). Achieving superior customer service through employee involvement. Academy of Management Best Paper Proceedings, 197–201.

Knoke, D., & Yang, S. (2008). *Social network analysis* (2nd ed.). Thousand Oaks, CA: Sage.

Kolb, D., & Frohman, A. (1970). An organization development approach to consulting. *Sloan Management Review, 12*(1), 51–65.

Kotter, J. P. (1982). *The general managers.* New York, NY: The Free Press.

Kotter, J. P., & Heskett, J. L. (1992). *Corporate culture and performance.* New York, NY: The Free Press.

Krantz, J. (2001). 6 dilemmas of organizational change: A systems psychodynamics perspective. In L. J. Gould, L. F. Stapley, & M. Stein (Eds.), *The systems psychodynamics of organizations: Integrating the group relations approach, psychoanalytic, and open systems perspectives* (pp. 133–156). London, England: Karnac Books.

Lawler, E. E. III. (1992). *The ultimate advantage: Creating the high involvement organization.* San Francisco, CA: Jossey-Bass.

Lawler, E. E. III. (1977). Reward systems. In J. R. Hackman & J. L. Suttle (Eds.), *Improving life at work* (pp. 163–226). Santa Monica, CA: Goodyear.

Lawler, E. E. III. (1973). *Motivation in work organizations.* Monterey, CA: Brooks/Cole.

Lawler, E. E. III, & Worley, C. G. (2006). *Built to change: How to achieve sustained organizational effectiveness.* San Francisco, CA: Jossey-Bass.

Lawrence, P. R., & Lorsch, J. W. (1969). *Developing organizations: Diagnosis and action.* Reading, MA: Addison-Wesley.

Lawrence, P. R., & Lorsch, J. W. (1967). *Organization and environment: Managing differentiation and integration.* Boston, MA: Division of Research, Harvard Business School.

Lawrence, W. G., Bain, A., & Gould, L. (1996). The fifth basic assumption. *Free Associations*, 6, Part 1 (No.37), 28–55.

Leadership Development Survey. Hogan Assessment Systems (www. hoganassessments.com).

Leahey, J., & Kotter, J. P. (1990). *Changing the culture at British Airways.* Harvard Business School Case No. 491–009.

Lennard, D. (2010). *Coaching models: A cultural perspective.* New York, NY: Routledge.

Lepore, J. (2014, June 23). The disruption machine. *The New Yorker*, XC (17), pp. 30–36.

Levinson, D. J., Darrow, C. N., Klein, E. B., Levinson, M. H., & McKee, B. (1978). *The seasons of a man's life.* New York, NY: Knopf.

Levinson, D. J., & Levinson, J. D. (1996). *The seasons of a woman's life.* New York, NY: Knopf.

Levinson, H. (1975). *Executive stress.* New York, NY: Harper & Row.

Levinson, H. (1972a). *Organizational diagnosis.* Cambridge, MA: Harvard University Press.

Levinson, H. (1972b). The clinical psychologist as organizational diagnostician. *Professional Psychology, 3,* 34–40.

Lewicki, R. J., & Alderfer, C. P. (1973). The tensions between research and intervention in intergroup conflict. *Journal of Applied Behavioral Science, 9,* 423–468.

Lewin, K. (1958). Group decision and social change. In E. E. Maccoby, T. M. Newcomb, & E. L. Hartley (Eds.), *Readings in social psychology* (pp. 163–226). New York, NY: Holt, Rinehart, and Winston.

Lewin, K. (1951). *Field theory in social science.* New York, NY: Harper.

Lewin, K. (1948). *Resolving social conflicts.* New York, NY: Harper.

Lewin, K. (1947). Group decision and social change. In T. M. Newcomb, E. L. Hartley, et al. (Eds.) *Readings in social psychology* (pp. 330-344). New York, NY: Henry Holt.

Lewin, K. (1946). Action research and minority problems. *Journal of Social Issues, 2,* 34–46.

Lewin, K. (1936). *Principles of topological psychology.* New York, NY: McGraw-Hill.

Lewis, M. (2004). *Moneyball: The art of winning an unfair game.* New York, NY: Norton.

Likert, R. (1967). *The human organization.* New York, NY: McGraw-Hill.

Likert, R. (1961). *New patterns of management.* New York, NY: McGraw-Hill.

Lippitt, R., & Lippitt, G. (1975). Consulting process in action. *Training and Development Journal, 29*(5) 48–54.

Lippitt, R., Watson, J., & Westley, B. (1958). *Dynamics of planned change.* New York, NY: Harcourt, Brace.

Litwin, G. H., & Stringer, R. A. (1968). *Motivation and organizational climate.* Boston, MA: Harvard Business School Press.

Lodahl, T. M., & Williams, L. K. (1978). An opportunity for OD: The office revolution. *OD Practitioner, 10*(4), 9–11.

Luthans, F., & Peterson, S. J. (2003). 360-feedback with systematic coaching: Empirical analysis suggests a winning combination. *Human Resource Management, 42*(3), 243–256.

Maccoby, M. (1976). *The gamesman: The new corporate leaders.* New York, NY: Irvington.

McCall, M. W., Jr. (2010). Recasting leadership development. *Industrial and Organizational Psychology: Perspectives on Science and Practice, 3*(1), 3–19.

McClelland, D. C. (1975). *Power: The inner experience.* New York, NY: Irvington.

McClelland, D. C., & Burnham, D. H. (1976). Power is the great motivator. *Harvard Business Review, 54*(2), 100–110.

McCollom, M. (1995). Group formation: Boundaries, leadership, and culture. In J. Gillette & M. McCollom (Eds.), *Groups in context: A new perspective on group dynamics* (pp. 34–38). Lanham, MD: University Press of America, Inc.

McCormick, D.W., & White, J. (2000). Using one's self as an instrument of organizational diagnosis. *Organization Development Journal, 18*(3), 49–61.

McGregor, D. (1967). *The professional manager.* New York, NY: McGraw-Hill.

McGregor, D. (1960). *The human side of enterprise.* New York, NY: McGraw-Hill.

Maltbia, T. E., Marsick, V. J., & Ghosh, R. (2014). Executive and organizational coaching: A review of insights drawn from literature to inform HRD practice. *Advances in Developing Human Resources, 16*(2), 161–183.

Mann, F. C. (1957). Studying and creating change: A means to understanding social organization. In *Research in Industrial Human Relations.* Industrial Relations Research Association, Publication No. 17.

Margulies, N. (1978). Perspectives on the marginality of the consultant's role. In W. W. Burke (Ed.), *The cutting edge: Current theory and practice in organization development* (pp. 60–69). La Jolla, CA: University Associates.

Marrow, A. J. (1969). *The practical theorist.* New York, NY: Basic Books.

Marrow, A. J., Bowers, D. G., & Seashore, S. E. (1967). *Management by participation.* New York, NY: Harper & Row.

Marshak, R. J. (2006). *Covert processes at work: Managing the five hidden dimensions of organizational change*. San Francisco, CA: Berrett-Koehler.

Maslow, A. H. (1965). *Eupsychian management: A journal.* Homewood, IL: Richard I. Irwin, and the Dorsey Press.

Maslow, A. H. (1954). *Motivation and personality.* New York, NY: Harper & Brothers.

Mayo, E. (1933). *The human problems of an industrial civilization.* Boston, MA: Harvard University Graduate School of Business.

Meggison, D., & Clutterbuck, D. (2006). Creating a coaching culture. *Industrial and Commercial Training, 38*(5), 232–237.

Michela, J. L., Boni, S. M., Schechter, C. B., Manderlink, G., Bernstein, W. M., O'Malley, M., & Burke, W. W. (1988). A hierarchically nested model for estimation of influences on organizational climate: Rationale, methods, and demonstration. Working Paper, Teachers College, Columbia University.

Miller, C. C. (2014, May 1). Yes, Silicon Valley, there is such a thing as not enough bureaucracy. *The New York Times,* p. B3. Retrieved from http://www.nytimes.com/2014/05/01/upshot/yes-silicon-valley-there-is-such-a-thing-as-not-enough-bureaucracy.html

Miller, E. C. (1978). The parallel organization structure at General Motors: An interview with Howard C. Carlson. *Personnel, 55*(4), 64–69.

Miller, E. J., & Rice, A. K. (1967). *Systems of organization.* London, England: Tavistock.

Mitchinson, A., Gerard, N. M., Roloff, K. S., & Burke, W. W. (2012). Learning agility: Spanning the rigor-relevance divide. *Industrial and Organizational Psychology: Perspectives on Science and Practice, 5,* 287–290.

Moeller, S. B., Schlingemann, F. P., & Stulz, R. M. (2005). Wealth destruction on a massive scale? A study of acquiring firm returns in the recent merger wave. *The Journal of Finance,* LX, 757–782.

Morrison, P. (1978). Evaluation in OD: A review and an assessment. *Group and Organization Studies, 3,* 42–70.

Morrison, T. (1992). *Playing in the dark: Whiteness and the literary imagination.* New York, NY: Knopf Doubleday, Inc.

Murphy, W., & Kram, K. E. (2014). *Strategic relationships at work: Creating your circle of mentors, sponsors, peers for success in business and life.* New York, NY: McGraw-Hill Education.

Myers-Briggs Type Indicator, Consulting Psychologists Press, Inc. (www. cpp.com).

Nadler, D. A. (1981). Managing organizational change: An integrative approach. *Journal of Applied Behavioral Science, 17*(2), 191–211.

Nadler, D. A. (1977). *Feedback and organization development: Using data-based methods.* Reading, MA: Addison-Wesley.

Nadler, D. A., Gerstein, M. S., Shaw, R. B., & Associates. (1992). *Organizational architecture: Designs for changing organizations.* San Francisco, CA: Jossey-Bass.

Nadler, D. A., & Tushman, M. L. (1989). Organizational frame bending: Principles for managing reorientation. *Academy of Management Executive, 3,* 194–204.

Nadler, D. A., & Tushman, M. L. (1977). A diagnostic model for organization behavior. In J. R. Hackman, E. E. Lawler, & L. W. Porter (Eds.), *Perspectives on behavior in organizations* (pp. 85–100). New York, NY: McGraw-Hill.

Naim, M. (2013). *The end of power.* New York, NY: Basic Books.

Naisbett, J. (1982). *Megatrends: Ten new directions transforming our lives.* New York, NY: Warner Books.

Naisbett, J., & Aburdene, P. (1985). *Re-inventing the corporation.* New York, NY: Warner Books.

Neuman, G. A., Edwards, J. E., & Raju, N. S. (1989). Organizational development interventions: A meta-analysis of their effects on satisfaction and other attitudes. *Personnel Psychology, 42*, 461–489.

Nicolis, G., & Prigogine, I. (1977). *Self-organization in nonequilibrium systems: From dissipative structures to order through fluctuations.* New York, NY: Wiley-Interscience.

Noumair, D. A. (2013). Cultural revelations: Shining a light on organizational dynamics. *International Journal of Group Psychotherapy, 63*(2), 153–176.

Noumair, D. A., Winderman, B. B., & Burke, W. W. (2010). Transforming the A. K. Rice Institute: From club to organization. *Journal of Applied Behavioral Science, 46*, 473–499.

Nowack, K. M., & Mashihi, S. (2012). Evidence-based answers to 15 questions about leveraging 360-degree feedback. *Consulting Psychology Journal: Practice and Research, 64*, 157–182.

O'Neill, M. B. (2007). *Executive coaching with backbone and heart: A systems approach to engaging leaders with their challenges* (2nd ed.). San Francisco, CA: Jossey Bass.

Obholzer, A., & Zagier Roberts, V. (Eds). (1994). *The unconscious at work.* London, England: Routledge.

Oreg, S., Vakola M., & Armenakis, A. (2011). Change recipients' reaction to organizational change: A 60 year review of quantitative studies. *Journal of Applied Behavioral Science, 47*, 461-524.

Orenstein, R. (2002). Executive coaching: It's not just about the executive. *Journal of Applied Behavioral Science, 38*, 355–374.

Orton, J. D., & Weick, K. E. (1990). Loosely coupled systems: A reconceptualization. *Academy of Management Review, 15*, 203–223.

Owen, H. (2008). *Open space technology* (3rd ed.). San Francisco, CA: Berrett-Koehler.

Parker, P., Hall, D. T., & Kram, K. E. (2008). Peer coaching: A relational process for accelerating career learning. *Academy of Management Learning & Education, 7*, 487–503.

Pasmore, W. (2014). Deconstructing OD: A closer look at the emergence of OD values and their impact on the field. *OD Practitioner, 46(4)*, 31-34.

Pate, L. E., Nielsen, W. R., & Bacon, P. C. (1977). Advances in research on organization development: Toward a beginning. *Group and Organization Studies, 2*, 449–460.

Pavur, E. J. (2013). Why do organizations want their leaders to be coached? *Consulting Psychology Journal: Practice and Research, 65,* 289-293.

Pearce, W. B., & Cronen, V. E. (1980). *Communication, action, and meaning.* New York, NY: Praeger.

Peltier, B. (2010). *The psychology of executive coaching: Theory and application* (2nd ed.). New York, NY: Routledge.

Peters, T. J. (1987). *Thriving on chaos: Handbook for a management revolution.* New York, NY: Alfred A. Knopf.

Peters, T. J., & Waterman, R. H., Jr. (1982). *In search of excellence: Lessons from America's best-run companies.* New York, NY: Harper & Row.

Peterson, D. B. (2011). Executive coaching: A critical review and recommendations. In S. Zedeck (Ed.), *APA Handbook of Industrial and Organizational Psychology, Volume 2: Selecting and developing members for the organization* (pp. 527–566). Washington, DC: American Psychological Association.

Pfeiffer, J. W., & Jones, J. E. (1978). OD readiness. In W. W. Burke (Ed.), *The cutting edge: Current theory and practice in organization development* (pp. 179–185). La Jolla, CA: University Associates.

Piderit, S. K. (2000). Rethinking resistance and recognizing ambivalence: A multidimensional view of attitudes toward an organizational change. *Academy of Management Review, 25,* 783–794.

Porras, J. I. (1979). The comparative impact of different OD techniques and intervention intensities. *Journal of Applied Behavioral Science, 15,* 156–178.

Porras, J. I., & Patterson, K. (1979). Assessing planned change. *Group and Organization Studies, 4,* 39–58.

Porras, J. I., & Wilkens, A. (1980). Organization development in a large system: An empirical assessment. *Journal of Applied Behavioral Science, 16,* 506–34.

Power, C. (1989, October 9). From "bloody awful" to bloody awesome. *Business Week*, p. 97.

Prigogine, I., & Stengers, I. (1984). *Order out of chaos: Man's new dialogue with nature.* New York, NY: Bantam.

Pucik, V., Tichy, N. M., & Barnett, C. K. (Eds.). (1992). *Globalizing management: Creating and leading the competitive organization.* New York, NY: Wiley.

Quinn, R. E., Heynoski, K., Thomas, M., & Spreitzer, G. (2014). Co-creating classroom experience to transform learning and change lives. In A. B. Shani & D. A. Noumair (Eds.), *Research in organizational change and development*, Vol. 22 (pp. 25–54). United Kingdom: Emerald Group Publishing.

Raven, B. H. (1993). The bases of power—origins and recent developments. *Journal of Social Issues, 49*(4), 227–251.

Rhinesmith, S. H. (1992). *A manager's guide to globalization.* Homewood, IL: Business One Irwin.

Rice, A. K. (1958). *Productivity and social organizations: The Ahmedabad experiment.* London, England: Tavistock.

Rioch, M. J. (1975a). Group relations: Rationale and technique. In A. D. Colman & W. H. Bexton (Eds.), *Group relations reader 1* (pp. 3–9). Jupiter, FL: A. K. Rice Institute.

Rioch, M. J. (1975b). The work of Wilfred Bion on groups. In A. D. Colman & W. H. Bexton (Eds.), *Group relations reader 1* (pp. 21–33). Jupiter, FL: A. K. Rice Institute.

Rioch, M. J. (1970). The work of Wilfred Bion on groups. *Psychiatry, 33,* 56–66.

Roethlisberger, F. J., & Dickson, W. J. (1939). *Management and the worker: An account of a research program conducted by the Western Electric Company.* Cambridge, MA: Harvard University Press.

Rosenthal, R. (1976). *Experimenter effects in behavioral research,* enlarged ed. New York, NY: Halsted Press.

Rubin, I. (1967). Increasing self-acceptance: A means of reducing prejudice. *Journal of Personality and Social Psychology, 5,* 233–38.

Rutan, J. S., Stone, W. N., & Shay, J. J. (2007). *Psychodynamic group psychotherapy* (4th ed.). New York, NY: The Guilford Press.

Saparito, B. (1986). The revolt against 'working smarter'. *Fortune, 114*(2), 58–65.

Sashkin, M. (1984). Participative management is an ethical imperative. *Organizational Dynamics, 12*(4), 4–22.

Sashkin, M., & Burke, W. W. (1987). Organization development in the 1980s. *Journal of Management, 13,* 393–417.

Sashkin, M., & Kiser, K. J. (1993). *Putting total quality management to work.* San Francisco, CA: Berrett-Koehler Publishers.

Schacter, S. (1959). *The psychology of affiliation.* Stanford, CA: Stanford University Press.

Schein, E. H. (2014). The role of coercive persuasion in education and learning: subjugation or animation. In A. B. Shani & D. A. Noumair (Eds.), *Research in organizational change and development*, Volume 22 (pp. 1–24). United Kingdom: Emerald Group Publishing Limited.

Schein, E. H. (2013a). *Humble inquiry: The gentle art of asking instead of telling.* San Francisco, CA: Berrett-Koehler.

Schein, E. H. (2013b). The role of art and the artist. *Organizational Aesthetics, 2,* 1–4.

Schein, E. H. (2004). *Organizational culture and leadership* (3rd ed.). San Francisco, CA: Jossey-Bass.

Schein, E. H. (2000). Coaching and consultation: Are they the same? In M. Goldsmith, L. Lyons, & A. Freas (Eds.), *Coaching for leadership: How the world's greatest coaches help leaders learn* (pp. 65–73). San Francisco, CA: Jossey-Bass.

Schein, E. H. (1999). *Process consultation revisited: Building the helping relationship.* Reading, MA: Addison-Wesley.

Schein, E. H. (1992). *Organizational culture and leadership* (2nd ed.). San Francisco, CA: Jossey-Bass.

Schein, E. H. (1991). Legitimizing clinical research in the study of organizational culture. Sixteenth Annual Frederick J. Gaudet Lecture, Stevens Institute, Hoboken, N.J. (April 30, 1991).

Schein, E. H. (1988). *Process consultation, Vol. 1: Its role in organization development* (2nd ed.). Reading, MA: Addison-Wesley.

Schein, E. H. (1987). *Process consultation, Vol. 2: Lessons for managers and consultants.* Reading, MA: Addison-Wesley.

Schein, E. H. (1985). *Organizational culture and leadership.* San Francisco, CA: Jossey-Bass.

Schein, E. H. (1980). *Organizational psychology* (3rd ed.). Englewood Cliffs, NJ: Prentice-Hall.

Schein, E. H. (1969). *Process consultation.* Reading, MA: Addison-Wesley.

Schein, E. H., & Bennis, W. G. (1965). *Personal and organizational change through group methods: The laboratory approach.* New York, NY: Wiley.

Schneider, B. (1990). The climate for service: Application of the construct. In B. Schneider (Ed.), *Organizational climate and culture* (pp. 383–412). San Francisco, CA: Jossey-Bass.

Schneider, B. (1980). The service organization: Climate is crucial. *Organizational Dynamics, 9*(2), 52–65.

Schneider, B., & Bowen, D. E. (1985). Employee and customer perceptions of service in banks: Replication and extension. *Journal of Applied Psychology, 70,* 423–433.

Schön, D. A. (1983). *The reflective practitioner.* New York, NY: Basic Books, Inc.

Schön, D. A. (1987). *Educating the reflective practitioner.* San Francisco, CA: Jossey Bass.

Schröder, M. (1974). The shadow consultant. *Journal of Applied Behavioral Science, 10,*579–594.

Schuler, R. S., & Harris, D. L. (1992). *Managing quality: The primer for middle managers.* Reading, MA: Addison-Wesley.

Seashore, S. E., & Bowers, D. G. (1970). Durability of organizational change. *American Psychologist, 25*(March), 227–33.

Seelye, K. Q., & de la Merced, M. J. (2014). Workers win supermarket president's job back. *The New York Times*, p. A17.

Seligman, M. E. P., & Csikszentmihalyi, M. (2000). Positive psychology: An introduction. *American Psychologist, 55*(1), 5–14.

Selznick, P. (1957). *Leadership in administration.* New York, NY: Harper & Row.

Senge, P. M. (1990). *The fifth discipline: The art and practice of the learning organization.* New York, NY: Doubleday.

Shapiro, E. R., & Carr, A. W. (1991). *Lost in familiar places: Creating new connections between the individual and society.* New Haven, CT: Yale University Press.

Shaw, P. (2002). *Changing conversations in organisations.* London, England: Routledge.

Shepard, H. A. (1960). Three management programs and the theory behind them. In *An action research program for organization improvement.* Ann Arbor, MI: Foundation for Research on Human Behavior.

Shull, A. C., Church, A. H., & Burke, W. W. (2014). Something old, something new: Research findings regarding the practice and values of OD. *OD Practitioner, 46*(4), 23–30.

Shull, A. C., Church, A. H., & Burke, W.W. (2013). Attitudes about the field of organization development 20 years later: The more things change, the more they stay the same. In A. B. Shani, W. A. Pasmore, R. W. Woodman, & D. A. Noumair (Eds.), *Research in organizational change and development, Volume 21* (pp. 1–28). United Kingdom: Emerald Group Publishing Limited.

Siefert, C., Yukl, G., & McDonald, R. (2003). Effects of multisource feedback and a feedback facilitator on the influence of behavior of managers toward subordinates. *Journal of Applied Behavior, 88,* 561–569.

Skinner, B. F. (1971). *Beyond freedom and dignity.* New York, NY: Knopf.

Skinner, B. F. (1953). *Science and human behavior.* New York, NY: Macmillan.

Skinner, B. F. (1948). *Walden two.* New York, NY: Macmillan.

Sloan, A. P. (1946). *My years in General Motors.* Garden City, NY: Doubleday.

Smith, K. K. (1995). On using the self as instrument: Lessons from a facilitator's experience. In J. Gillette & M. McCollom (Eds.), *Groups in context: A new perspective on group dynamics* (pp. 276–294). Lanham, MD: University Press of America, Inc.

Smither, J., London, M., Flautt, R., Vargas, Y., & Kucine, I. (2003). Can working with an executive coach improve multisource feedback ratings over time? A quasi-experimental field study. *Personnel Psychology, 56,* 23–44.

Sommer, J. (2014, June 22). For a shareholder, merger fever can be a menace. *The New York Times*, p. BU 3.

Sperry, L. (2013). Executive coaching and leadership assessment: Past, present, and future. *Consulting Psychology Journal: Practice and Research, 65,* 284–288.

Sperry, L. (2008). Executive coaching: An intervention, role function, or profession? *Consulting Psychology Journal: Practice and Research, 60,* 33–37.

Stacey, R. D. (2011). *Strategic management and organisational dynamics: The challenge of complexity to ways of thinking about organisations* (6th ed.). London, England: Pearson Education.

Stacey, R. D. (2001). *Complex responsive processes in organizations.* London, England: Routledge.

Stein, B. A., & Kanter, R. M. (1980). Building the parallel organization: Creating mechanisms for permanent quality of work life. *Journal of Applied Behavioral Science, 16,* 371–388.

Stiglitz, J. E. (2014, June 29). Inequality is not inevitable. *The New York Times*, SR 1, 7.

Stober, D. R., & Grant, A. M. (2006). *Evidence-based coaching handbook: Putting practices to work for your client.* Hoboken, NJ: John Wiley & Sons, Inc.

Sullivan, C. C. (2002). Finding the thou in the I: Countertransference and parallel process analysis in organizational research and consultation. *Journal of Applied Behavioral Science, 38,* 375–392.

Tagiuri, R., & Litwin, G. H. (Eds.). (1968). *Organizational climate: Explorations of a concept.* Cambridge, MA: Harvard University Press.

Tannenbaum, R., & Davis, S. A. (1969). Values, man, and organizations. *Industrial Management Review, 10*(2), 67–83.

Taylor, J., & Bowers, D. G. (1972). *The survey of organizations: A machine scored standardized questionnaire instrument.* Ann Arbor, MI: Institute for Social Research.

Tichy, N. M. (1983). *Managing strategic change: Technical, political, and cultural dynamics.* New York, NY: Wiley.

Tichy, N. M. (1978). Demise, absorption, or renewal for the future of organization development. In W. W. Burke (Ed.), *The cutting edge: Current theory and practice in organization development* (pp. 70–88). La Jolla, CA: University Associates.

Tichy, N. M. (1974). Agents of planned social change: Congruence of values, cognitions, and actions. *Administrative Science Quarterly, 19,* 164–182.

Tichy, N. M., & Devanna, M. A. (1986). *The transformational leader.* New York, NY: Wiley.

Tichy, N. M., Hornstein, H. A., & Nisberg, J. N. (1977). Organization diagnosis and intervention strategies: Developing emergent pragmatic theories of change. In W. W. Burke (Ed.), *Current issues and strategies in organization development* (pp. 361–383). New York, NY: Human Sciences Press.

Trist, E. (1960). *Socio-technical systems.* London, England: Tavistock Institute of Human Relations.

Trist, E., & Bamforth, K. (1951). Some social and psychological consequences of the long wall method of coal-getting. *Human Relations, 4*(1), 1–8.

Turquet, P. M. (1985). Leadership: The individual and the group. In A. D. Coleman & M. H. Geller (Eds.), *Group relations reader 2* (pp. 71–87). Washington, DC: The A. K. Rice Institute.

Tushman, M. L., & Nadler, D. A. (1978). Information processing as an integrative concept in organizational design. *Academy of Management Review, 3,* 613–624.

Vaill, P. B. (1989). *Managing as a performing art.* San Francisco, CA: Jossey-Bass.

Van de Ven, A. H., & Sun, K. (2011). Breakdowns in implementing models of organization change. *Academy of Management Perspectives, 25,* 58–74.

Van Eron, A. M., & Burke, W. W. (1992). The transformational/transactional leadership model: A study of critical components. In K. E. Clark, M. B. Clark, & D. P. Campbell (Eds.), *Impact of leadership* (pp. 149–167). Greensboro, NC: Center for Creative Leadership.

Van Knippenberg, D., & Schippers, M. C. (2007). Work group diversity. *Annual Review of Psychology, 58,* 515–541.

Vega, T. (2014, July 2). Census considers how to measure a more diverse America. *The New York Times,* A12, A16.

Vroom, V. (1964). *Work and motivation.* New York, NY: Wiley.

Wasserman, S., & Faust, K. (1994). *Social networks analysis: Methods and applications.* Cambridge, England: Cambridge University Press.

Watson, G. (1966). Resistance to change. In G. Watson (Ed.), *Concepts for social change,* Cooperative Project for Educational Development Series, Vol. 1. Washington, DC: National Training Laboratories.

Weick, K. E. (2001) *Making sense of the organization.* Malden, MA: Blackwell.

Weick, K. E. (1976). Educational organizations as loosely coupled systems. *Administrative Science Quarterly, 21,* 1–19.

Weisbord, M. R. (1978). *Organizational diagnosis: A workbook of theory and practice.* Reading, MA: Addison-Wesley.

Weisbord, M. R. (1977). How do you know it works if you don't know what it is? *OD Practitioner, 9*(3), 1–8.

Weisbord, M. R. (1976). Organizational diagnosis: Six places to look for trouble with or without a theory. *Group and Organization Studies, 1,* 430–17.

Weisbord, M. R. (1973). The organization development contract. *OD Practitioner, 5*(2), 1–4.

Wells, L. (1995). The group as a whole: A systemic socioanalytic perspective on interpersonal and group relations. In J. Gillette & M. McCollom (Eds.), *Groups in context: A new perspective on group dynamics.* Lanham, MD: University Press of America.

Wheatley, M. J. (1992). *Leadership and the new science.* San Francisco, CA: Berrett-Koehler Publishers.

Whitmore, J. (2009). *Coaching for performance: Growing human potential and purpose.* London, England: Nicholas Brealey Publishing.

Witherspoon, R. (2014). Double-loop coaching for leadership development. *Journal of Applied Behavioral Science, 50,* pp. 261–283.

Witherspoon, R., & White, R. P. (1996). Executive coaching a continuum of role. *Consulting Psychology Journal: Practice and Research, 48,* 124–133.

Worley, C. G., Williams, T., & Lawler, E. E. III. (2014). *The agility factor: Building adaptable organizations for superior performance.* San Francisco, CA: Jossey-Bass.

Yes, Silicon Valley, there is such a thing as not enough bureaucracy. *The New York Times,* p. B3. Retrieved from http://www.nytimes.com/2014/05/01/upshot/yes-silicon-valley-there-is-such-a-thing-as-not-enough-bureaucracy

Zaleznik, A. (1977). Managers and leaders: Are they different? *Harvard Business Review, 55*(3), 67–78.

Zand, D. W. (1974). Collateral organization: A new change strategy. *Journal of Applied Behavioral Science, 10,* 63–89.

Zikopoulos, P. C., Eaton, C., deRoos, D., Deutsch, T., & Lapis, G. (2012). *Understanding big data: Analytics for enterprise class Hadoop and streaming data.* New York, NY: McGraw-Hill.

Index